Studies in Emotion and Social Interaction

Paul Ekman
University of California, San Francisco

Klaus R. Scherer
Univerité de Génève
Justus-Liebig-Universität Giessen

General Editors

The mechanism of human facial expression

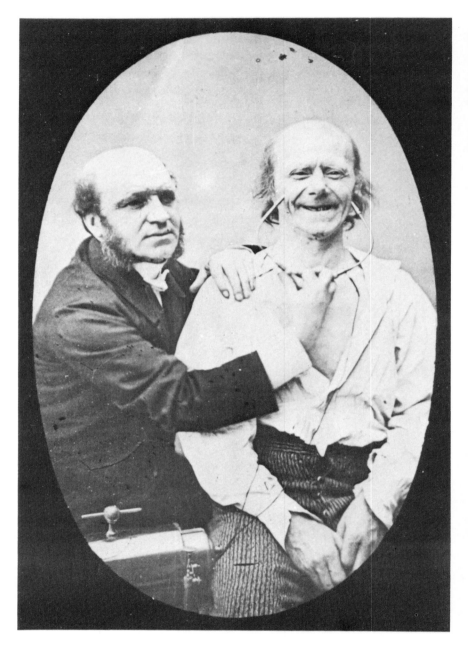

DUCHENNE (de Boulogne) phot.

SPECIMEN

D'UNE EXPÉRIENCE ÉLECTRO-PHYSIOLOGIQUE

MÉCANISME

DE LA

PHYSIONOMIE HUMAINE

OU

ANALYSE ÉLECTRO-PHYSIOLOGIQUE

DE L'EXPRESSION DES PASSIONS

APPLICABLE A LA PRATIQUE DES ARTS PLASTIQUES

PAR LE DOCTEUR

G.-B. DUCHENNE (de Boulogne)

Lauréat de l'Institut de France et de l'Académie de médecine de Paris (prix Itard).
Lauréat du concours Napoléon III sur l'électricité appliquée,
Membre titulaire de la Société de médecine de Paris,
Membre correspondant des Académies, Universités et Sociétés de médecine de Dresde, Florence, Gand,
Genève, Kieff, Leipzig, Madrid, Moscou, Naples, Rome, Saint-Pétersbourg, Stockholm,
Vienne, Wurtzbourg, etc.
Chevalier de la Légion d'honneur.

— — —

ALBUM

— — —

PARIS

Vᵉ JULES RENOUARD, LIBRAIRE

6, RUE DE TOURNON, 6.

1862

The mechanism of human facial expression

by G.-B. Duchenne de Boulogne

Edited and Translated by R. Andrew Cuthbertson

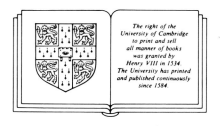

The right of the
University of Cambridge
to print and sell
all manner of books
was granted by
Henry VIII in 1534.
The University has printed
and published continuously
since 1584.

Cambridge University Press

Cambridge

New York   Port Chester   Melbourne   Sydney

Editions de la Maison des Sciences de L'Homme

Paris

Studies in Emotion and Social Interaction

This series is jointly published by the Cambridge University Press and the Editions de la Maison des Sciences de l'Homme, as part of the joint publishing agreement established in 1977 between the Fondation de la Maison des Sciences de l'Homme and the Syndics of the Cambridge University Press.

Cette collection est publiée en co-édition par Cambridge University Press et les Editions de la Maison des Sciences de l'Homme. Elle s'intègre dans le programme de co-édition établi en 1977 par la Fondation de la Maison des Sciences de l'Homme et les Syndics de Cambridge University Press.

Published by the Press Syndicate of the University of Cambridge
The Pitt Building, Trumpington Street, Cambridge CB2 1RP
40 West 20th Street, New York, NY 10011, USA
10 Stamford Road, Oakleigh, Melbourne 3166, Australia

© Cambridge University Press 1990

First published 1990

Printed in the United States of America

Library of Congress Cataloging-in-Publication Data
Duchenne, G.-B. (Guillaume-Benjamin), 1806–1875.
  [Mécanisme de la physionomie humaine. English]
  The mechanism of human facial expression / by Duchenne de Boulogne
  edited and translated by R. Andrew Cuthbertson.
    p.   cm. – (Studies in emotion and social interaction)
  Translation of: Mécanisme de la physionomie humaine.
  ISBN 0-521-36392-6
  1. Facial expression – Physiological aspects. 2. Face – Muscles.
I. Cuthbertson, R. Andrew. II. Title. III. Series.
QP327.D8313   1990
612'.92 – dc20   89-77825
                                                                         CIP

British Library Cataloguing in Publication Data
Boulogne, G.-B. Duchenne de
  The mechanism of human facial expression. – (Studies in
  emotion and social interaction).
  1. Man. Facial expressions
  I. Title II. Cuthbertson, R. Andrew III. Series.
  IV. Mecanisme de la physionomie humaine. *English*
  152.4

  ISBN 0-521-36392-6 hardback

To Paul Guilly, writer, neurologist, and psychiatrist of Paris, who published the first modern appreciation of Duchenne in 1936 and who offered kindness and encouragement to more recent discoverers of Duchenne de Boulogne.

Contents

Acknowledgments

This project has been enthusiastically supported from its inception to completion by John T. Hueston. The initial work was guided by Kenneth Russell in the Department of Medical History at the University of Melbourne.

The translation was prepared as a collaboration with Penny Hueston. Margaret Plant, Christobel Botten, and Penny Hueston kindly read and commented on parts of the text, and the index was prepared by Christobel Botten. The Maison generously provided financial assistance for the reproduction of Duchenne's original photographs from *Mécanisme de la Physionomie Humaine*. Access to essential library materials, and to patient records and photographs, has been gratefully acknowledged in the text. Lester Kaplan has improved the accuracy of the work through his excellent copy editing.

Finally, it is a pleasure to thank the co-editor of this series, Paul Ekman, for encouraging the production of a bound book from a thesis and a hand-written translation.

Contributors

Editor: R. Andrew Cuthbertson: Post-doctoral Fellow at the Howard Florey Institute of Experimental Physiology and Medicine, and Associate to the Medical History Unit, The University of Melbourne, Australia.

Now working in the Laboratory of Molecular and Developmental Biology, National Eye Institute, N.I.H., Bethesda, Maryland, U.S.A.

Co-translator: Penelope A. Hueston: Senior Editor, Pan Books, Australia, and former Associate Editor of the literary magazine *Scripsi.*

Chapter authors:
Jean-François Debord: Professor of Morphology, École Nationale Supérieure des Beaux Arts, Paris.

Paul Ekman: Professor of Psychology at the University of California in San Francisco, where he has been studying facial expression for the past thirty years.

John T. Hueston: Consultant Plastic Surgeon, Royal Melbourne Hospital, now living in St. Saturnin d'Apt, Provence.

Editor's preface

Mécanisme de la Physionomie Humaine was a rare book when it was published in Paris in 1862. Few copies were produced, as the text was accompanied by about 100 original photographic prints, each of which had to be pasted into the Album. The fascicule containing the Introduction appeared first, followed by the Scientific Section, and then an Aesthetic Section was published some months later. This sequential publication had the advantage that criticisms made by reviewers of, for example, the Scientific Section, were answered by Duchenne in the subsequent Aesthetic Section! Together, the three fascicules constituted the "Text" of *Mécanisme de la Physionomie Humaine*. They were either sold bound together or could be bought loose and bound by purchasers in their own preferred style.

Although important in the development of modern experimental psychology and physiology, original copies of this book have been restricted to a few major libraries. Our aim in producing this book was to make Duchenne's text and photographs more widely available for the first time. *Mécanisme de la Physionomie Humaine* is historically important as the first series of published physiological experiments to be illustrated by photography; it also has relevance to modern psychology, neurology, plastic surgery, and the study of fine arts, which is reflected in the four accompanying commentary chapters.

Duchenne's ideas were precise but his writing was rather verbose. We have always tried to reproduce his meaning accurately though sometimes stating it more precisely. We have used the Latinized anatomical names listed in *Nomenclature Anatomique Illustrée* by M. Guntz, Masson, Paris, 1975, which is based on the *Parisiensa Nomina Acta* (PNA) of 1955. In tables we have listed the current name, the nineteenth-century French name and the functional anatomical name given to each facial muscle by Duchenne. We have used Anglicized versions of proper names unless the original was French. Following the convention established by Duchenne, "left" and "right" refer to the sides of the individual photographed and not to the sides of the illustration.

R. Andrew Cuthbertson

PART 1

The mechanism of human facial expression or an electrophysiological analysis of the expression of the emotions

Preface

"When the spirit is roused, the human face becomes a living picture where the emotions are registered with much delicacy and energy, where each movement of the spirit is expressed by a feature, each action by a characteristic, the swift, sharp impression of which anticipates the will and discloses our most secret feelings."
[Buffon, *Histoire de l'homme*]

The spirit is thus the source of expression. It activates the muscles that portray our emotions on the face with characteristic patterns. Consequently the laws that govern the expressions of the human face can be discovered by studying muscle action.

I sought the solution to this problem for many years. Using electrical currents, I have made the facial muscles contract to *speak* the language of the emotions and the sentiments. "Experimentation," said Bacon, "is a type of question applied to nature in order to make it speak." This careful study of isolated muscle action showed me the reason behind the lines, wrinkles, and folds of the moving face. These lines and folds are precise signs, which in their various combinations result in facial expression. Thus by proceeding from the expressive muscle to the spirit that set it in action, I have been able to study and discover the mechanism and laws of human facial expression.

I will not limit myself to a formulation of these laws. Using photography I will illustrate the expressive lines of the face during electrical contraction of its muscles.

In short, through electrophysiological analysis and with the aid of

1

photography, I will demonstrate the art of correctly portraying the expressive lines of the human face, which I shall call the *orthography of facial expression in movement*.

DUCHENNE (de Boulogne)
Paris, 1st January, 1862

A. INTRODUCTION

1. A review of previous work on muscle action in facial expression

In this review I shall not confuse authors who were specifically concerned with facial expression in movement (the *symptomatology* of emotion) with those who have especially studied the signs of inclinations and habits, the study of the shape of the face at rest (properly called *physiognomy*).

The famous painter Lebrun is among the former,* who represented the diverse aspects of facial expression produced by the emotions but without worrying about their laws of motion. There are others who have tried to analyze the expressive movements of the face by identifying the actions of the muscles of this region. I am only going to refer to the work of the latter authors in order to make known how my research differed from theirs; I will speak only of the principal figures among them.

I. A historical survey

From earliest times anatomists recognized that the facial muscles govern the symptomatic expression of emotions; it was only toward the end of the last century and the beginning of this century that we have specifically studied the way each of these facial muscles contracts under the influence of emotion.

A. In 1792, the learned author of the *Dissertation on the Natural Variations that Characterize the Physiognomy of Men of Different Regions and Different Ages,* Camper,† who was also a talented painter, tried to determine the exact role of the facial muscles in the emotions; he studied the nature of the muscles to a lesser extent than the influence of the cranial nerves on facial expression.

---

*Lebrun has articulated a method for learning how to draw the passions in a speech at the Royal Academy of Painting and Sculpture.

†P. Camper, *Discours sur les moyens de représenter d'une manière sûre les diverses passions qui se manifestent sur le visage,* 1792.

3

He was not as happy in this type of research as in his other work. In fact, in attributing to the Vth cranial nerve a motor action similar to that of the VIIth, he placed the expressive movements of the face under the influence of either of these nerves. As he said:

In absolute sadness it is the Vth pair that act . . .

When a man is joyful, the only branches that act are those of the VIIth pair . . .

When we cry, the only difference is that all those muscles that are innervated by the Vth are even more strongly stimulated . . .

The VIIth makes us blush and blanch . . .

At the time when Camper was writing, the special properties of the VIIth and the Vth cranial nerves were unknown. Today we know the movements of the facial muscles are under the control of the VIIth, and that the Vth alone provides facial sensation; and that paralysis of the Vth does not disturb either the voluntary movement of the face, nor its expressive movements, whereas paralysis of the VIIth is necessarily followed by loss of facial mobility.

In Camper's discourse there is one single important proposition:

The folds of the face must necessarily cut at right angles the course of the muscle fibers.

He was the first author ever to make this remark, but he never proved it. I can prove that it is only applicable to certain facial muscles and that it is impossible to explain the formation of some folds or wrinkles during the play of facial expression based on this maxim.

B. Lavater devoted himself to the study of facial expression at rest, of *physiognomy* as such. His research was concerned with the difference between the combinations of contours and lines, the profiles and silhouettes that make up the static face. He certainly would not have neglected as much as he did of the study of facial expression in movement, which should serve as the basis for the examination of the physiognomy at rest, had he been either an anatomist or a physiologist or a doctor or even a naturalist.

The learned people who have undertaken the difficult task of collecting the different studies of this important observer, under the title of *Fragments,* understood that the study of facial expression in movement, entirely omitted by Lavater, should precede the study of physiognomy at rest.

In 1805, Moreau (de la Sarthe), Professor at the Faculty of Medicine at Paris University, and one of the principal collaborators in the great *Traité de la Physionomie* of Lavater, composed an important article for this publication about *the structure, the use, and the characteristics of the different parts of the human face.**

Incontestably, he acquitted himself with talent. He addressed the particular and detailed examination of the action and effect of each muscle on facial expression. He touched on physiological questions, which according to this author (and this is also my opinion), had never been tackled in the best treatises of anatomy and physiology published before him.

C. An English physiologist who became renowned for his research on the nervous system, Charles Bell, published a book entitled *The Anatomy and Philosophy of Expression*. If he had published this book before the work of Moreau, the physiology of facial muscles would certainly owe progress to him.

His ideas on the exact action of the facial muscles and the manner in which they interact to express the emotions are very similar to those of the French anatomist. We suppose, however, that at that time he had no knowledge of the great work of Lavater – published the preceding year in Paris.

A book written by a man whose experimental investigations were some years later to throw such light on certain aspects of the nervous system could not be an ordinary work, despite the fact that it lacked innovation. His basic science linked with his practical knowledge of drawing and painting – especially his love of the fine arts – makes reading this elegantly produced book as instructive as it is pleasant.†

D. After the works I have just quoted, most of the authors who dealt with the same questions only reproduced the work of Moreau and Charles Bell. I must nevertheless mention a paper by Sarlandières.§ This writer seems to have studied the action of the facial muscles a little more closely than his predecessors, but the preceding historical facts show that he was wrong to write in his preface: "Not a single author (those who preceded him), has examined the way each muscle contracts in isolation, either under the influence of the emotions, or under the influence of the will, or independent of this will, to produce expression or gestures by these isolated or combined movements."

* *L'art de connaître les hommes par la physionomie,* by Gaspard Lavater, 4th edition, 1820, vol. IV, art. 3.
† Charles Bell, who since his childhood was devoted to the art of drawing, had artistic talent. We find proof of this in his ink sketches, which he had reproduced by engraving in his treatises of great surgical operations (*Illustrations of the Operations of Surgery,* in-fol., 20 pl. colour, London, 1821).
§ *Physiologie de l'action musculaire appliquée aux arts d'imitation.*

Sarlandières attributed an influence on expression to the auricular muscles! It was certainly a new idea; unfortunately, the role he assigns them in this case is impossible.

I do not intend completely to analyze the works that I have mentioned; it will be more opportune to return to this subject when I deal with particular facts. It will then be easy for me to show that the authors of these works, some of whom have acquired great fame, have committed numerous errors; it could not be otherwise – as I shall explain.

II. Critical consideration of the various means of investigation used in myology

Following a description of each muscle, the treatises in myology offer us more or less detailed study of their actions. Several methods have been employed to determine the action of the contractile elements; here they are according to Professor Bérard:

1. Sometimes the outline of the muscle during the production of certain movements displays the muscular action itself. The *m. biceps* and *m. brachialis* swell while the forearm flexes; obviously they are the flexors of this region. My temple bulges when my jaws come together; without a doubt *m. temporalis* above is pulling on the coronoid process of the mandible.

2. Sometimes the configuration of the articular surfaces indicates the use of the neighboring muscles. Never will a muscle passing over a ginglyform articulation determine the lateral movements; it will be a flexor or an extensor according to whether it approaches more to either side of the opposing planes in which the movements are made.

3. Furthermore, we refer to the excellent criteria that I shall describe, the true touchstone of muscular action.

   Accepting the notion that a muscle shortens during its action, or rather that its fibers shorten (it's not exactly the same thing), we may dissect a muscle on a corpse, make different movements of the part and observe the movement when fibers stretch and the movement when they slacken. By this technique, you can determine almost certainly that in the living person the muscle at least contributes to bringing the limb into the position in which you see the fibers relaxed in the corpse. This simple method – so useful that I wouldn't know who invented it, nor even who taught it to me – must have been obvious to the first anatomist who saw a muscle shortening during its contraction.

4. Finally, when lively controversies arise about the actions of certain muscles, it is not rare to call up vivisectionists to arrive at a solution.

These techniques are perfectly applicable to the myology of the limbs and the trunk and I recognize, with Bérard, that thanks to them, we had advanced in the knowledge of the particular action of each muscle; but I don't think as he does, however, that there are only a few remaining sections to complete and a few opinions to rectify with regard to the myology of the limbs.*

Without being unjust toward my predecessors, without sacrificing all past knowledge for the greater glory of modern progress, we may affirm today that before my electrophysiological research, we had very incomplete ideas of the actions of the muscles of the hand, and that it was impossible to explain even the simplest movements of the hand.

How, for example, in everyday use of the hand (as when one writes, and so forth), do we move the phalanges in opposite directions. It is of facts like this that we were ignorant – correct physiological theories being equally lacking for the muscles that move the foot and for those of other regions. The same will probably apply to those regions I have yet to explore.

If then, in spite of using the diverse methods of investigation common in myological studies, it was not possible to determine the individual action and the function of most of the muscles in the limbs, the difficulty is much greater in the face, where these techniques are not for the most part applicable.

First, in the face, we only recognize the action of a few of the muscles by their swelling or their outline; second, in this region there are no articular surfaces whose configuration can guide us to the action of the neighboring muscles; third, this veritable touchstone of myology, of *approximating the two extremities of a muscle to relax it*, is not applicable to the myology of the face. What use can such experimental methods be to studying the true actions of the muscles of the face, the wrinkles, the folds, the outlines numerous and infinitely varied that can all be imprinted on the skin? They could not, in fact, show the influence that these muscles exert on expression.

One really has to admire the observational talent of those who have been able to guess, so to speak, the expressive action of certain muscles

---

*When Bérard wrote these lines, my electrophysiological research on the hand, the shoulder, the foot, and the diaphragm were not yet published. He later recognized that his muscle physiology left a lot to be desired.

of the face in spite of being deprived of all means of experimentation and control. Nevertheless, the opinions they have expressed in this regard were nothing but assertions that needed to be studied by direct experimentation.

One must also understand that these observers committed many more errors than they realized because of the optical illusions produced by movements limited to certain points of the face. I will shortly demonstrate, for example, that seeing a slight movement of muscles of the eyebrow one experiences a mirage that gives the impression of a general contraction of the face.

Live dissections, if practicable on man, would not resolve the problems in question, for it would be necessary to sacrifice the skin on which the signs of the expressive language of facial expression are drawn.

Let us examine the value of the system recommended by Camper. According to this celebrated observer, the folds and wrinkles of the face are necessarily perpendicular to the direction of action of the muscles. Does it follow then that in all expressive movements we can recognize the muscles that are acting by the direction of the wrinkles? Is the muscle that crosses the direction of a wrinkle produced by an expressive movement necessarily in contraction?

This seems to be the opinion of Camper. It has also been the method employed after him by other workers to explore the motor agents involved in particular expressions. Ah well! Nothing is less certain, or rather, nothing is more deceptive than this method!

To prove it, I shall make a comparison. If one exerts a vertical or oblique traction above and below a point on a curtain, one sees, depending on the suppleness and age of the material, folds form in various directions and sometimes at different points of this surface.

Similarly, with a simple traction on the skin of the face, one sees wrinkles and furrows form in diverse directions and in places more or less removed from one another. Moreover, the skin surface is not uniform; in the relaxed state it displays the furrows and reliefs due to the tonic predominance of such and such a muscle of this region, a predominance that is inifinitely variable, depending on the age of the subject and the habitual play of emotions. This is what constitutes the individual facial expression.

So! All traction limited to a point on the face changes these furrows and outlines, either exaggerating or effacing them, or altering their direction.

An example to develop my ideas further. Supposing a force acts from the corner of the lips to the external side of the cheekbone (as with *m.*

zygomaticus major), then the nasolabial fold creases, curving in a diverging manner, and the wrinkles seem to radiate, in most cases, from the external angle of the eye.

Here is how we must explain these movements, according to Camper's theory that the folds and wrinkles of the face are necessarily perpendicular to the direction of the responsible muscles. The corner of the mouth has been moved by *m. zygomaticus major*; the nasolabial fold is creased by the action of *m. levator labii superioris alaeque nasi*; the wrinkles radiating from the external angle of the eye are due to the action of *m. orbicularis oculi*. I shall demonstrate that this explanation is completely erroneous and that *m. zygomaticus major* alone produces all the wrinkles and all the furrows.

What I have said of *m. zygomaticus major* is applicable to most of the expressive muscles of the face.

III. The background to my electrophysiological research on facial expression in movement

All movements, both voluntary and instinctive, result from simultaneous (synergistic) contraction of a more or less large number of muscles. Nature has not given man the ability to localize the action of the nervous fluid to an individual muscle to provoke an isolated contraction. This ability, functionally useless, would have exposed man to accidents and deformities, as I have already demonstrated elsewhere.*

As we cannot break down the movements and thus analyze the individual actions of muscles, how may we study them? How are we to arrive at a precise knowledge of the true action of these muscles?

If we were able to master the electrical current, an agent so analogous to the nervous fluid, and could limit its effect to individual muscles, we could certainly shed some light on their localized actions. In the face in particular, one could determine the isolated actions of the muscles with ease! Armed with electrodes, one would be able, like nature herself, to paint the expressive lines of the emotions of the soul on the face of man. What a source of new observations!

For a dozen years, this has been the fundamental idea of my electrophysiological research, an idea with a rich future that inflamed my imagination.

This is not the place to report the long series of physical and anatomical experiments through which I had to pass, and the difficulties I have

---

* *De l'électrisation localisée et de son application à la physiologie, à la pathologie et à la thérapeutique.* Paris, 1855; 2nd edition, 1861.

had to surmount before proving my idea. After several years of experimentation, I can apply electrical power to the surface of the body, in a controlled manner, and then make it traverse the skin without burning or cutting it and concentrate its action in one muscle or in a muscle bundle, in a nerve trunk or in a nerve branch.

The first application of the method of electrization that I invented was in the study of the face. "Localized electrization" has helped me resolve the problem, both so difficult and so interesting, stated in the previous paragraph; it permitted me to see the tiny radiations of the muscles occurring under the influence of the instrument. The muscular contraction revealed their direction and their anatomical situation more clearly than the scalpel of the anatomist. At least this is true in the face, where one inevitably sacrifices, in anatomical dissections, the terminal portions of the muscle fibers that have their crucial insertion into the skin.

This is then a new sort of anatomy, to which one can apply the two words by which Haller described physiology: it is *animated anatomy – anatome animata;* Soemmerring would have without doubt called it *contemplatio musculi vivi.*

By 1850, I had enough new facts for me to present a series of papers entitled "Functions of the muscles of the face demonstrated by localized electrization" to the Academies of Science and of Medicine of Paris, based on my electrophysiological experiments. This work provoked the brilliant discussion of Professor Bérard, member of the Academy of Medicine, in 1851.* I take the liberty of affirming that this electromuscular method had not been used before my experiments.

No one thought that the study of myology could benefit from gross experiments by a physician who provoked convulsions on the faces of his tortured subjects using electrical currents.

It has been suggested that C. Bell and Sarlandières tried to study the muscles of the face using galvanization. These authors don't mention this in their writings; furthermore, if they had used this method of exploration, they would certainly not have committed the errors I have had to rectify.

It will be recognized, I hope, that the honor of revealing the mechanism of human facial expression, this anatomical analysis of the emotions, was reserved for the method of electrization, which alone permitted the exact determination of the isolated action of the muscles and the dissection of their movements.

My initial research was not and could not be anything but a rough

---

*Meeting of 18 March 1851, *Bulletin de l'Académie de médecine,* t. XVI, p. 609.

sketch. The electrophysiological facts I originally observed did not give me a complete idea of the physiological movements of the face. And which actions should one give to each of the muscles of the face to see how they act in the play of facial expression? I was far from answering these complex and difficult questions, whose surface I had barely scratched.

Today, based on long and continuing experimentation, I believe that I can reveal my research to the public. I hope it will shed great light on these questions.

2. Principal facts that emerge from my electrophysiological experiments

In order to know and judge the influence on expression of the facial muscles, I have produced contractions of the latter with electrical currents. I always started with the face in repose, when it showed internal calm; the gaze of my subject was initially fixed and directed forward.

First I put each of the muscles into isolated contraction, on one side and then both sides of the face at the same time; then, progressing from the simple to the composite, I combined these isolated muscle contractions in all the variations possible, by making the different named muscles contract, two by two and three by three.

I will describe concisely, in the following paragraphs, the principal facts that have come to light by these isolated contractions and by the combined contractions of the muscles of the face.

I. Isolated contractions of the muscles of the face

The experimental study of isolated contractions of the muscles of the face shows that they are either *completely expressive, incompletely expressive, expressive in a complementary way,* or *inexpressive.*

A. Isolated contractions that are completely expressive

There are muscles that produce an expression of their own by their isolated action.

At first glance this assertion appears paradoxical. Although a small number of muscles have been accorded a special influence on facial expression, one would at the same time imagine that all expression depends on the harmonious working and synergy of at least several other muscles.

I must confess that I shared this opinion until my view was changed in an instant by electrophysiological experimentation.

12

From early in my research I had noticed that the isolated contraction of one of the muscles moving the eyebrow always produced a complete expression on the human face. It was the muscle that portrays *suffering*. Now then! No sooner had I induced the electrical contraction than not only the eyebrow took on the form that characterizes this expression of suffering, but the other parts or features of the face, principally the mouth and the nasolabial fold, appeared also to undergo a profound change, in order to harmonize with the eyebrow, and portray, like it, this suffering of the soul.

In this experiment only the eyebrow region had undergone a very obvious contraction, and I was not able to verify the much slighter movements of the other parts of the face. Yet I was forced to conclude that the generalized modification of the features I had seen was produced by the synergistic contraction of a large number of muscles, although I had excited only one. This was also the opinion of those before whom I repeated my experiments.

What then was the mechanism of this apparently generalized movement of the face? Was it due to a reflex action? Whatever the explanation of this phenomenon, it appeared to be evident to everyone that localized muscular electrization would never be possible in the face.

And then a fortunate accident occurred that showed me that I had been the victim of an illusion.

One day I was exciting the *muscle of suffering*, and at the moment when all the features appeared to be contracted expressing pain, the eyebrow and the forehead were suddenly accidentally masked (the veil of the person on whom I was experimenting falling over her eyes.) Imagine my surprise in seeing that the lower part of the face was not displaying the least contraction!

I repeated this experiment several times, covering and uncovering the forehead and the eyebrow alternately; I repeated it on other subjects, and also on a fresh cadaver, and always got identical results. That is to say, I saw complete immobility of the features of those parts of the face below the eyebrows; but at the instant the eyebrows and forehead were uncovered, so that one could see the whole facial expression, the features of the inferior part of the face seemed to take on an attitude of suffering.

This was a moment of revelation: this apparent general contraction of the face was only an illusion produced by the influence of the lines of the eyebrow on the other features of the face.

It is certainly impossible not to be deceived by this illusion, which is, as I have previously stated, a kind of mirage exerted by the isolated movements of the eyebrows, if it were not disproved by direct experiment.

Any propositions that contravene popular opinion, or that look like physiological heresy, must be backed up by proof. So I must now present the facts that are the complete and physical proof of the preceding assertions; but I must invert the order that I was forced to follow in my research. It is fitting that in these general and preliminary considerations I outline the principal facts to give an idea of the importance and the basis of my experimental research on facial expression in movement.

By what means can a movement confined to a point in the upper part of the face seem to produce such changes on the other features?

An analogy may be the optical illusions produced by bringing certain colors together. M. Chevreul, Director of the tapestry makers Gobelins, and a member of the Institute, has published a work of very great merit on this subject, and which is of practical use in painting.* This learned man has demonstrated that colors and even shades of colors, when placed next to one another, change in such a way that the eye sees them quite differently to when they are isolated. Put, for example, a layer of orange next to a grey color; if the grey is bluish, it looks more pale; if it leans toward yellow, it seems greenish.

This optical illusion produced by the simultaneous contrast of colors eludes all forms of scientific explanation. It is a similar sort of mirage that we experience in some circumscribed movements of the face.

The utility of this illusion produced by certain features of the face should be recognized. Here, I think, are the principal points:

1. If, in order to portray each emotion or each sentiment, it were necessary to put all the muscles simultaneously into play to change in general the features of the face, the nervous action would have to be much more complicated.
2. If the features that represent one emotion are reduced to one or a small number of muscles and limited to certain parts of the face, their significance becomes easier to grasp.
3. These traits, although circumscribed, exert a generalized influence; but as the emotions expressed are fairly numerous, there must not be an excessive number of contractions of this limited number of muscles that produce the traits.

Let us recognize here that the ingenious artifice employed by nature to these ends deserves our admiration. When we see a limited move-

---

* *Traité du contraste simultané des couleurs.*

ment and recognize the perfect image of an emotion, it seems to us that the face has changed in an overall way. When we experience such illusions, it is by virtue of our organization, by virtue of a faculty we have possessed since birth.

B. Isolated contractions that are incompletely expressive

Of the muscles below the eyebrow, there are those that produce their own expression and influence facial expression in a general manner, but this expression is incomplete.

These muscles are highly expressive; their individual action betrays a particular movement of the soul; each of them, in short, is the unique representative of an emotion. When they are successively brought into play, one sees appear, in turn, the expressive lines of *joy,* from simple contentment to foolish laughter, of *sadness,* of *vexation,* of *weeping,* and so forth.

This is the first impression one always receives on viewing these isolated contractions; nonetheless one then notices that the expression is not natural, that it is artificial, and ultimately that it lacks something.

What is the feature that is lacking and that is necessary to complete the expression? It is not always easy to find, judging by the opinions that I have heard from the people who assist in my experiments.

The experiments have taught me which muscles must synergistically contract to complete the expression. I will return soon to this important subject.

C. Isolated contractions that are expressive in a complementary way

Some muscles inferior to the eyebrow do not express anything by themselves, although they have the property of specifically representing certain emotions by combining with other muscles. They come into play in certain expressions to complete them or to communicate an added character.

I will cite an example. It is a muscle that attaches obliquely above to all the skin of the lower part of the face, and distends the anterior part of the neck, without the slightest trait that would contribute a recognizable facial expression. This muscle certainly deforms the features and the instant one couples it with the action of such and such another one, we see the most violent passions with an exactness that is striking: dread, terror, fright, torture, and so forth.

D.   Isolated contractions that are inexpressive

There is not a single muscle of the face that may not be synergistically put into action by an emotion; but some of them (a very small number) do not produce a single apparent expressive line, even though their isolated contraction produces a very appreciable movement. From the point of view of facial expression, these muscles can be considered inexpressive.

II.   Combined contractions of the muscles of the face

We can study combined facial muscular contractions by exciting several muscles of different names simultaneously, on one side or both sides at the same time. These combined contractions may be *expressive, inexpressive* or *discordantly expressive*.

A.   Combined contractions that are expressive

Experimental study of isolated muscular contractions of the face has revealed to me the origin of a large number of facial expressions, just as I have shown in the previous section. Some of these expressions are perfectly drawn by the isolated contraction of certain muscles, whereas other expressions, which are also specifically represented by a particular muscle, need the synchronous assistance of one or more other muscles to be completed.

I have stimulated each of the facial muscles conjointly with the muscles that are incompletely expressive. Exploring these muscular combinations taught me the complementary muscles for all of these incompletely expressive ones. I learned that a complementary muscle cannot be replaced by any other muscle and that it is always the necessary auxiliary to a particular incompletely expressive muscle. Finally, I learned that in her mechanism for the expression of the emotions, nature proceeds, as always, with simplicity. In these expressive muscular combinations it was rare that I had to activate more than two muscles simultaneously to reproduce completely any of the expressions that man can show on his face.

The original expressions of the face (produced either by the isolated contraction of a completely expressive or by the combination of incompletely expressive with the complementary expressive muscles), are primordial, for they can produce a harmonious ensemble and give rise to other more profound expressions, that is, to *complex* expressions.

An example to explain my idea. The *attention* produced by the isolated contraction of *m. frontalis,* and the *joy* caused by the synergistic contraction of *m. zygomaticus major* and *m. orbicularis oculi,* are primordial expressions. Altogether, the face announces that the soul is alive to new happiness, to an unexpected pleasure: It is a complex expression. If to these two primordial expressions one adds *lasciviousness* or lust, by making *m. nasalis* contract synergistically with the previous muscles, the sensual traits belonging to this last emotion will show the special character of *attention* brought on by something that excites lubricity. It will portray perfectly, for example, the faces of the lewd old men spying on the chaste Susanna.

Combinations of primordial expressions may produce complex expressions and in their progress they are complemented by the successive appearance of the lines belonging to each primordial expression. These combinations of primordial expressions do not give perfect complex expressions except where they occur in accordance with the laws of nature.

B.   *Combined contractions that are inexpressive*

It is rational to think that muscles that represent directly opposite emotions will not act synergistically and that their combined action will give only inexpressive contractions. In fact I have not been able to achieve a natural, harmonious combination from the union of expressions of opposite emotions or affections, above all when these have been accentuated. Not only did the face appear to be grimacing, but the spirit of the observer was left with a great uncertainty as to its real significance.

Thus associating the movements that belong to the expressions of *joy* and *pain* gives a strange facial expression that is more and more removed from reality as the expressive contractions become stronger. It is the same with other opposite expressions, where an artificial union produces a falseness in the facial expression, to the point where it is hard, sometimes nearly impossible, to make any meaningful interpretation.

It often happens in these delicate experiments that the electrode meets a nerve trunk that sets off a large number of muscles. The "en masse" contraction that results never produces anything but a grimace that resembles no expression. This "en masse" contraction mimics the convulsive spasms one sees in a chronic nervous affliction called *tic indolent de la face.*

C.   Combined contractions that are discordantly expressive

One should not conclude from the preceding facts that there is always absolute antagonism between contrary primordial expressions.

I have seen the lines that signify *joy* associated marvelously with those of *pain*, provided that the contraction was moderate; the image being that of a melancholy smile. It was a flash of *contentment*, of *joy*, where the subject was unable to dissipate the traces of a recent *pain* or the signs of habitual *sadness*. I thought to myself of a mother smiling down at her child, at the same time mourning the loss of a dear one, of her husband.

Smiling does not just indicate an inner contentment, it also shows *kindliness*, that happy disposition of the soul that makes one sympathetic to the trials of others, sometimes to the point of *pity*. We link, for example, a smile with moderate crying, or even better with the slight contraction of the *muscle of suffering*, and obtain an admirable expression of *compassion*, a most sympathetic emotion.

These composite contractions by opposite expressions, and that portray what one might call a forced sentiment, I call *combined expressive contractions that are discordant*.

III.   The muscular synergy of the expressive movements of the face

The facts in the two preceding paragraphs lead to a conclusion that will not have escaped any astute reader: Muscular synergy in the physiological movements of the limbs and the trunk is not at all comparable with that seen in the expressive movements of the face. This requires some explanation.

There is no physiological movement of the trunk or the limbs that is not a result of the synergistic contraction of a fairly large number of muscles. The voluntary elevation of the arm (of the humerus) is produced by the contraction of a muscle (*m. deltoid*); we feel it harden under our hand during this movement, and we imagine that it is the only one that is acting, because we are not conscious of other muscular contractions. Yet this is not the case. If we make *m. deltoid* contract in isolation, using an electric current, we see the scapula detach itself from the trunk – in the manner of a wing. I have explained elsewhere the mechanism of this deformity.* To prevent it, nature puts another muscle (*m. serratus anterior*) into synergistic action during the voluntary contraction of *m. deltoid*, which powerfully fixes the spinal border of the scapula against

---

* De l'électrisation localisée et de son application à la physiologie, à la pathologie et à la thérapeutique, second part, chapter II, articles 4 and 5, 1st edition, 1855.

the thorax, without our conscious knowledge and beyond our ability to stop it.

I can give many other convincing examples concerning the synergistic movements of the hand and the foot, movements that are marvelous mechanical combinations.

These synergistic contractions are necessitated by the laws of mechanics and this proposition can be further demonstrated by observing examples of human pathology. I have elsewhere studied this important question at length.* Is it necessary to say that the same need for mechanical equilibrium does not apply to the expressive movements of the face?

In the face, our Creator was not concerned with mechanical necessity. He was able, in his wisdom, or – please pardon this manner of speaking – in pursuing a divine fantasy, to put any particular muscles into action, one alone or several muscles together, when he wished the characteristic signs of the emotions, even the most fleeting, to be written briefly on man's face. Once this language of facial expression was created, it sufficed for him to give all human beings the instinctive faculty of always expressing their sentiments by contracting the same muscles. This rendered the language universal and immutable.

It would certainly have been possible to double the number of expressive signs by only putting muscles on one side of the face into play at any time, as one may see me doing in my experiments. But one senses how such a language would be ungainly; it was probably in the interest of a harmonious presentation that nature put bilateral muscles (of the same name) at the service of each emotion, and that we were deprived of the faculty of making them act unilaterally.

*Ibid.

3. The reliability of these experiments

I must anticipate a number of objections that, if they had foundation, would diminish and even cancel the worth of my experiments. I do not raise these objections for the pleasure of refuting them but advance them in all seriousness.

The sensitiveness of the face is such that one is not able to spare the subject submitting to this type of experiment a disagreeable sensation and even a little pain. Now this sensation can cause involuntary movements. How do we distinguish these latter movements from those that are actually appropriate to the muscle excited?

In general, these involuntary movements are only seen upon the first application of the electrodes, and not in those individuals who are used to the electrical sensation. Besides, we will see later, in order to dissipate doubts that could be raised by this objection, I chose as the principal subject for my experiments a man whose facial sensibility was poorly developed. Finally, these same experiments were repeated on a fresh cadaver and gave absolutely identical results.

Could not the isolated contraction of a muscle that presides over a particular emotion enable it to react on the soul, and produce an internal feeling that would provoke other involuntary contractions in sympathy? Two facial muscles might contract, for example, one of which draws the fundamental lines of an emotion, while the other completes the expression (I will demonstrate this at an opportune time). So! Might not the artificial excitation of the first muscle create an internal sensation, and this sensation, in its turn, lead to the contraction of the second muscle? This is called a sympathetic phenomenon in physiology. It would result in us not being able to put a facial muscle into isolated contraction without provoking synergistic action in other muscles: common satellites of the emotion of which the first muscle was the principal representative.

This argument, like the preceding one, is somewhat specious. A weight of experimental evidence contradicts it, however. I have induced contraction of the facial muscles in recently dead subjects and produced expressive movements that resemble absolutely those I have produced in the living.

Some colleagues raised the possibility that the facial contractions were reflexes, provoked by all external excitation and that localized muscular electrization was only an illusion.

It is useful to recall the circumstances in which we see the phenomenon called reflex muscular contraction. When one pricks an extremity of an animal whose head has been separated from its trunk, one sees movements leading to flexion of the different segments of the excited limb at the same time. The peripheral stimulation travels up the sensory nerves as far as the point of the medulla corresponding to the origin of the motor nerves of the excited limb. In this manner certain muscles react and contract. One sees then that the will is completely divorced from these contractions and that they appear in the region that has been stimulated. They are due, therefore, to a process justifiably called reflex.

"Is it possible," critics asked, "that the expression produced during the electrical excitation of a facial muscle results from a collection of reflex contractions analogous to those that we have just discussed and not the product of an isolated muscular contraction?" I knew that this objection cast doubt on the value of my electrophysiological research where it dealt with muscular action in not only the face but also the limbs. It has been soundly refuted by the numerous experiments that I have published elsewhere* and that I will simply summarize again here.

I have shown that this reflex phenomenon, which develops in certain pathological conditions, cannot occur in a normal state. Moreover, I have made isolated contractions of human muscles, exposed in some freshly amputated limbs and proven that the movements were quite the same as those obtained when I excited the homologous muscles of limbs not separated from the trunk. Finally, I have performed experiments on animals where I excited the facial muscles and the movements were absolutely identical whether or not the head was separated from the trunk.

From these facts collected from my experiments on healthy subjects, it is evident that localized muscular electrization does not provoke reflex contractions that complicate the isolated muscle action.

*Ibid., 1st ed., 1855, p. 30, and 2nd ed., 1862, p. 34.

4. The purpose of my research

Assuredly, nobody will contest the originality of my electrophysiological experiments on facial expression. I will try to summarize their use from the anatomical, physiological, and psychological points of view, and to indicate their happy or fortunate applications to the study of the Fine Arts.

I. The application to anatomy and physiology

A. Most of the facial muscles seem to continue one into the other, especially when you study them from the inside. M. le professeur Cruveilhier has been good enough to show me some figures depicting anatomical preparations that he had made with the object of studying the "inner view" of the muscles, after having detached the soft tissue of the face, en masse, from the bones. In these preparations all the muscular fibers seem to merge, one with the other, so that one is not able to assign exact limits to most of the facial muscles.

If this fibrillar continuity of the facial muscles were real, their independence would be highly compromised, if not annulled. Does a muscle contract in a portion of its length or in its entirety? And what then should one take as the fixed point? In brief, this continuous fibril doctrine,* which converts all the muscles of the face into a mask of facial expression, cannot explain the mechanism of this crowd of tiny independent movements that write the numerous feelings of the soul on the face in characters that are always identical.

The principal aim of morbid anatomy is to guide us in our research into the mystery of life by helping us learn the functions of the organs. It seemed in this case, on the contrary, to be intent on misleading us. It was only by using the true living anatomy of electromuscular explora-

*The doctrine of fibrillar continuity was conceived by Bellingeri, the celebrated Italian anatomist.

22

tion that we were able to demonstrate that this fibrillar continuity was an illusion.

Without anticipating later chapters I can say that I have discovered the limits of some muscles that were considered to continue one into the other. Some of these, since then, have been confirmed by dissection to be one muscle (for example, *m. pyramidalis*).

B. Electrophysiology demonstrates the existence in the face of muscles that are neither classified nor named. I shall cite some examples.

An electrode, placed on the ala of the nose, dilates the nostril, as happens in the more profound emotions. Anatomists had to look again to find a muscle responsible for this movement and they went so far as to deny the existence of muscular fibers in the ala of the nose.* I shall show that this muscle has been confused with one called *myrtiforme*, which itself was composed of several muscles of opposing actions.

Anatomy has grouped under the same name some muscles that possess independent actions when electrically stimulated, just as muscles for voluntary and instinctive involuntary movements may be confused, although their functions are essentially different.

In *m. orbicularis oculi,* for example, which we call a single muscle, we find four independent muscles that preside over some diverse expressions. It is evident to all the world that physiology must dictate to anatomy. Thus it would be wrong to continue to confuse the science of life, and above all the study of facial expression, under the pretext of simplifying classical studies.

My experimental research also helped correct some physiological errors committed in attributing to some muscles movements that are not theirs and in failing to recognize some that are. These errors confused us as to the role that they played in expression.

Thus we included *m. zygomaticus minor* in the movement of *joy*, whereas my experiments make it clear that it is the only muscle representing *sorrow* and *moderate pain*. Similarly with *m. platysma*, until now forgotten or badly studied as an expressive muscle. It contributes a striking accentuation to the most violent movements of the soul: *terror, wrath, torture,* and so forth.

I can say as much again of some other virtually unknown muscles, principally those that move the eyebrow and play a most important role in facial expression, as we will soon see.

---

*C. Sappey, *Traité d'anatomie descriptive*, p. 627.

II.   The application to psychology

That the muscular physiology of the human face is intimately linked to psychology cannot be denied. I have seen on the face of a cadaver the exact image of most of the emotions listed by the philosophers. I shall demonstrate this link in the following paragraphs:

A.   A summary of the expressive muscles stimulated and the expressions obtained in my electrophysiological experiments

a) I have shown in Chapter 2 that there is a hierarchy of the expressive muscles of the human face because they do not all share the same degree of importance in the play of facial expression. In the first tier are the independent muscles that express diverse passions or states of the spirit, by their isolated contraction, in a most complete way.

A second group comprises muscles that designate the expressive lines of an emotion for which they are the unique representative, as in the first group, but which they are not able to portray completely.

Finally, in a third group are muscles that, in association with others, specifically express certain emotions or complete them. These muscles are, however, inexpressive in isolation.

Here is a list of these expressive muscles arranged in their hierarchy:

Synoptic table

1. Completely independent expressive muscles

Current name	19th century French	Name used by Duchenne
m. frontalis	frontal	muscle of *attention*
superior part of *m. orbicularis oculi*	orbiculaire palpébral supérieure	muscle of *reflection*
m. corrugator supercilii	sourcilier	muscle of *pain*
m. procerus	pyramidal du nez	muscle of *aggression*

II. Incompletely expressive muscles and muscles that are expressive in a complementary way

m. zygomaticus major	grand zygomatique	muscle of *joy*
m. zygomaticus minor	petit zygomatique	muscle of *moderate crying* or *weeping*
m. levator labii superiorus	elévateur propre de la lèvre supérieure	muscle of *crying*

1. Completely independent expressive muscles

Current name	19th century French	Name used by Duchenne *
m. levator labii superiorus alaeque nasi	elévateur commun de l'aile du nez et de la lèvre supérieure	muscle of *crying with hot tears*
transverse part of *m. nasalis*	transverse du nez	muscle of *lust*
m. buccinator	buccinateur	muscle of *irony*
m. depressor anguli oris	triangulaire des lèvres	muscle of *sadness*, of *disgust*, and complementary to *aggressive expressions*
m. mentalis	muscle de la houppe du menton	muscle of *disdain* or *doubt*
m. platysma	peaucier	muscle of *fear*, *fright*, and *torture*, and complementary to *wrath*
m. depressor labii inferiorus	carré du menton	muscle complementary to *irony* and *aggressive feelings*
alar part of *m. nasalis*	dilateur des narines	muscle complementary to *violent feelings*
m. masseter	masséteur	muscle complementary to *wrath* and *fury*
palpebral part of *m. orbicularis oculi*	palpébraux	muscle of *contempt* and complementary to *crying*
inferior part of *m. orbicularis oculi*	orbiculaire palpébral inférier	muscle of *benevolence* and complementary to *overt joy*
outer fibers of *m. orbicularis oris*	fibres excentriques de l'orbiculaire des lèvres	muscle complementary to *doubt* and *disdain*
inner fibers of *m. orbicularis oris*	fibres concentriques de l'orbiculaire des lèvres	muscle complementary to *aggressive* or *wicked passions*
upward gaze	regard en haut	movement complementary to *recollection*
upward and lateral gaze	regard oblique en haut et latéralement	movement complementary to *ecstasy* and to *sensual desire*
downward and lateral gaze	regard oblique en bas et latéralement	movement complementary to *defiance* or *fear*
downward gaze	regard en bas	movement complementary to *sadness* and *humility*

There is a final group of muscles that, without doubt, are activated by some emotions but do not show any expressive lines on the face: These are the muscles that move the external ear. I would also place *m. levator anguli oris* (canine) in this category. I could not make this muscle contract in an isolated fashion and consequently cannot exactly describe its action.

b) It is apparent from my electrophysiological research and the findings given in preceding sections that facial expressions can be divided into two classes: primordial and complex.

Primordial expressions are produced by isolated contractions of muscles that are completely expressive, or by the combination of muscles that are incompletely expressive with muscles that are expressive in a complementary way.

Complex expressions result from the association of different primordial expressions.

I shall outline a classification of primordial and complex expressions derived from electrophysiological experimentation.

Synoptic table

Primordial expressions	Muscles that produce them
1. Produced by the isolated contraction of muscles that are completely expressive:	
Attention	m. frontalis
Reflection	superior part of m. orbicularis oculi, moderately contracted
Meditation	same muscle, but strongly contracted
Intentness of mind	same muscle, but very strongly contracted
Pain	m. corrugator supercilii
Aggression or Menace	m. procerus
2. Produced by the combined contraction of muscles that are incompletely expressive with those that are expressive in a complementary way:	
Weeping with hot tears	m. levator labii superiorus alaeque nasi plus the palpebral part of m. orbicularis oculi
Moderate weeping	m. zygomaticus minor plus the palpebral part of m. orbicularis oculi
Joy	m. zygomaticus major
Laughter	same muscle plus palpebral part of m. orbicularis oculi
False laughter	m. zygomaticus major alone
Irony, ironic laughter	m. buccinator plus m. depressor labii inferiorus
Sadness or Despondency	m. depressor anguli oris plus flaring of the nostrils and downward gaze

Primordial expressions	Muscles that produce them
Disdain or Disgust	m. depressor anguli oris plus palpebral part of m. orbicularis oculi
Doubt	m. mentalis plus the outer fibers of m. orbicularis oris (either the inferior portion or the two portions at the same time) plus m. frontalis
Contempt or Scorn	palpebral part of m. orbicularis oculi plus m. depressor labii inferiorus plus m. transversus plus m. levator labii superiorus alaeque nasi
Surprise	m. frontalis plus muscles lowering the mandible to a moderate degree
Astonishment	same combination of muscles and lowering of the mandible, but of a stronger contraction
Stupefaction	same combinations, maximally contracted
Admiration, agreeable surprise	the muscles of astonishment associated with those of joy
Fright	m. frontalis plus m. platysma
Terror	m. frontalis plus m. platysma and lowering of the mandible, maximally contracted
Terror, with Pain or Torture	m. corrugator supercilii plus m. platysma and muscles lowering the mandible
Anger	superior part of m. orbicularis oculi plus m. masseter plus m. buccinator plus m. depressor labii inferiorus plus m. platysma
Carried away by ferocious anger	m. procerus plus m. platysma and muscles lowering the mandible, maximally contracted
Sad reflection	superior part of m. orbicularis oculi plus m. depressor anguli oris
Agreeable reflection	superior part of m. orbicularis oculi plus m. zygomaticus major
Ferocious joy	m. procerus plus m. zygomaticus major plus m. depressor labii inferiorus
Lasciviousness	m. transversus plus m. zygomaticus major
Sensual delirium	same muscles as lubricious pleasure, with gaze directed above and laterally, with spasm of the palpebral part of m. orbicularis oculi, the superior portion of which covers part of the iris

Synoptic table

Primordial expressions	Muscles that produce them
Ecstasy	same muscles as sensual delirium, but without *m. transversus*
Great pain, with tears and affliction	*m. corrugator supercilii* plus *m. zygomaticus minor*
Pain with despondency or despair	*m. corrugator supercilii* plus *m. depressor anguli oris*

We see that in general the more superiorly the facial muscles are found in the face, the more likely their expression is to be complete when they contract in isolation.

These muscles not only represent the image of emotions, sentiments, and passions; higher understanding can also be reflected in the face. Perhaps this is why these facial signs may be written with such clarity in the facial expression of man, by, for example, the isolated contraction of one of the muscles that move the eyebrow! *Intellectual reflection*, the most important, most noble, and most abstract state of the spirit, and *meditation*, which is the mother of great ideas, are the dominant passions in certain men.

The expressions in the above table are those that can be obtained artificially and recorded with the aid of photography. I will certainly be able to augment this number later on, by producing subtle nuances of these principal expressions.

Without doubt, however, the expressions produced by electrophysiological experimentation are already fairly numerous.

Perhaps it isn't given to man to express all his emotions on his face, especially when we consider the many different emotions that have been named and arbitrarily classified by the philosophers.*

I cannot be accused of enumerating them arbitrarily, for the expressions I induce are produced by the soul itself, as it paints them on the face of man. One day, perhaps, these electrophysiological studies on the different modes of expression of human "physionomie" will serve as the foundation for a better classification of the emotions founded on the observation of nature.

*There is, according to M. Lélut, nothing more varied, more multifarious, more complex, or more difficult to grasp in the diversity of its designations than the emotions. "We should refer," he says, "to the following list, whose items are borrowed from the best sources, from Plato, from Aristotle, from Cicero, from Descartes, and Hobbes, etc., a list

B.   *Facial expression*

The study of facial expression is that part of psychology dealing with the different ways man manifests his emotions by the movements of the face.

As man has the gift of revealing his passions by this transfiguration of the soul, should he not equally be able to understand the very varied expressions successively appearing on the face of his fellow men? What use is a language one cannot understand? To express and to monitor the signs of facial expression seem to me to be inseparable abilities that man must possess at birth. Education and civilization only develop or modify them.

The union of these two faculties makes the play of facial expression a universal language. To be universal, the language must always be composed of the same signs, or, in other words, depends on muscular contractions that are always the same.

Such reasoning is clearly proven by my research. In my experiments I

that could have been even longer and that we have left in the disorder of alphabetic order.

abjectness	drunkenness	mockery
admiration (the first of the passions according to Descartes)	emulation	mourning
	enmity	overwhelmed
amour-propre	enthusiasm	pain
anger	envy	pity
anguish	esteem	pride
audacity	evilness	pusillanimous
avarice	fear	rapture
avidity	fickleness	recognition
baseness	fright	regret
boredom	fury	remorse
chagrin	generosity	repentance
charity	glory	resilience (aggression)
cheerfulness	gluttony	resolution
confidence	greed	sadness
courage	hate	scorn
crying	hope	security
cupidity	humility	self-satisfaction
curiosity	indignation	sensuality
defensiveness	jealousy	shame
desire	joy	surprise
desolation	lamentation	temerity
despair	lasciviousness	timidity
disagreement	laughter	vanity
disdain	laziness	veneration
disgust	love	vengeance
	magnanimity	worry

have established that it is always a single muscle that executes the fundamental movement, representing a movement dictated by the soul. This law is so strict that man cannot change it or even modify it. If it had been otherwise, the language of facial expression would have had the same fate as that of spoken languages created by man: Each region, each province would have its way of portraying emotions on the face; perhaps this caprice would have gone so far as to vary infinitely facial expression in each town, in the case of each individual.

The language of facial expression had to be immutable, a condition without which it could not be universal. Because of this the Creator placed facial expression under the control of instinctive or reflex muscular contractions.

We know the regularity with which all instinctive movements are executed. I will only mention as a comparable example those of walking, during which the infant resolves the most complicated mechanical problems, with a facility and precision that the will would never be able to achieve. In the same way each emotion is always represented on the face by the same muscular contractions, which neither fashions nor whims can change.

"In general," said Descartes, "all the appearances, whether of face or eyes, may be changed by the soul when, deciding to hide an emotion, it vigorously calls up the image of a contrary one; so that we may make use of these actions as well in dissimulating our emotions as in evidencing them."* It is very true that certain people, comedians above all, possess the art of marvelously feigning emotions that exist only on their faces or lips. In creating an imaginary situation, they are able, thanks to a special aptitude, to call up these artificial emotions. But it will be simple for me to show that there are some emotions that man cannot simulate or portray artificially on the face; the attentive observer is always able to recognize a false smile.

The patterns of expression of the human face cannot be changed, whether one simulates them or actually produces them by an action of the soul; they are the same in all people, in savages and civilized nations, differing in the latter only by their moderation or exaggeration of certain traits.

C. The face at rest

During muscular relaxation, in the interval between the movements caused by voluntary or instinctive nervous action, the muscles still have

---

Les Passions de l'âme, 2nd part, art. 113.

a power that never sleeps, which is only lost with life itself. This power is called *tonicity*. This tonic power causes the free ends of a cut muscle to retract in a living person.

Muscles are like springs, which in the interval between contractions tend to equilibrate themselves. Thus the facial tissues, principally the skin, are drawn in the direction of the strongest muscles.

In the newborn, the soul is bereft of all emotion and the facial expression at rest is quite neutral; it expresses the complete absence of all emotions. But, from the time that the infant can experience sensations and starts to register emotions, the facial muscles portray the various passions on his face. The muscles most often used by these early gymnastics of the soul become better developed and their tonic force increases proportionately.

The face in repose must undergo some modification by the tonic force of these muscles, or as in my simple analogy I have just made, by the force of the springs that maintain them in equilibrium. Facial expression is formed in repose in the individual face, which must be the image of our habitual sentiments, the *facies* of our dominant passions. (This fact is well known and generally admitted.)

Yet Diderot, a celebrated philosopher, seems to have reservations on this subject. "In a sense we make (he says) our own physiognomy. The visage, accustomed to taking the character of the dominant emotion, retains it; sometimes also, we receive a contribution from nature, and we may retain what we have received. *It may have pleased him to make us good and to give us the face of an evil person, or to make us evil, and to give us the face of kindness.*"*

If it were true that goodness could be masked by the facial features of wickedness, then we would have to reduce the admiration that we owe to the masterpiece of nature that is facial expression.

Diderot's assertion, happily, is not accurate. If we observe the newborn, we always find an identical neutral expression, as I have said previously. It is only with time that we see their individual facial expressions forming: good or bad depending on the predominance of good or bad emotions. If a good man can be born with a wicked face, this monstrosity would sooner or later be effaced by the incessant influence of a good soul.

It is always the local afflictions of the face (contractions, partial paralyses, tics) that permanently alter the natural traits of individual facial expression. We must gain a knowledge of this cause of deformity.

---

* *Oeuvres complètes de Diderot: Essai sur la peinture*, p. 500.

III.   The application to painting and sculpture

The anatomical and electrophysiological analysis of the mechanism of human facial expression, which explains the lines, wrinkles, projections, and hollows of the face, is of great use in the practice of painting and sculpture.

A.   A comparison of the usefulness of morbid and live anatomy, from the point of view of painting and sculpture

The experimental study of the mechanism of facial expression requires exact anatomical concepts of the muscle distribution and innervation of the face. Anyone wanting to repeat my experiments, to satisfy their scientific curiosity as to the mechanism of human facial expression, must possess this special anatomical knowledge.

Yet the artist can neglect them entirely; for practical purposes all he needs to know are the laws of expressive movement, which followed from my research.

To justify this opinion, I will describe the usefulness of anatomical knowledge in general for those interested in the fine arts.

In ancient times, the study of anatomy consisted of two parts, called "morbid anatomy" and "living anatomy." The first, concerned mainly with the conformation of the organs, was inseparable from the second, which dealt with their functions; in other words, the study of morbid anatomy was only a preparation for the study of the organs in action.[*] We find proof of this in a book entitled *Of the Uses of the Parts*, a magnificent monument by Galen to the experimental physiology of the ancients.[†]

It would be hard to contest the usefulness of morbid anatomy to painting or sculpture. The greatest masters of the Renaissance, Leonardo da Vinci, Michaelangelo (whom we could reproach for having abused it), and many others where genius was supported by science, show us the advantage of an anatomical knowledge.

Yet I do not believe that these studies made on the cadaver were absolutely indispensable to art, as it appears that the Greeks ignored human anatomy. It was contrary to their religion and customs. Even in Galen's time human dissection was considered a sacrilege. Thus this

---

[*]This is what we call these days vivisection, a mode of experimentation reintroduced by modern physiology, in imitation of the ancients, whom we have not always equaled in this branch of research.

[†]*Oeuvres anatomiques, physiologiques et médicales de Galien*, translated by Ch. Paremberg, 1854, vol. 1.

great anatomist, taking the example of his predecessors, never dissected anything but apes. And he then extrapolated from this animal to man! Such knowledge would obviously not be of use in the study of human morphology; consequently it was not applicable to the plastic arts.

From which school then came the magnificent masterpieces of antique statuary the debris of which we admire today? If one didn't know, one could suppose that a profound anatomical science existed to aid the masters who produced these works.

The study of the nude was singularly favored by the Greeks; the artist had many occasions to study the play of muscles on their subjects. They observed the strength and the beauty of the human form – qualities then held in honor. And with what severity and wisdom did they define the reliefs and the depressions that depict movement and give life to the limbs of their subjects!

This precious science of the living model, indispensable to all artists, was born solely from observation of man in movement. It was a true *study of living anatomy, without which the knowledge of morbid anatomy would only have produced anatomical models or deformities.* At least this is what experimentation taught later. Isn't the exaggeration of morbid anatomical science one of the principal causes of the decline of art?

In summary, though the study of morbid anatomy may be of incontestable use and though it aids the understanding of the muscular workings of the limbs and trunk, we can conclude the following: (1) that it is not absolutely indispensable; (2) that the study of exterior form, above all the study of the state of movement, needs to be cultivated much more specifically in the practice of painting and sculpture.

If the study of morbid anatomy is not absolutely necessary to understand the movements of the limbs and trunk for the plastic arts, one can see that it is of even less use in the face, where, with few exceptions, the contracting muscles do not show under the skin.

If it is sufficient for an artist to observe men experiencing these emotions in the normal run of life to paint these diverse emotions exactly, then it may be of little importance for the artist to know the situation, the form, and the orientation of the muscles of the face, or to know that a particular muscle presides over the expression of joy, of dissatisfaction, of anger, and so forth.

B.   The impossibility of studying the expressive movements of the face in the same manner that one studies the voluntary movements of the limbs

The movements of facial expression are not controlled by the will, as are those of the limbs or trunk. Only the soul has the faculty of producing them truly. The movements are so fleeting that it has not always been possible for even the greatest masters to grasp the sum total of all their distinctive features, as they have the movements of other regions of the body. I will furnish proof of this from some of the celebrated works of antiquity. Please forgive me for my boldness; I will try to justify it later by a strict scientific analysis.

The rules governing the expressive lines of the moving face, which I would like to call the *orthography* of facial expression, have not been formulated before today, although for a long time we have tried to describe the whole collection of traits that make individual expressions.

It is not that talent has been lacking in this field of study; for among the authors who have dealt specifically with this important subject we find names illustrious in the history of the fine arts (I recall again here the name of that celebrated painter Lebrun). Unfortunately, each of them has followed their own inspirations, rather than exactly observing nature.

Lucky is the artist who, following only his genius or inspiration, does not sometimes miss the point! Studying the works of the great masters from this position, I have made some observations.

The traits belonging to a particular expressive movement are composed of *fundamental* lines, which make up their pathognomic signature, and lines which I call *secondary*. Secondary lines may be missing in certain conditions; and if they appear, it is only as satellites of the fundamental lines, adding to their significance, altering the degree of the emotion, hinting at the age of the subject, and so forth.

Great artists have not always recognized these fundamental lines: Sometimes after instinctively and accurately sketching them, they have lost them in finishing the work, without being able to rediscover them; at other times, they only knew how to portray them on one side of the face. I will demonstrate, by giving examples, that these faults are due to a lack of sufficient knowledge of the mechanism of human facial expression.

However, these men of genius have, in general, had a marvelous sense of the fundamental lines of expression. When they erred in accurately painting an emotion, it was nearly always due to the secondary expressive lines. Thus, when viewing their masterpieces, I am sometimes surprised to see secondary lines belonging to the most touching sympathetic passions drawn beside the fundamental lines of the very worst passions, even though nature makes such associations mechanically impossible.

Were the secondary expressive lines merely an ornament, with which the Creator decorated the fundamental lines, they would be no less sa-cred. This sole consideration would forbid the artist from capriciously effacing these lines whatever the degree of his genius. But they are not a simple ornament, a fantasy of nature. They enrich the fundamental lines and furnish further significant information.

Oh well! In spite of the incontestable usefulness of these secondary lines, artists have had no qualms about forgetting or eliminating them. Thus I will later examine whether ancient Greek artists, who rarely imi-tated details, sacrificed too much to the standards of artistic beauty by neglecting the secondary traits; and whether modern artists, following their example, are not similarly led astray by a false fashion. In addition, modern artists may not have recognized the importance of these lines, because of the difficulty in observing the expressive movement of the face.

In summary, until today, the artist has lacked a sure strategy in the study of the expressive lines of the face.

C. *The rules of the mechanism of facial expression, deduced from electromuscular experimentation, enlightening the artist without shackling the freedom of his genius*

Localized electrization can provoke the isolated contraction of the facial muscles singly or in groups. This freezes the traits of the face and tells us the exact cause of all the wrinkles and ridges, building up a represen-tation of both primitive and complex expressions. I have formulated rules to guide the artist in the true and complete portrayal of the movements of the soul, the rules of the *orthography* of facial expression, using this method of exploration.

We need not fear that these rules will menace the liberty of art, suf-focating the inspirations of genius; they do not, for example, provide any more shackles than the laws of perspective. Each expression does not come, as one might once have thought, from a single mold; the play of facial expression cannot be either as simple as that or as dreadfully monotonous.

It is established by my experiments that the degree of accentuation and development of the fundamental and secondary traits of facial expression are not only in proportion to the muscular contraction (which in turn relates to the strength of the emotion that provokes it), but also depend on a number of other conditions.

Here, in summary, are some of these conditions:

The fundamental traits that appear during the movements of facial expression after birth become more distinctive, deeper, and extensive with age and the continuing play of the emotions; in general, it is only at a certain stage of life that the secondary lines, satellites of the fundamental lines, arise and develop.

These phenomena are further subordinated to the stoutness or slimness of the subject, and gender also exercises an influence over their final form.

Furthermore, the background on which all the signs of the mute language of the soul are painted is never the same; in other words, the individual facial expression must conserve its own identity in the midst of the fleeting transfigurations that the incessant agitations of the emotions make it undergo. This individual facial expression depends not only on the contours of the face, upon which Lavater founded a doctrine; there is also a contribution from the permanence of the features arising from the habitual sentiments of the subject. This is especially true of their violent passions, and the predominance of some muscles that are most exercised in the *gymnastics of the passions.*

This suffices, I think, to allow an infinite variety of the features of the same emotion.

To follow the rules deduced from a study of the mechanism of expression demands great finesse of observation in the artist. Evidently these rules cannot take the place of genius; but in teaching the art of *correctly* painting the movements of human facial expression and by making the natural harmony of its expressive lines known, these rules can prevent or modify errors of the imagination.

IV.   A plan for the exposition of these studies

The findings from my electrophysiological experiments on the mechanism of facial expression can only be judged by seeing them. I have repeated these experiments several hundred times before numerous witnesses, and they have always believed what they have seen.

Skillful artists have tried in vain to represent the faces of my subjects; for the contractions provoked by the electrical current are of too short a duration for an exact reproduction of the expressive lines that develop on the face to be drawn or painted.

Only photography, as truthful as a mirror, could attain such desirable perfection. Photography allowed me to compose an album of figures that illustrate my lectures on the electrophysiological experiments I have performed on the face of man.

A spiritual writer, Töpffer, has demonstrated in a very original manner the existence of a new kind of literature, which he has called *literature in pictures*.

"One can write," he said in his *Essay in facial expression*, "stories with chapters, with lines and with words: this is literature as we understand it. One can also write stories with a succession of scenes represented graphically: this is the *literature in pictures*. . . .

"Literature in pictures has several advantages; it allows, with its richness of detail, a comparative conciseness; one or two volumes written by Richardson himself, would have great difficulty in saying with as much power the same things as those ten or twelve plates by Hogarth, which, under the title of "A Modern Marriage," has presented us with the sad fate and the miserable end of a dissolute . . .

"It also has the advantage of being somehow intuitive, and yet marked with great precision. . . .

"Finally, there are far more people who look at pictures than those who read."

The judicious remarks of Töpffer are perfectly applicable to our scientific and artistic subject. Photographic figures that represent, as in nature, the expressive traits assigned to the muscles that interpret the emotions, teach a thousand times more than extensive written descriptions.

I could have just published the album of these electrophysiological photographs of the face, with a few explanatory notes, and still showed the accuracy of my new and important propositions outlined above. My task would have been much easier; but I am obliged to discuss some anatomical and physiological findings that could not be placed in the captions to the plates of the album. These details would be essential, moreover, to those wishing to repeat my experiments or who would like to apply the results to painting or sculpture.

I have therefore composed an album of photographic plates from nature, which represent my electrophysiological experiments on the mechanism of facial expression, and, in the captions to these plates, I have reviewed the principal facts that emerged from my experiments.

I will then publish a more detailed text to accompany the album in which I propose:

(1) to give some anatomical findings on each of the muscles of facial expression; (2) to describe the isolated action of these muscles; the prominences, the hollows, the furrows, the folds, the wrinkles, and the variable movements to which they give birth, according to their degree of contraction, the age of the subject, and various anatomical conditions;

(3) to demonstrate the part that they play in individual expressions, either by their isolated action or by their various combined actions; and (4) finally to deduce the laws or rather the rules of the mechanism of human facial expression.

B. SCIENTIFIC SECTION
Foreword

The facts brought to light by my electrophysiological research on the mechanism of human facial expression are of considerable importance; they are, in general, so unexpected or in opposition to certain prejudices and to general opinion that experimental demonstration is the only way to make them acceptable to science.

Photography, as true as a mirror, can illustrate my electrophysiological experiments and help to judge the value of the deductions that I have made from them.

From 1852, convinced of the impossibility of popularizing or even of publishing this research without the aid of photography, I approached some talented and artistic photographers. These first trials were not, and could not be, successful. In photography, as in painting or sculpture, you can only transmit well what you perceive well. Art does not rely only on technical skills. For my research, it was necessary to know how to put each expressive line into relief by a skillful play of light. This skill was beyond the most dextrous artist; he did not understand the physiological facts I was trying to demonstrate.

Thus I needed to initiate myself into the art of photography.

I photographed most of the 73 plates that make up the Scientific Section of this Album myself, or presided over their execution,* and so that none shall doubt the facts presented here, I have made sure that not one of the photographs has been retouched.

If from the technical point of view these photographs leave something to be desired, I hope my readers will take into account the difficulties presented by this method. Although my electrical induction apparatus is of great precision and was adjusted for each of these electrophysiological experiments, it was still impossible to maintain these muscular con-

---

*M. Adrien Tournachon, a photographer whose ability is known to everyone, has been kind enough to lend me the sum of his talent to execute some of the negatives for this scientific section.

tractions at the same degree for a long time; the irritability of a muscle, after some seconds of continuous contraction, seemed to weaken under the influence of a current of high frequency. Therefore, I needed to photograph rapidly the expressions produced by the electrophysiological stimulus.

At the time when most of my negatives were taken (from 1852 to 1856), the photographic apparatus in use was less perfect than those of today.* I needed to obtain German objective lenses, which were the only ones able to operate with enough speed. Unfortunately, these lenses produced slight distortions and lacked so much depth of field that if, for example, the eye of my subject was in focus, the nose and the ear would be slightly out of focus. Often, if I wanted to highlight certain expressive traits and show them with distinctness, I was forced to sacrifice others, which in terms of photography were *blurred*.

On the other hand, with the object of obtaining more of the total picture, I could focus on an intermediate point so that none of the features in the photographic image was quite sharp.

With the apparatus that we possess today, it would be easy for me to avoid these minor faults.† But it would be a great pity if these photographs had to be sacrificed because of some imperfections; for they all have a scientific and artistic interest.

In actual fact, these photographic imperfections do not alter the truth and clarity of the expressive lines. Moreover, we will see that generally the distribution of light is quite in harmony with the emotions that the expressive lines represent. Thus the plates that portray the somber passions, the sinister ones: *aggression, wickedness, suffering, pain, fright, torture mingled with dread*, gain singularly in energy under the influence of chiaroscuro; they resemble the style of Rembrandt (see Plates 18, 20, 60, 65). Other plates, taken in plain sunlight where the exposure time could be very short, display the finer details, the shadows showing great complexity; there is again chiaroscuro, but after the style of Ribera (see among others, Plates 22, 40, 41, 42). And there are also some very brightly and evenly illuminated photographs. These are the ones that portray *astonishment, amazement, admiration, gaiety* (see Plates 11, 31, 32, 33, 56, 57). All the plates of the Album are fairly big so that one can see the expressive lines very distinctly: They are one-quarter natural size.

These details disappear at a certain distance, and I thought that it would be useful, above all for teaching, to enlarge photographs of the

---

*[About 1862.]

†I use an objective made by M. Dérosier, of short focal length, great speed, and of great depth of field.

heads, which could demonstrate the fundamental principles of the facial expression doctrine that I had established. These heads, enlarged to nearly natural size, were about 50 in number.*

The complete Album for the Scientific Section is made up of 73 photographic plates. They are devoted to the study of the muscles of *attention* [*m. frontalis*], of *reflection* [superior part of *m. orbicularis oculi*], of *aggression* [*m. procerus*], of *pain* [*m. corrugator supercilii*], of *joy* [*m. zygomaticus major*], of *kindness* [inferior part of *m. orbicularis oculi*], of *scorn* [palpebral part of *m. orbicularis oculi*], of *lasciviousness* [*m. transversus*], of *sadness* [*m. depressor anguli oris*], of *crying* [*m. zygomaticus minor* and *m. levator labii superiorus*], of *sniveling* [*m. levator labii superiorus alaeque nasi*], and finally of the muscles complementary to *surprise* or *astonishment* [the muscles lowering the mandible] and complementary to fear and terror [*m. platysma*].

I could not show the individual action of a few facial muscles photographically and these will be described in the corresponding text.

I have summarized, in the captions, the electrophysiological studies to which the plates of the Album relate. But reading these captions alone would have been too dry. I have therefore added a more detailed text, which defines the principles of my studies on the mechanism of human facial expression.

---

*From 1856 to 1857, I had made these large-scale negatives, after some positive intermediate enlargements, which themselves had been made from my original negatives of one-quarter natural size. I don't know whether this kind of photography has been done by anyone else before me. [Collections of these enlarged plates were advertised for sale by Duchenne's publisher, but I know of none in existence today except on the walls of the École des Beaux Arts in Paris.]

5. Anatomical preparations, and portraits of the subjects who underwent electrophysiological experiments

Plates 1, 2a, 2b, 3, 4, 5, 6

Plate 3: The face of an old man who served in numerous electrophysiological experiments, photographed in repose.*

Plate 4: The face in repose of a young man who appears in later photographs showing facial expressions produces both naturally and electrophysiologically.

Plate 5: Photograph of a young girl frowning, on whom several electrophysiological experiments were performed.

Plate 6: To show that when an electrode is applied to a nerve trunk that supplies several muscles only a grimace is produced. In this electrization of the temporofacial trunk we see contraction of all the muscles supplied by it; the grimace produced is similar to a tic of the face.

Further notes on these plates

The individual I chose as my principal subject for the experiments shown in this album was an old toothless man, with a thin face, whose features, without being absolutely ugly, approached ordinary triviality and whose facial expression was in perfect agreement with his inoffensive character and his restricted intelligence.

The reasons that determined my choice were:

1. In the elderly, facial muscle contractions produce all the expressive lines of the face (both fundamental and secondary lines).
2. The thinness of my subject favored the development of these expressive lines, and at the same time facilitated localized electrization of the muscles of his face.
3. I have preferred this coarse face to one of noble, beautiful features, not because in order to be true to nature one must show her imperfections; I simply wanted to prove that, despite defects of shape

*The Plates 3–84 are collected on pages 129–210 as in the original Album.

and lack of plastic beauty, every human face can become spiritually beautiful through the accurate rendering of emotions. I will support this contention by separately stimulating the motor units of the face – whose principal function is to portray our passions.

4. Finally, this man showed a very favorable condition that I had not recognized in other subjects. There are few people who are willing to submit to this type of experiment, because, without being extremely painful, electrization of the facial muscles often provokes involuntary movements resulting in contortion of the facial features. This subject had reduced sensation. He was suffering from a complicated anaesthetic condition of the face.* I was able to experiment on his face without causing him pain, to the extent that I could stimulate his individual muscles with as much precision and accuracy as if I were working with a still irritable cadaver.

I preferred not to choose my models as artists often do, when they select subjects with facial features suiting a particular expression. I thus deprived myself of a powerful means of increasing the interest of my experiments; moreover, not wanting to combine gestures with the facial expressions of my subjects, I have given all my models in this scientific section the same pose.

In spite of these restrictions and the unfortunate presence of electrodes and the hands which held them in my plates, the artificial expressions that I photographed remain grippingly true.

I have also produced some expressions on other subjects; taking the opportunity to collect the conditions that aesthetically constitute beauty.

I experimented on subjects of differing ages: on children (see Plates 5, 10, 28, 29), on a young man (see Plates 4, 15, 16, 24, 25), on a young woman (see Plates 35 and 36), and finally on an older woman whose skin had been tanned by the sun (see Plates 11, 26, 27).

My experiment could not be complete without comparing natural expressive movements with those produced by localized electrization. The muscles that move the eyebrows, of all the expressive muscles, are least under the control of the will; in general, only the emotions of the soul can move them in an isolated fashion. Unfortunately, the old man referred to above (see Plate 3) was of too low intelligence or too poorly motivated to produce himself the expressions that I have produced artificially on his face. Happily, I met a subject who, after much practice,

---

*He also had a spasm of the right rotator muscles of the head, a spasm that only showed itself when he wanted to do his work as a shoemaker. (I have described this condition under the name "functional muscular spasm.") I have cured it by electrizing the antagonist muscle.

could perform a large range of eyebrow movements. He was an artist of talent and at the same time an anatomist who was interested enough to undergo this study on himself. By calling on his feelings, he could produce perfectly most of the expressions portrayed by each of the muscles of the eyebrow. He was good enough to consent to these experiments and to allow me to record the results with photography. We see his face in repose in Plate 4.

I have also made the muscles of his eyebrow move individually, using faradization, and have established that these artificial movements resemble the expressive movement provoked by the emotions. I could have recorded these electromuscular movements in the Album, but this would have unnecessarily multiplied the number of figures. I therefore restricted myself to photographing some of the expressive movements of the eyebrow that he was able to produce himself.

Only one of the eyebrow muscles was beyond his control; I have therefore shown its isolated action obtained by localized electrization.

Finally, he conforms to the requirements of physical beauty; this is evident in his portrait (Plate 4), where, in repose, his features are handsome and regular.

These initial plates allow me to show the differences between the expressive movements in a young man and an old man.

Frontispiece A to this text volume illustrates the method of electrization that I have used to obtain an isolated contraction of the facial muscles. The electrodes, held in my right hand, communicate with my induction apparatus* via some conducting wires and are positioned to stimulate the muscles of *joy*, (I, Plate 1). The expressive lines of *joy* would have appeared on the face of the subject if I had sent current through my apparatus. But I must say that in this case the laughter is natural! I merely wanted to show a simulation of one of my electrophysiological experiments in this figure.

These experiments were not as easy as one might suppose from just looking at this plate. They required a perfect knowledge of the method, which I invented, for limiting the electrical excitation to each individual organ.

We should recall the principles required to perform electrization of the muscles of the face† to understand better the electrophysiological photographs that make up this Album:

---

*This precise apparatus, which I preferred for these experiments, is better represented in Plate 2b.

†Electricity produced by an induction apparatus is the only type applicable to this kind of

(continued on p. 47)

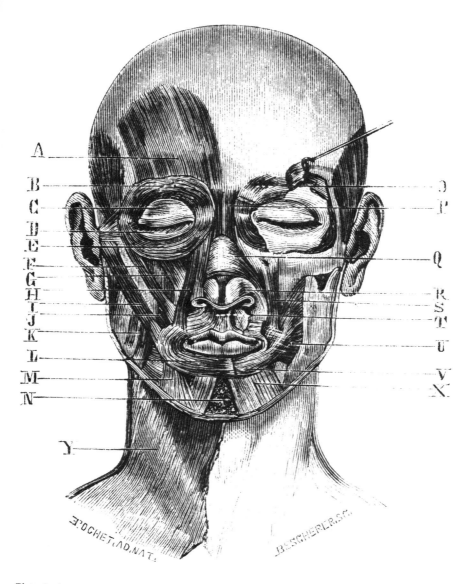

Plate 1: An anatomical preparation of the muscles of the face. A. *m. frontalis,* muscle of *attention;* B. superior part of *m. orbicularis oculi,* muscle of *reflection;* C, D. palpebral part of *m. orbicularis oculi,* muscle of *scorn* and complementary to *crying;* E. inferior part of *m. orbicularis oculi,* muscle of *kindness* and complementary to *overt joy;* F. *m. zygomaticus minor,* muscle of *moderate crying* and of *affliction;* G. *m. levator labii superiorus,* muscle of *crying;* H. *m. levator labii superiorus alaeque nasi,* muscle of *sniveling;* I. *m. zygomaticus major,* muscle of *joy;* K. *m. masseter;* L. *m. orbicularis oris;* M. *m. depressor anguli oris,* muscle of *sadness* and complementary to *aggressive feelings;* N. *m. mentalis;* O. *m. corrugator supercilii,* muscle of *pain;* P. *m. procerus,* muscle of *aggression;* Q. transverse part of *m. nasalis,* muscle of *lasciviousness* and *lubricity;* R. dilator portion (pars alaris) of *m. nasalis,* complementary muscle to passionate expressions; S. *m. caninus;* T. *m. depressor septi;* U. *m. buccinator,* muscle of *irony;* V. deep fibers of *m. orbicularis oris,* which are continuous with *m. buccinator;* X. *m. depressor labii inferiorus,* complementary muscle to *irony* and of *aggressive passions;* Y. *m. platysma,* muscle of *fear,* of *terror* and complementary to *anger.*

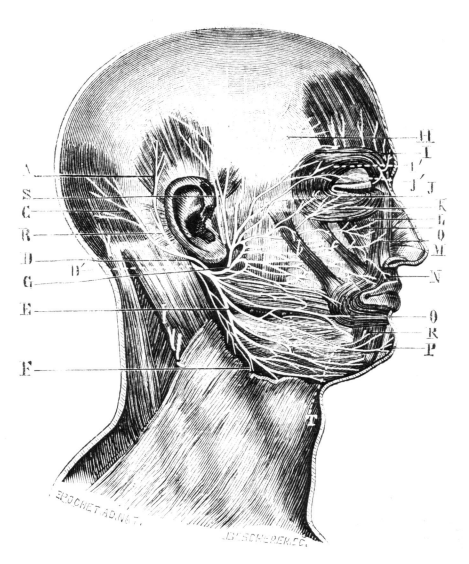

Plate 2a: An anatomical preparation of the motor nerves of the face (of the VIIth nerve). A., B. motor branches to *m. auricularis superior and posterior;* C. motor branch to the occipital belly of *m. occipitofrontalis;* D. turn of the facial nerve at its exit from the facial canal; E. cervicofacial branch; F. motor branch to *m. platysma;* G. temperofacial branch; H. motor branch to *m. frontalis;* I. motor branch to *m. corrugator supercilii;* I'. motor branch to the outer superior part of *m. orbicularis oculi;* J. motor branch to the inferior part of the palpebral portion of *m. orbicularis oculi;* J'. motor branch to the superior part of the palpebral portion of *m. orbicularis oculi;* K. motor branch to the inferior part of *m. orbicularis oculi;* L. motor branch to *m. levator labii superiorus alaeque nasi;* M. motor branch to the transverse part of *m. nasalis;* N., O. motor branch to *m. orbicularis oris;* P. motor branch to *m. mentalis;* Q. motor branch to *m. levator labii superiorus;* R. motor branch to *m. depressor labii inferiorus;* S. auriculotemporal branch of the trigeminal nerve; T. motor nerves to the inferior portion of *m. orbicularis oris, m. depressor labii inferiorus, m. mentalis,* and *m. depressor anguli oris.*

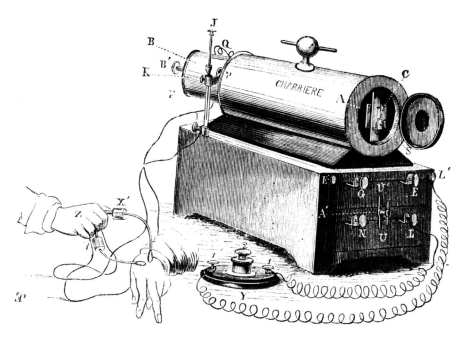

Plate 2b: The double current volta-faradic apparatus of Doctor Duchenne (de Boulogne). A description of this apparatus and the manner in which it was used has appeared in my book *Localized electrization and its application to pathology and therapeutics*, chapter IV, art. 1, §1, 2nd edition.

1. The induction apparatus must be adapted to these types of experiments: The oscillations of its current must be rapid and regular

experiment; I have called it *faradism*, and its use *faradization*. I justify this new name in the following way:

"The word *electrization* can only be used in a general sense.

"The electricity produced by rubbing can be called *static electricity*, and the electricity produced by *contact* of different substances should keep the name *galvanization*. But under this latter name we have, in the past, indifferently designated, in medical practice, both contact electricity and electricity of induction. The annoying consequences of such confusion may be understood after reading further in this work.

"It is necessary to create a word that exactly designates inductive electricity or its application. Should we not, therefore, take the name of the savant who discovered this type of electricity? So, just as Galvani has given his name to contact electricity, in my opinion we should give the name of *Faraday* to inductive electricity. This electricity should be called *faradism*, and its application designated by the word *faradization*. This name seems to me to be a very happy one also, as it establishes a clear distinction between the electricity of induction and contact electricity, and at the same time consecrates the name of a scientist to whom medicine owes a discovery even more precious for therapy than that of Galvani. (Today this distinction is universally accepted within medical practice.)"

enough to avoid the muscle trembling during contraction; gradation of the current must be very precise and adjusted to suit the
differing excitability of each of the facial muscles.

2. The electrodes should be as small as possible, so as not to obscure the
facial features. They are covered with a damp material and placed
on the *motor points*. In the face, these motor points are simplistically
the points under which the motor nerves enter the facial muscles.
We see them in Plate 2a, where the motor nerve fibers of the facial
muscles have been dissected with the greatest care, and in which
the sensory nerves (from the Vth Nerve) have been cut away. I
have indicated these motor points in the captions to the plates in
the following Scientific Section.

Those who would like to verify my experimental results will find these
data insufficient. To initiate them completely into this art of localizing
electrical currents in the muscles of the face, I would have to describe
the anatomical and practical details that are beyond the scope of these
notes.* This type of experiment also demands a lot of experience, for it
is hard to find the motor points through the skin.

The experiment shown in Plate 6 is striking proof. The electrode placed
to stimulate *m. zygomaticus major* produces a contraction of this muscle,
as we also observe in Plate 30; but the current is too intense, with the
effect spreading to the temporofacial branch of the facial nerve (see G,
Plate 2a), provoking the contraction en masse of the muscles supplied
by this nerve trunk. The result is only a grimace.

*These details are set out in my *Monographie sur les muscles de la face* [presented to the
Academies of Science and Medicine in 1850], and in my *Traité de l'électrisation localisé* [1st
ed. 1855, 2nd ed. 1861, 3rd ed. 1872, Paris].

6. The muscle of attention

(m. frontalis, A, Plate 1)

Plates 7, 8, 9, 10, 11
(Alternate and compare the two sides of Plates 7, 9, 10, and 11 by masking the opposite side.)

Plate 7: A study of the mechanism of action of m. frontalis in an old man (see his photographic portrait, Plate 3).
 On the right, a moderate degree of electrical excitation of m. frontalis; fundamental lines (elevation and curvature of the eyebrow) and secondary lines (frontal folds, rounded and concentric with the arch of the eyebrow): attention.
 On the left, a relaxed face.

Plate 8: Showing how the secondary expressive lines of attention join and are continuous at the midline during contraction of the right m. frontalis.*

Plate 9: A study of m. frontalis in maximum contraction.
 On the right maximal excitation of m. frontalis: profound attention.
 On the left, a relaxed face.

Plate 10: Showing the expressive lines of m. frontalis in a young girl (see her portrait, Plate 5).
 On the left, electrization of m. frontalis, with development of the fundamental line (elevation and curvature of the eyebrow, without frontal folds): attention.
 On the right, spontaneous lowering of the eyebrow, due to very bright light.

Plate 11: Showing the secondary lines (frontal ridges, which are both irregular and numerous) produced by strong electrical excitation of m. frontalis, in a woman aged 41 years whose skin was tanned by the sun.
 On the right the electrization of m. frontalis; elevation and curvature of the eyebrow; frontal ridges are irregular and numerous: attention. On the left, a relaxed face.

Further notes on these plates

A.   Technical details

Localized electrization of m. frontalis (A, Plate 1) was achieved by placing one of the electrodes at the point of insertion of the motor nerve (H, Plate 2a) as in Plates 7, 8, 9, 10, and 11.

*There is a discrepancy here in Duchenne's original book. He apparently intended Plate 8 to show bilateral contraction of mm. frontalis (as it does in part 8 of the first Synoptic Plate), [Ed].

In Plate 7, the right *m. frontalis* must have been moderately stimulated, via its motor nerve (N, Plate 2a), when the face was relaxed. We see, on the excited side (the right): (1) that not only is this muscle elevating the eyebrow to a considerable extent, but it is also producing a very pronounced curvature of the eyebrow; (2) that the forehead is wrinkled with curved furrows concentric with the curvature of the eyebrow.

Plate 8 shows moderate electrical stimulation of the right *m. frontalis*. This may be compared to Plate 33, where both *mm. frontalis* are stimulated. In the latter figure, the wrinkles extend right across the forehead. On each side they describe curves with inferior facing concavities that join at the midline. This makes a new curve, with a superior concavity, in which the lines and the radius are smaller than those of the preceding curves. In Plate 33 we notice that the frontal wrinkles are slightly less numerous and less pronounced on the right than on the left. This is the result of a slightly weaker excitation produced by the positive pole of the current.

In Plate 9, where *m. frontalis* is shown in maximum contraction, the eyebrow and the forehead wrinkles no longer describe curves as regular as those in Plates 7 and 8; they are more strongly drawn up on the lateral side. The enlargement of the palpebral fissure, on the excited side, shows that the contraction of *m. frontalis* exerts a noticeable action on the elevation of the upper eyelid.

The young girl in whom I produced a moderate contraction of *m. frontalis* (Plate 10) was 9 years old. Note that her eyebrow is elevated without producing the slightest wrinkle on her forehead; it is the privilege of youth and of adolescence to draw only the fundamental lines during the play of facial expression. Nevertheless, with the maximum contraction of *m. frontalis*, I have produced one or two secondary expressive forehead lines on her forehead.

B.   *Expression*

If you mask the right side of Plate 7 or of Plate 9 with a piece of card, so as to leave only the left side of the face visible, you will notice the profound darkness that envelopes the eye and the orbit of this side, darkness that spreads over the entire cheek.

Rapidly slide the card from right to left so that the forehead and the right cheek stay exposed from the medial extremity of the artificial forehead wrinkles; is the contrast not surprising between these two sides of the face! On the right, the orbit is illuminated, the pupil is sparkling with light; especially in Plate 9, where the contraction is maximal.

And then see the difference between the right cheek and the left cheek. On the left there is darkness, a heaviness of the features, inner calm, and the most complete indifference of expression. On the right, on the contrary, the light of the eye and the orbit shines right across the whole cheek, and the features appear lengthened and their relief modified. What a marvelous transformation of facial expression! It is the awakening of the spirit.

My readers may think that I exaggerate the truth by saying that *the eye sparkles with its own fire, under the influence of an ardent passion,* but the preceding experiment is the incontestable proof of my assertion. Having actually seen this flash in the right eye, this luminous point that sparkles from the pupil, you could be led to believe that this eye has undergone a profound organic modification, under the influence of psychic activity, of a violent emotion. But as soon as you return your gaze to the left side of the face, you note the dull age, which represents the true state of the soul of the subject. It follows from all the evidence therefore that this sparkle of the eye, this fire in the gaze, depends on a specific movement of the eyebrows. If you now compare Plates 7 and 9, you will see that both are expressing a similar state of the spirit, yet they strike the observer with their different appearances. Thus, they announce that (on the right side) the spirit is kept alert by an external cause; they express *attention.*

But we feel that the subject experiences a significantly stronger emotion in Plate 9 than in Plate 7. Plate 9 shows very great attention, almost an expression of surprise or admiration. In Plate 7 the facial expression is more tranquil, the subject being merely attentive.

7. The muscle of reflection

(superior part of *m. orbicularis oculi*, that part of the muscle called the sphincter of the eyelids, B, Plate 1)

Plates 12, 13, 14, 15

(Alternate and compare the two sides of Plates 12 and 14 by masking the opposite side.)

Plate 12: Showing, as does Plate 13, a study of the contraction of and the expression produced by the superior part of *m. orbicularis oculi* (B, Figure 1), in an old man (also shown in Plates 3, 7, 8, 9).
On the right, moderate electrization of the superior part of *m. orbicularis oculi: reflection.*
On the left: *attention.*

Plate 13: Stronger electrization of the superior part of *m. orbicularis oculi,* with slight lowering of the labial commissures: *meditation, mental concentration.*

Plate 14: Designed to show a comparison between the maximal contraction of the superior part of *m. orbicularis oculi* and *m. corrugator supercilii,* in the same individual.
On the left, very strong electrization of the superior part of *m. orbicularis oculi: dissatisfaction, somber thoughts.*
On the right, electrization of *m. corrugator supercilii.*

Plate 15: To demonstrate that the mechanism of voluntary contraction of the superior part of *m. orbicularis oculi* is exactly the same as when it occurs under the influence of the electric current.
A strong voluntary contraction of the superior part of *m. orbicularis oculi* in a young subject (see his photographic portrait, Plate 4): *meditation, mental concentration.*

Further notes on these plates

A. Technical details

At the moment the photograph in Plate 12 was taken, my subject was looking opposite him, at an object on which I had strongly secured his attention; his left eyebrow was raised; his forehead was transversely creased across its whole breadth; his *mm. frontalis* were lightly acting and expressed the state of his spirit: *attention.* Masking the right side of this figure, you recognize on the left the characteristic signs of this expressive movement, signs that have been described in relation to Plates 7 and 8.

If you then uncover the right side, where the superior part of *m. orbicularis oculi* is contracting, you see: (1) that the whole eyebrow is lowered, removing the wrinkles from the forehead; (2) that the eyebrow has become linear; (3) that the eyebrow looks molded, because the hairs that normally sit obliquely from the medial to lateral and from superiorly to inferiorly are standing up. This is the group of movements of the eyebrow always produced by the moderate and isolated contraction of the superior part of *m. orbicularis oculi*.

The vertical line that we can see in Plate 12, medial to the head of the right eyebrow, exists even when the face of this subject is relaxed, as we can see from his portrait in Plate 3. (I have explained the reason for this anomaly elsewhere.) This vertical line usually only appears with a very pronounced molding of the eyebrow, a movement barely induced in the previous experiment, because I had only provoked a moderate contraction of the superior part of *m. orbicularis oculi*.

In Plate 13, the superior part of *m. orbicularis oculi* is contracting on each side more strongly than in Plate 12. The molding is very pronounced and two deep vertical lines have been produced between the heads of the eyebrows. I must say that our old man is not the best subject for studying these vertical lines, which are one of the characteristic signs of a more forceful action of the spirit, of the thinking process.

We usually see them developed beautifully and purely in the space between the eyebrows, where the cutaneous surface is smooth during muscular repose in those of less advanced age.

These vertical lines between the eyebrows are well shown in the young man photographed (see Plate 15) while indulging in a great effort of thinking. This expressive movement of the eyebrow, produced by meditation and arising from the soul, is absolutely the same as the one in the preceding experiment (see Plate 13) that was produced by the electrical contraction of the superior part of *m. orbicularis oculi*. The differences between these two figures are entirely due to the individual conditions of the two subjects, above all their difference in age. One is old and ugly (see his portrait, Plate 3); the other young and handsome (see his portrait, Plate 4); the skin of the brow and of the space between the eyebrows of the latter is perfectly smooth, due to his youth; his forehead is high, the curvature of it is quite pronounced and tends to be rectilinear, which suggests the habit of reflection. Finally, in the space between his eyebrows, two beautiful vertical lines have been created by the efforts of meditation.

When the contraction of the superior part of *m. orbicularis oculi* is at a maximum, the molding of the eyebrow is such that in certain slender and elderly people we see some radiating vertical folds in the skin form above the medial portion of the eyebrow: this is evident on the left side of Plate 14, where I have induced an energetic contraction of the superior part of *m. orbicularis oculi*.

B.   Expression

Let us return to the experiment studying the movements of the superior part of *m. orbicularis oculi*, shown in Plate 12. Look alternately and compare the different parts of the face. What do we feel when viewing these two different facial expressions?

We see on the right that the attention of the subject has just been caught by an external cause. This was the state of his spirit at the moment of the experiment, as I have already said. On the left, he seems to be collecting his thoughts, gathering his concentration, in order to reflect on the object that, on the opposite side, had taken his attention: It is a picture of reflection without exertion. The presence of an electrode tells us that his spirit has nothing to do with it, that it is all artificial; that the electrical current alone has made the muscle contract that portrays reflection and thinking.

The old man whose portrait appears in Plate 3 is, we know, a fairly simple-minded character. Yet, if we look only at the right side of his face in Plate 12, we see a profound thought, which transforms and ennobles all the features of the face – they seem distinguished and spiritual. Seeing such a reflective air, one would credit this man with great intelligence.

Such is the magical effect of this movement imprinted on the eyebrow by the superior part of *m. orbicularis oculi*.

We could object that the eyebrow is naturally lowered in the subject undergoing these experiments, singularly favoring the expression of reflection. This observation seems legitimate; for it would clearly be impossible to express reflection or meditation to such a high degree, with an eyebrow that is naturally held very high and where the superior part of *m. orbicularis oculi* is poorly developed. Yet, in the very cases where I have encountered these unfavorable conditions for the development of this expression, I have always seen that moderate contraction of this muscle imprints the seal of reflection on the face.

It would have been easy for me to furnish the proof, even by choosing a model in which the eyebrows are naturally elevated, showing flippancy or thoughtlessness. We would have seen the *muscle of reflection*, under the influence of my electrodes, fix, so to speak, an expression that is normally fleeting and spread a serious and reflective expression across the face. This artificial state of one side of the face would have formed a striking contrast with the normal state on the opposite side, where I would not have influenced the superior part of *m. orbicularis oculi*.

Compare Plate 13 with Plate 12. They show the same muscle contracting in the same individual, but to different degrees. Plate 12, as I have just demonstrated, shows calm reflection because the muscular contraction is moderate. In Plate 13, we recognize meditation requiring effort. These strongly lowered eyebrows, linear, puckered, inclined medially, draw the night around the eye, one might say. These eyebrows have distended heads and the space between them is creased by vertical lines; these eyebrows, tormented by thought, declare the laborious work of the spirit.

8. The muscle of aggression

(*m. procerus*, P, Plate 1)

Plates 16, 17, 18

Plate 16: Showing that *m. procerus* terminates superiorly in the skin at the level of the heads of the eyebrows. Electrical contraction of both *mm. procerus* in a young man of gentle character (see his portrait, Plate 4): expression of *severity*.

Plate 17: A study of the expressive action of *m. procerus* in an old man (also shown in Plates 3, 7, 8, 9, 12, 13, and 14). On the right, electrization of *m. procerus*: *severity, aggression*. On the left: *attention*.

Plate 18: Strong electrization of both *mm. procerus*: *aggression, wickedness*.

Further notes on these plates

A.   Technical details

The experiment shown in Plate 16 sheds light on a previously unknown anatomical fact: The superior termination of *m. procerus* (P, Plate 1) is in the skin between, and at the level of, the heads of the two eyebrows, explaining the complete independence of this muscle. The electrodes have been placed on the root of the nose and we see that the skin of the inter-eyebrow space is drawn from above and below. A transverse furrow is thus formed at the level of the head of the eyebrow. This furrow does not exist in Plate 4, which shows the face of the same individual in repose.

The electrodes have not produced any muscular movement at the point corresponding to this transverse furrow; this is a new proof that the neutral point of the transverse furrow marks the insertion of *m. procerus*.

Immediately below the line traced by this transverse ridge, the electrodes have pulled the skin from below upward in an opposite sense to *m. procerus*; this shows that this muscle is not only independent of *m. frontalis* but that it is also its antagonist.

In order to understand the importance of these facts, I recall that

56

anatomists have professed up until this day that *mm. procerus* are the continuation of *mm. frontalis*, of which they constitute the pillars. Mr. Ludovic Hirschfeld, guided by my experiments, has verified by dissection that there is a point of termination of *m. procerus* before the continuation of *m. frontalis*. I have called this termination a neutral point, which consists of an aponeurosis. It is seen well in Plate 6.

When the skin of the forehead above the space between the eyebrows yields to the action of *m. procerus* easily, we no longer see the transverse ridge, denoting the superior termination and the cutaneous insertion of this muscle, drawn in such a pronounced manner as in the subject in Plate 16.

Thus, in the old man shown in Plates 17 and 18, the mobile skin of his forehead has been pulled down by the electrical contraction of *m. procerus* and the skin of the root of the nose, compressed inferiorly, is ridged by many transverse folds.

Finally, in Plates 16, 17, and 18, the head of the eyebrow is drawn downward by *m. procerus,* and the skin of the forehead is yielding to the action of this muscle. The eyebrow no longer describes its natural curve; its medial half has an oblique direction downward and inward, and the skin of the central part of the forehead is rendered tight and smooth.

B.   Expression

Despite the weakness of the action of *m. procerus* on the head of the eyebrow and the space between the eyebrows, it still gives a certain severity to the most pleasant look and announces *aggression.*

We see this phenomenon in Plate 16. The *mm. procerus* are in energetic contraction and yet the lowering of the head of the eyebrow is moderate, as is the puckering of the inter-eyebrow space.

I have said that the skin of the central part of the forehead resists the action of *mm. procerus* in this subject, to the point where their superior terminal fibers have created a deep groove in the inter-eyebrow space. And in spite of the habitual pleasantness of his countenance (see his portrait in a relaxed state, Plate 4), his face has taken on a harsh expression, if not one of wickedness, solely through the light action of *m. procerus* on his eyebrow. But the potential of *m. procerus* is limited in this subject. As much as I tried, by tormenting these muscles, I could not create a completely wicked expression, one of hatred, which I could in others obtain easily, by the energetic contraction of *m. procerus.*

There is another curious fact that may shed some light. This subject has practiced moving the muscles of his eyebrows. He is such a master of it that not only can he give his eyebrow various expressions, but he can move the muscles in opposite directions. Yet, in spite of his control over the muscles that move the eyebrow, he cannot voluntarily move *m. procerus* in the slightest. Whatever he does, he cannot give his face an expression of hardness, of aggression, or of wickedness. This fact may be explained by the paucity of development of the muscles that represent this emotion – muscles that, in his case, obey only the electrodes. This young man is a very pleasant character but probably, if his worst emotions came to dominate, their repetitive exercise would very quickly develop *m. procerus* and change the habitual expression of his face.

Returning to our old man (the main subject of our experiments), whose pleasant and inoffensive character is recognized in his portrait (Plate 3). We know that his eyebrow is very mobile in all directions and easily obeys the muscles that move it. We have already seen with what power his eyebrow can be lowered as a whole, how the head of the eyebrow is puckered and wrinkled, while at the same time two deep identical lines form creases between the heads. This ensemble of movements and lines results from the energetic contraction of the superior part of *m. orbicularis oculi*. With the contraction of this muscle, we have seen the appearance of somber thoughts (Plate 13), without traces of wickedness.

But the moment that I produce strong contraction of *m. procerus*, his look becomes wicked or menacing.

The right side of Plate 17 can serve to analyze the general influence of *m. procerus* on facial expression, although the action of this muscle, which is only contracting on one side, is less complete than when the two *mm. procerus* are excited simultaneously.

If we alternately cover each of the sides of this figure, one is struck by the contrast between their expressions.

On the right, due to the contraction of *m. procerus*, the medial extremity of the eyebrow is lowered, causing a decrease in the angle of the medial canthus of the eye covering the lachrymal caruncle, and the root of the nose has many transverse wrinkles. His face has taken on an expression of severity and this expression modifies the other features.

This phenomenon can be demonstrated by covering and uncovering the eye on the right side. This man has a habitually good posture of the mouth (see Plate 3). One can verify this in Plate 17, when the right eye is covered; but at the instant when this eye is uncovered the lips seem to tighten under the influence of a wicked thought.* On the left, to the contrary, the facial expression remains calm.

---

*It is difficult to limit the action of a muscle as small as *m. procerus* to one side very precisely. This is why the space between the eyebrows on the left side of this figure is deformed by the contraction of *m. procerus* of the right side. For the same reason, the transverse lines of the root of the nose extend a little to the left; and the wrinkles of the

Plate 18, where the two *mm. procerus* of the same subject are contract-ing simultaneously and energetically, reveals an expression of wicked-ness, of hatred, which is repulsive. We all fear this look; only one with a cruel and ferocious nature has the power to give naturally such an expression.

I must pause for a moment to describe an accident that occurred dur-ing this experiment.

We see, in Plate 18, that the labial commissures are much lowered, which adds to the expression belonging to *m. procerus*. The commissures of this individual fall naturally (see Plate 3), as in old people generally. Left to itself, this sagging will go a long way, as in Plate 18. This habitual feature, which is in harmony with his old man's face, only makes him seem older. When his face was relaxed, I was often forced to rouse his attention, or to make him open and close his mouth alternately before photographing him, to prevent this exaggerated sagging of the commis-sures. I had neglected to take this precaution during this last experi-ment; and as a result the commissures are lower down than in the other figures.

The expression in Plate 18 is so characteristic that I have kept the pho-tograph. It is useful, moreover, for studying the combined contraction of *m. procerus* and *m. depressor anguli oris*. This latter muscle (I can say this in anticipation), expresses only *sadness* by itself; but we see, in this Plate, that the sagging of the labial commissures adds to the expression of wickedness belonging to the isolated action of *m. procerus*.

In spite of the accident that complicated this experiment, we can fur-ther analyze the expressive influence of *m. procerus* by hiding the inferior part of the face including the upper lip. Is it possible to see a more wicked look? It proclaims a ferocious instinct: It is the eye of a tiger.

forehead on the left side, above all the first, are dragged a little inferiorly and medially. If we wish to understand exactly the normal expression of the subject, we must mask these deformities by covering the right side of the face up to the beginning of the left eyebrow. These precautions taken, we see that the left side of his face does not portray any inner agitation, and that his countenance has nothing hard in it, in spite of the thickness of his eyebrows.

9. The muscle of pain

(*m. corrugator supercilii*, O, Plate 1)

Plates 19, 20, 21, 22, 23, 24, 25, 26, 27, 28, 29

(Compare each of the sides of Plates 19, 21, 22, 24, 27, and 28 while covering the opposite side.)

Plate 19: A study, as in Plate 20, of both the fundamental and secondary expressive lines produced by the moderate electrical contraction of *m. corrugator supercilii*, in an old man (also shown in Plates 3, 6, 7, 8, 9, 12, 13, 14, 17, and 18).

On the right, the electrical contraction of *m. corrugator supercilii* to a moderate degree: *suffering*.

On the left, the face is relaxed, with a lost look (the subject was in this state at the time of the experiment).

Plate 20: Electrical stimulation, to a moderate degree, of *m. corrugator supercilii: profound suffering, with resignation*. (The face was relaxed at the time of the experiment, as in the preceding figure, but the face has been illuminated in such a way as to throw a strong shadow across its lower half.)

Plate 21: Showing the antagonism between *m. corrugator supercilii* and *m. frontalis* in the same individual.

(At the time of the experiment the gaze of the subject was directed upward and his forehead was furrowed across its whole breadth, as seen in the left side of this figure.)

On the right, moderate electrical stimulation of *m. corrugator supercilii* and an upward gaze: *painful recollection*. On the left, a voluntary contraction of *m. frontalis* and an upward gaze: *recollection* or *calling something to mind*.

Plate 22: Beyond a certain degree of contraction, and in some conditions, *m. corrugator supercilii* is no longer expressive.

On the left, maximal electrical stimulation of *m. corrugator supercilii*: no painful expression; it only looks like a spasm of *m. corrugator supercilii* under the influence of a very strong light.

On the right, a relaxed face (photographed in full sunshine).

Plate 23: The expressive lines produced by *m. corrugator supercilii* contracting to a moderate degree in a young subject (also represented in Plates 4, 15, and 16). A moderate degree of voluntary contraction of *m. corrugator supercilii* and an upward gaze: *painful recollection or painful thoughts*.

Plate 24: A stronger degree of voluntary contraction than in Plate 23, in the same subject

60

seen full face, in whom the eye is obliquely turned superiorly and laterally, compared to the contraction of *m. frontalis*, with the same movement of the eye. On the left, the voluntary contraction of *m. corrugator supercilii* to a stronger degree than in Plate 23, the gaze upward and outward, the mouth half open: *extreme pain* to the point of exhaustion; the subject seems to succumb to suffering: *the head of Christ*.

On the right, the voluntary contraction of *m. frontalis* with the gaze a little obliquely superiorly and medially and with the mouth a little opened: *memory of love* or *ecstatic gaze*.

Plate 25: Very strong spasm of *mm. corrugator supercilii*, produced by shining a strong light, in the same subject seen in profile: *not an expression of pain*.

Plate 26: The median forehead wrinkles produced by the contraction of *m. corrugator supercilii*, in a 52-year-old woman, shown also in Plate 11, whose skin is thin and burned by the wind and sun.

On the right, moderate electrical stimulation of *m. corrugator supercilii* with a lateral gaze: expression of *painful attention*. On the left, a light voluntary contraction of *m. frontalis*, with a slightly lateral gaze: *attention, attentive gaze*.

Plate 27: Same experiment as in the preceding plate; but, in this one, the electrical stimulation of *m. corrugator supercilii* on the right is stronger and the expression proportionally more pained.

Plate 28: To study the fundamental expressive lines, produced by the gentle contraction of the *m. corrugator supercilii*, in a 6-year-old girl (previously shown in Plates 5 and 10). On the right, gentle electrical contraction of *m. corrugator supercilii*: *pain*. On the left, spasm causing lowering of the whole eyebrow, produced by shining a light into the eyes.

Plate 29: Stronger electrical stimulation of *m. corrugator supercilii* with an upward gaze, in an 8-year-old girl: *painful memories* – an unnatural expression for this age.

Further notes on these plates

(The action of *m. corrugator supercilii* is poorly known; yet it plays such an important role in facial expression and the practical application of the new notions revealed by my electrophysiological study that I have chosen a greater number of figures for this than for the other muscles moving the eyebrow.)

A. Technical details

The *m. corrugator supercilii* (O, Plate 1), covered by the superior part of *m. orbicularis oculi*, can only be excited by its motor nerve, outside the peripheral fibers of the superior part of *m. orbicularis oculi*. This nerve comes from the upper eyelid and is subcutaneous at two points (see I, Plate 2a). We see that the electrode is applied at the first point in Plates 19, 20, 21, and 22, and at the second point in Plates 26, 27, 28, and 29.

Plate 28 represents the first degree of contraction of *m. corrugator su-*

percilii on the right in a 6-year-old girl. The head of her eyebrow is puckered and is gently elevated. In an adult, this movement is the same, but a little more accentuated.

In Plate 19, the right *m. corrugator supercilii* is energetically contracting in an old man who often served in my experiments (see his portrait, Plate 3). We note: (1) that the head of his eyebrow is puckered and elevated, forming an outline that extends a little onto the forehead; (2) that the eyebrow has become oblique downward and outward as a sinuous line made up of two curves, one medial, with a superior concavity, the other lateral, with an inferior concavity; (3) that several transverse skin folds have developed on the central part of the forehead, on the stimulated side, and that lateral to these folds the skin has flattened above the medial part of the eyebrow; (4) finally, that the skin is stretched at the level of the head of the eyebrow and the inter-eyebrow space, while it is pushed down beneath the lateral two-thirds of the eyebrow.

These lines, reliefs, and planes are more regular and better accentuated in Plate 20, where *m. corrugator supercilii* is seen contracting on each side. The central wrinkles of the forehead reunite and describe at the midline a small curve that has a superior concavity. Finally they end laterally at an imaginary vertical line that would fall at the union of the medial third of the eyebrow with its middle third.

These furrows are about four in number in Plates 20, but in the woman shown in Plates 26 and 27, the central lines of the forehead are more numerous. I have counted up to eight or ten of them, when I have energetically stimulated both *mm. corrugator supercilii* at the same time. This is what happens in aged subjects in whom the skin is very delicate or has been exposed to the air and the sun for a long time, as in the woman I have just been talking about (she is Roumanian, and lived in Naples for a long period).

In her case these central lines of the forehead are closer together and are intersected often by little oblique wrinkles. During muscular relaxation, this woman's forehead is furrowed in all its breadth by wrinkles so numerous that on the lateral part of the forehead they cannot be erased entirely by the strong contraction of *m. corrugator supercilii* (see Plate 27). In Plate 26, where the contraction of *m. corrugator supercilii* is less strong, these forehead wrinkles are also retained.

The little vertical wrinkles that we see below the electrode in Plates 26 and 27 would not have existed if the location of the current had been precisely limited to the motor point of the nerve to *m. corrugator supercilii*. The electrode has touched some of the most lateral fibers of the superior portion of *m. orbicularis oculi,* which has contracted and produced these wrinkles.

Plates 23, 24, and 25 show us that in a young adult, the central furrows of the forehead produced by *m. corrugator supercilii* are less numerous; and that the lines are not interrupted by little cracks or wrinkles, as in Plates 19 and 20. Two of them are seen in Plate 23, where the eyebrow is moderately puckered; and in Plates 24 and 25, we can distinguish a third, but only very lightly, because the production of these central lines is stronger. The curvature of these median lines of the forehead is graceful and more pronounced than in Plate 20. The skin folds between these lines are more full, more rounded, and form a wavelike pattern.

In two little girls, aged 6 and 8 years, shown in Plates 28 and 29, the moderate contraction of *m. corrugator supercilii* has not produced the central lines of the forehead. Maximum excitation in the older child produced a slight central fold that we would have seen in Plate 29, if she had been photographed full face.

In all the preceding figures, the direction of the eyebrow has become more oblique as the contraction of *m. corrugator supercilii* has become stronger. We notice that the eyebrow is more oblique in Plate 22 than in Plates 19 and 20, in Plate 25 than in Plates 23 and 24, in Plate 27 than in Plate 26, and in Plate 29 than in Plate 28. The reason for this is the varying degree of contraction of *m. corrugator supercilii.* There are, however, subjects in whom *m. corrugator supercilii,* even at its maximum contraction, does not give much obliquity to the eyebrow, because the head of their eyebrow is held back by a powerful *m. procerus* muscle.

The anatomical arrangements of *m. corrugator supercilii* perfectly explain the movements imprinted by this muscle on the eyebrow; the bulges, the planes, and the lines that develop under its influence.

Its fibers play in all directions; some pull the head of the eyebrow up, while others pull the outer two-thirds of the eyebrow obliquely down and in.

We should remember that the superior portion of *m. orbicularis oculi* lowers the whole eyebrow and stretches the skin of the forehead above it, that is, it acts on the head of the eyebrow in the opposite sense to *m. corrugator supercilii,* while it is synergistic with this latter muscle in the lateral two-thirds of the eyebrow.

Thus *m. corrugator supercilii* is antagonistic to *m. procerus* and to the superior portion of *m. orbicularis oculi* for the head of the eyebrow.

Finally, this muscle is equally antagonistic to *m. frontalis* for the lateral third of the eyebrow and is synergistic for the medial third.

I asked my subject to wrinkle his forehead strongly, which he could do without gazing upward; then, at the moment when *mm. frontalis* had raised his two eyebrows en masse and creased his forehead across all its breadth, I stimulated his right *m. corrugator supercilii*. With moderate stimulation of this muscle the modeling of the eyebrow and the forehead did not change; but with a greater intensity of current, the contraction of *m. corrugator supercilii* overcame that of *m. frontalis*.

We see the results of this experiment in Plate 21. On the left, his eyebrow is elevated en masse and the skin of his forehead is furrowed by wrinkles across all its breath by *mm. frontalis*. This movement was produced by the subject's will and was therefore produced equally on both sides. But on the right, where I have stimulated the more energetic contraction of *m. corrugator supercilii*, the arch of the eyebrow is replaced by a sinuous curve passing obliquely down and outward. Furthermore, the skin of the forehead is furrowed only in its central part; in the outer sections the long transverse wrinkles caused by *m. frontalis* have disappeared.

To sum up, wrinkles that spread across the whole breadth of the forehead cannot coexist with either a downward and outward direction or with a sinuous form of the eyebrow. Conversely, the archlike elevation of the whole eyebrow cannot produce wrinkles limited to the central part of the forehead.

B.   *Expression*

The slightest contraction of *m. corrugator supercilii*, in childhood, always gives the face an acute expression of suffering. One cannot look at the right side of Plate 28, where this muscle is weakly stimulated, without being touched by the pain the young girl seems to experience. To really experience the expression in this plate take care to cover the left side. During repose the eyebrows of this child usually describe a beautiful curve, a little like the left side of Plate 10 (the right eyebrow is however more elevated than its usual state by the electrical excitation of *m. frontalis*). This curve, which reflects innocence and interior calm, was present when I commenced my experiment and contrasts with the painful movements of the right eyebrow. Unhappily, my little model was unable to tolerate the strong light of the studio for long and frowned (as we see in her portrait, Plate 5, and on the right side of Plate 10), without, however, being able to modify the sinuous and painful movement artificially given to her right eyebrow.

But a child quickly forgets pain. No moral suffering for her. The expression of Plate 29, which portrays a painful memory, a sadness of the soul, is far less touching than that of Plate 28. This is because the expression of mental anguish is not natural at this age. It is obtained in this other little girl by the association of *m. corrugator supercilii* with the voluntary elevation of the eyes.

We again recognize a distressing memory, a bitter thought, in Plate 23. This expression may be true and natural in this young man. His pained gaze, so constantly turned to the sky, may indicate that his soul is drawn toward God from whom he implores help in his suffering or unhappiness.

His sorrow is even more pronounced in Plate 24. His eyebrow has become sinuous and more oblique and the outlines and planes of his forehead more accentuated, with the more energetic contraction of *m. corrugator supercilii*. The association of this strong muscular contraction with an upward and slightly oblique gaze has given an expression of severe and sharp pain; but this expressive movement is seen only on the left, and without the use of electrical stimulation.

There may be an explanation for this strange phenomenon.

I have said that this young man, shown in Plates 23 and 24, and whose portrait is seen in Plate 4, practiced contracting the individual muscles of his eyebrow to such an extent that he could move his eyebrows in opposite directions. This is why he was able to contract *m. frontalis* on one side and *m. corrugator supercilii* on the other, as we see in Plate 24. Plate 23 proves that he can also independently move his *m. corrugator supercilii*. I have repeated this experiment by electrically stimulating these same muscles and seen these movements reproduced exactly with the lines and reliefs seen in Plate 24. So we can understand how and why the eyebrows in this last figure have performed different movements. Of course, to assess properly the painful influence of *m. corrugator super-cilii* in Plate 24, we must mask the right eye.

The subject in Plates 26 and 27, who was specially photographed to study the central, "painful" lines of the forehead, is middle-aged and her skin is very delicate and damaged by long exposure to the elements. These two plates show us another nuance of pain. The direction of the gaze of the woman shows that her emotions are aroused by an outside cause. When I took these photographs, I fixed her attention on a point in front and a little to the side of her. By masking the stimulated side of these plates we can see that the natural expression of this woman was *attention*. If then we uncover the excited side, we see the expression of *pain*. It seems that the object that has secured her attention has affected her painfully. These two plates only differ in the degree of pain that they express, in the direction of their gaze, and in the manner in which they are lit. Thus, in Plate 26, where the electrical excitation of *m. corrugator supercilii* is much less strong than in Plate 27, the expression is correspondingly less pained.

I have made the two eyebrows of the aged man contract in Plate 20, starting when his features were in complete repose, as in his portrait (Plate 3). We notice that this photograph is more strongly lit. I have used chiaroscuro in Plate 20 to illuminate the region on which I was experimenting better and to bring it into relief. Consequently, the lower two-thirds of the facial oval have been plunged into shadow, *without his face undergoing modification*. It stayed just as calm, just as indifferent as in Plate 3. We can confirm this by covering the forehead and the eyebrows of the figure. But at the instant *m. corrugator supercilii* was stimulated, the face, as in Plate 20, took on an expression of *suffering*, which became more pronounced with the stronger stimulus.

In fact, this is the expression of profound pain. On seeing this figure we know that this man is very unhappy. Is his heart broken? Is he tormented by mental anguish or by a physical ailment? His expression cannot tell us. However, although all his features seem wracked by pain, he suffers it with resignation.

We can now examine the general and specific influence of *m. corrugator supercilii* on the features of the face.

I mentioned, in the general introduction, that "there are some muscles that depict exclusively a particular expression, by their own isolated action: These are the muscles that move the eyebrow."

It was only by analyzing the anatomy and physiology of the muscles of the face that I shed light on this most interesting unexpected fact; its accuracy had already emerged from the experiments on the other muscles that move the eyebrow. It remained for me to complete the demonstration using the plates that demonstrate *m. corrugator supercilii*.

If we cover the forehead in Plate 19 to just below the eyebrow, we see that the expression is neutral and that the two sides of the face are equal. If we can cover, say, the left half of this same figure, it seems that all the features of the other half (the mouth, the nasolabial fold) are painfully contracted, putting themselves in harmony with the eyebrow and the forehead.

This general movement, which apparently operates in the areas situated below the eyebrow, is easier to show in Plate 20, where the *muscle of pain* has been excited bilaterally. I have already said that the face of my subject was absolutely in repose at the start of the experiment; we have verified this by covering his forehead and his eyebrows. Then we have seen that, at the moment when the forehead and the eyebrows have been uncovered, all the features of the face seem to show the subject in pain.

Every time I have publicly repeated this experiment on this subject, the illusion has been such that I could not convince the spectators that a general movement was not operating in the rest of the face at the same time as the eyebrow. But with this photograph doubt is dispelled, for it would be absurd to say that the features can be thus changed on paper.

These facts become even more evident when we cover the forehead of this same plate, after having studied it uncovered.

I have performed this experiment a great number of times, in the presence of distinguished artists. So as not to influence them, I did not explain my object. In seeing this face in its entirety, they attributed his expression of suffering to a general contraction of all the facial features. The mouth and the nasolabial fold in particular held their attention. "How obviously suffering and yet how resigned is this mouth," they said to me! "And this nasolabial fold, how it seems to be pulled by the pain!" Their surprise was profound when I covered the eyebrows of my subject and made a calm expression fall across these lower features.

This experiment showed them that they had been deceived by an error of the senses. It was then easy for me to convince them that the movement of the eyebrow alone had disturbed the general tranquility of the facial features. The same experiment, performed on the other figures where the *muscle of pain* has been excited, gave identical results.

In summary, the expressive movements of the *muscle of pain* create an illusion that is inherent in our senses, and to which I referred in the general introduction that preceded the study of the individual facial muscles.

We can repeat this experiment in another way: by alternately uncovering and comparing each eye, and we see, on the side where *m. corrugator supercilii* is contracting, that all the features of the face appear to contract painfully.

Plates 22 and 25 prove that there is a degree of contraction beyond which *m. corrugator supercilii* loses its expressive property. Under these conditions it is nothing more than a violent spasm of the muscle, produced, for example, by a blinding light. The subject in Plate 22 has been photographed in full sunlight and his right eye does not seem uncomfortable. If we look at the left side, after masking the right, we do not see an expression of pain, though his *m. corrugator supercilii* was being stimulated. I always noticed this when the contraction of the muscle was forced, as in this plate, and when the eye and the forehead were very well lit.

We frequently see this spasm of *m. corrugator supercilii* in people who are disturbed by a very bright light. I wanted to show this natural spasm in Plate 25. I asked my subject to look at a wall lit by the sun and which brightly reflected it. He was contracting his *mm. corrugator supercilii* in a strong and involuntary way as I photographed him. Compare this picture to Plates 23 and 24, and you will see that none of them expresses pain; we recognize only that *mm. corrugator supercilii* are in spasm.

10. The muscles of joy and benevolence

(*m. zygomaticus major* and the inferior part of *m. orbicularis oculi*, I and E, Plate 1)

Plates 30, 31, 32, 33, 34, 35, 36

(Compare alternately the two sides of Plates 30, 35 and 36, by masking the opposite side.)

Plate 30: To study the fundamental and secondary expressive lines produced by the contraction of *m. zygomaticus major* in an old man (shown also in Plates 3, 6, 7, 8, 9, 12, 13, 14, 17, 18, 19, 20, 21, and 22). On the right, electrical excitation, which is strong but quite limited to *m. zygomaticus major*, showing development of the fundamental and secondary lines of this muscle: *false joy* or *laughter*. On the left, a relaxed face.

Plate 31: Slightly stronger electrical excitation of both *mm. zygomaticus major*: development of the same fundamental and secondary expressive lines of *joy*, with mild contraction of some fibers of the muscle called the sphincter of the eyelids: *false laughter*.

Plate 32: The same subject as in Plates 30 and 31, showing that natural laughter really is constituted by the association of *m. zygomaticus major* and the inferior part of *m. orbicularis oculi*. *Natural laughter*, by the voluntary contraction of the two *mm. zygomaticus major* and of the inferior part of *mm. orbicularis oculi*.

Plate 33: The same subject, showing that the wrinkles radiating from the lateral canthus of the eyelids, due to the action of *mm. zygomaticus major*, disappear when *mm. frontalis* is stimulated at the same time. Maximal stimulation of *mm. zygomaticus major* and of *mm. frontalis*: a false incomplete expression of *agreeable surprise*, or *admiration*.

Plate 34: Showing, in the same subject, that the combination of the muscles of *joy* and *pain*, at certain degrees of contraction, will only produce a grimace. Strong electrical contraction of *m. zygomaticus major* and of *m. corrugator supercilii: grimace*.

Plate 35: To study the expressive lines produced by the strong and isolated contraction of *m. zygomaticus major* in a young woman. (This woman was depressed at the time of the experiment, which we can see from the slight lowering of the angle of the mouth on the left side). On the right, the fairly strong electrical excitation of *m. zygomaticus major* and mild excitation of the palpebral part of *m. orbicularis oculi*: fundamental lines belonging to the *muscle of joy: false laughter*.

Plate 36: To study the association of either *m. zygomaticus major* or *m. depressor anguli oris*, its antagonist, with the palpebral part of *m. orbicularis oculi*. (This woman was confronted by a light that was too bright at the moment of the experiment, and was spasmically contracting the palpebral parts of her *m. orbicularis oculi*.) On the right, stimulation of *m.*

69

zygomaticus major associated with a slight voluntary contraction of the palpebral part of *m. orbicularis oculi: scornful laughter.* On the left, strong electrical stimulation of *m. depressor anguli oris* associated with a moderate voluntary contraction of the palpebral part of *m. orbicularis oculi: scornful disgust.*

Further notes on these plates

A.   Technical details

The insertion of the motor nerve (see Plate 2a) of *m. zygomaticus major* is made a little below the superior attachment of this muscle, that is, 2½ centimeters to 3 centimeters inferomedial to the external angle of the eye. It is approximately at this point that the electrodes have been placed in all the electrophysiological experiments that I have done on *m. zygomaticus major* (see Plates 30, 31, 33, 34, 35, 36). On the left side of Plate 31, where the two *mm. zygomaticus major* were simultaneously put into action, the electrode corresponding to the negative pole, which excites more than the positive pole, has been positioned inferior to the motor point of *m. zygomaticus major,* so that the muscular contraction would be equal on each side.

Sometimes I was able to localize the stimulus exactly within the muscle, as in the right side of Plate 30. This exact localization was fairly difficult, for the electrical current often spread to one or two motor filaments that supplied neighboring muscle fascicles, when the current was a little too intense or when an unrecognized anatomical anomaly existed. We see an example on the right side of Plate 35, where the current has lightly stimulated the palpebral parts of *m. orbicularis oculi,* at the same time as *m. zygomaticus major.*

Plate 30, where the electrical excitation is perfectly localized to *m. zygomaticus major,* shows the ensemble of the fundamental and secondary lines that, at an advanced age, develop with energetic contraction of this muscle.

I have said elsewhere: (1) that these fundamental lines, which develop at all ages, in an old man as in a young adult, are constituted by the superolateral oblique movement of the nasolabial fold, by bulging of the cheeks, and finally by the slight elevation of the lower eyelid; (2) that the secondary lines consist of the wrinkles radiating from the lateral canthus of the eyelids. These latter only appear in the adult becoming even more numerous and deeper as age advances, especially if the skin has been burned by the sun.

All the lines and the reliefs produced by *m. zygomaticus major* are shown in Plate 31.

In this figure, the muscles are stimulated on both sides at the same time and more strongly than in Plate 30; consequently, we see the lines radiating from the lateral canthus of the eye are deeper and the convexity of the nasolabial curve is more pronounced.

On the right side of Plates 35 and 36, where *m. zygomaticus major* is as strongly stimulated as in Plate 30, we don't see the secondary lines at the lateral canthus of the eyelids. This is because the subject of these experiments had not reached the age when these lines habitually appear in our climate.

The first wrinkle appears at the lateral canthus of the eye and the rest follow; increasing in length and in depth, in direct relation to age and general build of the subject. In the old man photographed in Plates 30 and 31, six or seven wrinkles radiate on each side. I have counted greater numbers in other subjects.

The origin, insertion, and orientation of *m. zygomaticus major* and the condition of the skin, would account perfectly for the formation of the fundamental and secondary lines so well shown in Plates 30, 31, and 33. The tugging of the labial commissure obliquely in a superolateral direction results in (1) the inferior part of the nasolabial fold describing a slight curve with an inferior convexity; (2) the skin of the cheek being forced back superolaterally to form a more pronounced contour, and slightly elevating the lower eyelid; and (3) the formation of folds and wrinkles at the lateral canthus of the eyelids, which occurs more rapidly when the skin has been burned by the elements, and when the muscle is frequently exercised by habitual gaiety.

B. Expression

The *m. zygomaticus major* is the only muscle that expresses *joy* to all its degrees and in all its nuances, from the simple smile to the raucous laugh. It never portrays any other expression.

The best name that we could find from its expressive action is the *muscle of joy*, though this is not completely justified when it contracts in isolation.

See the subject in Plates 30 and 31: His *mm. zygomaticus major* are at maximum contraction. At first glance, he seems to be abandoned to the most frank and open laughter, but a moment's attention shows that his gaiety is false; the more you look at this laughing mouth, the more it strikes you by its falseness. Don't accuse the exaggeration of the laugh for its falseness; for if I show you the subject smiling, the isolated contractions of *m. zygomaticus major* will seem just as unsympathetic. Nor blame the ugliness of his face, for the same experiment done on the most beautiful visage would offend you just as much and excite your defiance.

Compare Plates 30 and 31, in which the laughter is false and deceptive, with Plate 32, which shows this man when I had made him spontaneously laugh; you sense that in the latter his laugh is honest and open. We notice, however, in all these plates, the same curved line separating the lips, the same sinuosity of the nasolabial folds, the same projection of the cheeks, and the same lines radiating from the lateral canthus of the eye. It is only a particular movement of the lower eyelid that makes these figures different. Indeed, cover the upper part of the figure just to the inferior border of the orbit, and you will see that they laugh just as well as one another, and even that Plate 31 expresses the wildest gaiety. But the moment the eye is uncovered, you can see, in Plate 32, that it is in perfect harmony with the labial commissures and completes the expression of pleasure and gaiety. Whereas in Plates 30 and 31 (more so in the former) the indifference of the eye contrasts strikingly with the widespread joyous expansion and gaiety of the inferior part of the face.

This movement of the lower eyelid, without which no joy could be painted on the face truthfully, needs to be studied fully. In Plate 32, about 4 mm from the margin of the lower eyelid, a transverse depression has formed, with a superior concavity, and above this depression the skin of the eyelid is slightly swollen and bunched, whereas beneath the depression it is taut.

Experimentation, coupled with observation of naturally expressed movements, has shown me that this particular modeling of the lower lid develops from emotions that agreeably affect the soul and that it completes the expression of smiling and of laughing.

The muscle that produces this depression on the lower eyelid does not obey the will; it is only brought into play by a genuine feeling, by an agreeable emotion. Its inertia in smiling unmasks a false friend.

The will can only mask its action with difficulty, if the action has been awoken by a heartfelt emotion.

Not only does it brighten up the eye and is complementary to *m. zygomaticus major* in expressing a smile or laughter, but also, in certain circumstances, it contracts by itself under the influence of pleasant sentiments. It then gives a kindly gaze, so we can also call it the *muscle of kindness*.

Anatomically, I have called it the inferior part of *m. orbicularis oculi* (see E, Plate 1); it is separated laterally from the superior part of *m. orbicularis oculi* by an aponeurotic intersection.

All of these facts will be developed and demonstrated in the article on this muscle, but because of their relevance I had to review them here.

The inferior part of *m. orbicularis oculi* is so hard electrically to stimulate in an isolated fashion that I have not been able to maintain an isolated contraction long enough to photograph it. I happened to hit on its motor nerve (see K, Plate 2a) while exciting *m. zygomaticus major*, as in the left side of Plate 31, where we see that this tricky muscle is slightly contracted, which gives this side a laugh that is a little less false than the opposite side. The expressive function of this muscle cannot be replaced by the palpebral part of *m. orbicularis oculi;* Plate 35 and, more strikingly, Plate 36 furnish the proof.

In the former (Plate 35), the electrode has been positioned at the point where the motor nerve of *m. zygomaticus major* emerges. The muscle is contracting, producing the furrows and fundamental outlines assigned to it, without any secondary lines, just as we would expect to see in subjects of this age. But we also see, in comparing their palpebral fissures, that on the right side, where the experiment is carried out, the upper eyelid is lowered, and that the lower eyelid is, on the contrary, elevated.

Now, this last movement indicates that the palpebral parts of *m. orbicularis oculi* are contracting; this can only happen if the motor nerve of these muscles is stimulated. I could have easily localized the electrical excitation to *m. zygomaticus major* as in the right side of Plate 30 by moving the electrode or decreasing the intensity of the current; but I preferred to photograph this combination of *m. zygomaticus major* with the palpebral parts of *m. orbicularis oculi,* a combination that produced *scornful laughter.*

This effect is even stronger in Plate 36, because of the stronger contraction of the palpebral parts of *m. orbicularis oculi* produced by the spasm of the eyelids.

11. The muscle of lasciviousness

(transverse part of *m. nasalis,* Q, Plate 1)

Plates 37, 38, 39, 40, 41, 42

Plate 37: Portrait of the old man seen in profile (also shown in Plates 3, 6, 7, 8, 9, 12, 13, 14, 17, 18, 19, 20, 21, 22, 30, 31, 32, 33, 34, 35, 36). Compare this with Plates 38 and 39.

Plate 38: To study the isolated contraction of the transverse part of *m. nasalis* in the same subject. Contraction of the transverse part of *m. nasalis* is not generally produced in isolation during natural expressive movements, but contributes to the shape of the nose in those subjects of a lascivious temperament or those who are habitually lustful. (It exists in various anatomical variants, depending on the shape of the nose.)

Plate 39: To study the combined contraction of the transverse part of *m. nasalis* and *m. zygomaticus major* in the same individual. Combined contraction of the transverse part of *m. nasalis, m. zygomaticus major,* and *m. frontalis:* the *attention* attracted by an object that *provokes lascivious ideas and desires.*

Plate 40: A portrait, seen in profile, of a man 42 years old, stupefied by the abuse of alcohol; his nose is aquiline. It serves to study the expressions produced by the transverse part of *m. nasalis.* Compare this to Plates 41 and 42.

Plate 41: To demonstrate the movement of the alae of the same man's nose by the transverse part of *m. nasalis,* and the morphology of this muscle when the nose is aquiline; also to study the expression it gives when associated with the palpebral part of *m. orbicularis oculi.*
    Electrical contraction of the transverse part of *m. nasalis* and voluntary gentle contraction of the palpebral part of *m. orbicularis oculi* in such a way as to maintain the eyelids half-open: *bad humor, malcontentment.*

Plate 42: To show the grossness and the cynicism of the expression of *lust* in the same individual in whom the transverse part of *m. nasalis* is very well developed. Combined electrical contraction of the transverse part of *m. nasalis* and *m. zygomaticus major: gaiety* expressed by the ideas of *lustfulness, cynicism,* and *lewdness.*

Further notes on these plates

A.   Technical details

Isolated stimulation of the transverse part of *m. nasalis* (Q, Plate 1) can be obtained by placing the electrodes over the fleshy body of this muscle, as in Plates 38, 39, 41, and 42. The anatomical disposition of this muscle makes this experiment easy.

Plates 38 and 41 show the pattern of expressive lines, fundamental and secondary, produced by the energetic contraction of the transverse part of *m. nasalis* in two subjects in whom the skin of the lateral part of the nose creased or wrinkled easily. We see that the ala of the nose is drawn obliquely upward and forward; that the upper portion of the nasolabial fold follows the same direction; that the nostril, in being elevated, is turned up in such a way that its opening looks outward instead of downward; that the skin crease that shapes the nostril posteriorly is more accentuated; and finally that the skin of the lateral part of the nose is folded parallel to the direction of the nasal spine.

The general form of the nose is considerably modified by the transverse part of *m. nasalis,* which is characteristic. To understand this properly, compare the form of the nose in repose in Plates 37 and 40, with the nose during contraction of the transverse part of *m. nasalis* in Plates 38, 39, 41, and 42.

The posterior part of the ala of the nose, where the inferior portion of the transverse part of *m. nasalis* inserts, and which is mobile, is inevitably drawn toward the nasal spine, which is the origin of this muscle. It is clear to everyone why the skin of these lateral parts of the nose, pressed superoanteriorly, is covered with little wrinkles parallel to the direction of the nasal spine.

The movement of the ala of the nose and the lines and the reliefs that are caused by it are much more pronounced in Plates 41 and 42 than in Plates 38 and 39.

B. Expression

Plate 38 shows us that the isolated contraction of the transverse part of *m. nasalis* gives the face an expression of bad humor, which announces hostility; but this muscle never contracts by itself and in order to render this expression of discontent, it acts in concert with other muscles.

Plate 41, where the transverse part of *m. nasalis* is contracting while the eyelids are slightly closed (by the palpebral part of *m. orbicularis oculi*), and where the labial commissures are lowered (by *m. depressor anguli oris*), offers a mixture of *discontent* and *scorn.*

The man shown in this last figure was an intelligent workman, 42 years old, who so much abused alcohol beverages that he fell into *delirium tremens.* He was taken to hospital and treated with success with a large dose of opium (he was given a gram of opium gum extract). When

I did these electrophysiological experiments on his face, he was still under the influence of the narcotic. Thus, we notice that his features express depression in place of his habitual gaiety, his labial commissures sag, and in order to open his eyes I had to strongly attract his attention, as we see in Plate 40.*

I used this prostration of the features produced by opium, and above all the drooping of the labial commissures, to study the expressive effect of combining the transverse part of *m. nasalis* with *m. depressor anguli oris*. The signs of discontent were much more strongly portrayed here than in Figure 38, but this expression was still not an exact imitation of nature. I then allowed him to half close his eyes, as if the light were hurting them, and I repeated the preceding experiment; I saw a true mixture of discontent and scorn appear on his face: I photographed this electrophysiological expression in Plate 41.

The transverse part of *m. nasalis* is also associated with *m. levator labii superioris alaeque nasi* in portraying a suggestion of the same expression. I will return to this later.

The photographic experiments in Plates 39 and 42 show that the combination of the transverse part of *m. nasalis* with the *muscle of joy* (*m. zygomaticus major*) produces the expression of *lascivious pleasure*, of *gay lust*. It is the most important function of the transverse part of *m. nasalis*; consequently I have called it the *muscle of lasciviousness, of lust*.

The old man shown in Plate 39 is far from lascivious; he is on the contrary of such a cold temperament he vows that women have never inspired him in the least: He is even proud to have conserved his innocence. Moreover, we notice in his photographic portrait, from the shape and flattening of his nostrils (Plates 3 and 37) it is clear that the expressive muscle of lascivious pleasure is in his case poorly developed.

In spite of these unfavorable conditions, we see in Plate 39 that by electrically exciting the transverse part of his *m. nasalis* united with stimulation of his *m. zygomaticus major*, we can portray the expression of lascivious pleasure that nature has refused him. You will notice that I also stimulated his *m. frontalis* at the same time to indicate that this emotion was awakened by an exterior cause; that nudity, for instance, grabbed at his lascivious attention. I wanted it to represent the lewd old men and the chaste Susanna; but it was impossible for me to give him such a lustful air, because the muscle that represents this emotion was not developed enough in his case. However that may be, this powerful laugh and ribald air contrast singularly with his usually simple laugh!

---

*He succumbed to delirium tremens ten days after this experiment.

Plate 42 shows us libidinous gaiety at its most gross stage. This man, before his features were sunken by opium, had a face that was totally different to that which we see in Plate 40; these features proclaimed a habitual gaiety, and the form and attitude of his nostrils declared a very lascivious temperament. The information I have gathered on this point convinced me that I was not mistaken! The experiment shown in Plate 42 proved that the muscle of lubricity was well developed in this man. Thus I could create this brutal passion on his facial features that were momentarily masked by the narcotic.

12. The muscle of sadness

(m. depressor anguli oris, **M, Plate 1)**

Plates 43, 44, 45

Plate 43: To study the movements, lines, and skin folds produced by the isolated action of *m. depressor anguli oris* compared with the opposite side, which is in repose, in an old man (also shown in Plates 3, 7, 8, 9, 12, 13, 14, 17, 18, 19, 20, 21, 22, 30, 31, 32, 33, 34, 37, 38, and 39). On the right, strong electrical contraction of *m. depressor anguli oris: disgust.* On the left, a relaxed expression.

Plate 44: To study the expressive qualities of maximally contracting both *mm. depressor anguli oris* in the same subject.
   Very strong electrical contraction of *mm. depressor anguli oris: disgust.*

Plate 45: To study the combined contraction of *mm. depressor anguli oris* and *mm. corrugator supercilii,* in the same individual.
   Strong electrical contraction of *mm. depressor anguli oris* and of *mm. corrugator supercilii: pain and despair.*

Further notes on these plates

A. Technical details

The localized electrical stimulation of *m. depressor anguli oris* (M, Plate 1) is performed by positioning the electrodes, as in Plates 43, 44, and 45, over the muscle (2 cm inferior and 1 cm lateral to the angle of the mouth). If the current is so intense as to traverse the thickness of this muscle, it can reach the motor branch that supplies *m. mentalis, m. depressor labii inferioris,* and *m. orbicularis oris,* and consequently stimulate all these muscles at once.

   The *mm. depressor anguli oris* pull the commissures obliquely inferiorly and laterally. Plates 44 and 45 show that at maximal contraction, the interlabial cleft describes a curve with an inferior concavity, that the lower lip is dragged a little forward, and that the nasolabial fold is enlongated,

78

tending to become straight and more vertical. The half of the upper lip on the side where *m. depressor anguli oris* is stimulated is drawn obliquely down and out and the nostril is lowered and is a little less open. This last fact is shown better in Plate 43, where, on the side of the face that remains relaxed, the nostril is a little more elevated than on the stimulated side. Finally, there are some wrinkles and folds beneath the labial commissures, caused by the skin being pushed back, which are much more pronounced and more numerous as the subject becomes older.

B. Expression

We know that the labial commissures of my old male subject are naturally lowered when his face is relaxed, which we see at rest in his portrait (Plate 3). This drooping of the labial commissures is found in old age, regardless of all moral causes.

But in young people, the gentlest contraction of *mm. depressor anguli oris* will cause a slight lowering of the corners of the mouth, giving the face an expression of sadness and of depression. We see an example in the left half of Plate 35. This young woman's commissures were habitually elevated and her normal expression one of gaiety; but she was very moody, and on the day I performed the experiment on the right side of her face, she was sad and gloomy. This latter expression is seen on the left side of Plate 35, due only to a slight lowering of the left labial commissure; in other words, to a feeble contraction of *m. depressor anguli oris* on that side.

In Plate 35, we can compare contrary movements of the labial commissures and appreciate the enormous influence they have on human facial expression. When this woman was sad, it was reflected in her *m. depressor anguli oris* and a consequent lowering of the labial commissures. I elevated the corner of her mouth, on the right side, by exciting the antagonist of the right *m. depressor anguli oris* (*m. zygomaticus major*), causing *joy* to be expressed artificially on this side of her face.

I did the opposite experiment in this woman when she was in a good humor. Her mouth was smiling and I gently stimulated one of the *m. depressor anguli oris,* and at once the lowering of the corresponding commissure, although feeble, altered the facial expression on that side.

Yet the expressive action of *m. depressor anguli oris* changes completely at maximal contraction, expressing *disgust,* as we see on the right side of Plate 36. Spasm of the eyelids, which is combined with this expression, has modified it a little and I will come back to this point.

Plate 44 is a better demonstration of this fact, as the maximal contraction of *m. depressor anguli oris* is quite isolated. This face expresses a profound *disgust*, which comes from the heart and indicates great aversion.

Other plates in this album show that diverse associations of other muscles with *m. depressor anguli oris* modify or change its expressive action. The slightest lowering of the labial commissures (by a feeble contraction of *m. depressor anguli oris*), associated with a subtle closing of the eyelids (by the palpebral part of *m. orbicularis oculi*), as when one is disturbed by light, gives the face an expression of *scorn*. This expression is seen on the left half of Plate 36. The extreme contraction (perhaps slightly exaggerated and grimacing) of *m. depressor anguli oris* portrays this expression to its highest degree and grossest form; showing us a mixture of *scorn and disgust*.

Drooping of the labial commissures, in the relaxed face of the subject in Plate 3, is a sign of age and augments the expressions of most of the movements of his eyebrow, with which it is combined in other figures. This drooping renders the *reflection* expressed by the superior part of *m. orbicularis oculi* more serious on the right half of Plate 12; and if it were at its maximum, as in Plate 45, this state of the spirit would take on a character of *sadness and dejection*.

Meditation, imparted in Plate 13 by the fairly strong contraction of the superior part of *m. orbicularis oculi*, becomes an expression of somber thoughts in Plate 14 by combining this with a slight lowering of the labial commissures.

In Plate 18, considerable lowering of the commissures adds to the hardness of the gaze produced by *m. procerus*, the muscle of *aggression*. Certainly the isolated contraction of *mm. procerus* results in a gaze that is already unpleasant, confirmed by masking the mouth of this figure. But the combination of lowering the commissures of the lips with *mm. procerus* gives this figure a harder and more menacing air.

The slight drooping of the corners of the mouth in Plate 20 gives the subject an air of sadness that is well suited to the expression of suffering portrayed by *mm. corrugator supercilii*.

The same muscular combination in Plate 45 expresses a mixture of *pain and depression:* It is the image of *despair*.

13. The muscles of weeping and whimpering

(*m. zygomaticus minor* and *m. levator labii superioris*, F and H, Plate 1)

Plates 46, 47, 48, 49, 50, 51, 52, 53

(Compare each side of Plates 46, 47, 48, 49, 50 and 51 by masking the opposite side.)

Plate 46: To study the lines that characterize weeping, with feelings of pity, in an old man (also shown in Plates 3, 6, 7, 8, 12, 13, 14, 17, 18, 19, 20, 21, 22, 30, 31, 32, 33, 34, 37, 38, 39, 43, 44, 45).
   Quite strong electrical stimulation of *m. zygomaticus minor* on the left side: *weeping, tears of pity*.

Plate 47: To study the differential action of *m. zygomaticus minor* and *m. levator labii superioris* in the same subject. On the left, electrical stimulation of *m. zygomaticus minor* and voluntary contraction of the palpebral part of *m. orbicularis oculi: weeping openly, with hot tears*. On the right, electrical stimulation of *m. levator labii superioris* and voluntary contraction of the palpebral part of *m. orbicularis oculi: a suggestion of this same weeping*.

Plate 48: To study the differential expressive lines of *m. zygomaticus minor* and of *m. zygomaticus major* in the same subject seen full face. On the left, electrical stimulation of *m. zygomaticus minor: mild weeping; pity*. On the right, moderate electrical stimulation of *m. zygomaticus major: feeble false laughter*.

Plate 49: To study the association of *m. zygomaticus minor* and *m. corrugator supercilii* in the same subject. On the left, electrical excitation of *m. zygomaticus minor* and of *m. corrugator supercillii: painful weeping*. On the right, the face in repose with fixed gaze and forward looking.

Plate 50: To study the expressive function of *m. zygomaticus minor* in a young woman (also shown in Plates 35 and 36). On the right, electrical stimulation of *m. zygomaticus minor* and the palpebral part of *m. orbicularis oculi: affected weeping*. On the left, the face in repose.

Plate 51: To study the isolated action of *m. levator labii superioris alaeque nasi*. On the right, isolated contraction of *m. levator labii superioris alaeque nasi: discontent, bad humor*. On the left, the relaxed face.

Plate 52: To show the expressive action of *m. levator labii superioris alaeque nasi* associated with the retraction of the lower lip by *mm. depressor labii inferioris*. Electrical contraction of *m. levator labii superioris alaeque nasi* and voluntary retraction of the lower lip; same expression as on the left side of Plate 51 but more pronounced.

Plate 53: Showing, on one side, the expressive action of *m. levator labii superioris alaeque nasi*, combined with those of the palpebral part of *m. orbicularis oculi*, compared to the expression of *m. zygomaticus major* on the opposite side. On the left, electrical stimulation of *m. levator labii superioris alaeque nasi* and of the palpebral part of *m. orbicularis oculi: whimpering*. On the right, contraction of *m. zygomaticus major: false laughter*.

Further notes on these plates

A.   Technical details

In all the studies of *m. zygomaticus minor*, the electrode is applied above the most external fibers of the inferior part of *m. orbicularis oculi*, that is to say about 2½ cm beneath the free border of the lower eyelid, vertically below its lateral canthus. Here we find the superior portion of *m. zygomaticus minor* (see F, Plate 1), which is attached superiorly to the lateral aspect of the maxilla; this is also the point where the motor nerve inserts into this muscle (see K, Plate 2a).

On the right side of Plate 47, the electrode is placed at the same level, but more medially, opposite the middle of the lower eyelid. In this region a part of the upper portion of *m. levator labii superioris* (see G, Plate 1) and its motor nerve (see L, Plate 2a) are subcutaneous.

It is not always easy or even possible to localize the electrical stimulation in *m. zygomaticus minor* exactly: The experiment photographed in Plate 50 is proof of this. It was impossible for me to make *m. zygomaticus minor* contract without closing the subject's eye by exciting the palpebral part of *m. orbicularis oculi*, although the electrode was placed very low, far from this latter muscle.

Here is the anatomical reason: "The *m. zygomaticus minor* starts," says Professor Cruveilhier, "from several roots *of which one is often constituted by the external fibers of the palpebral part of m. orbicularis oculi*. In some cases *m. zygomaticus minor* is exclusively formed by some detached fibers of this muscle. In other cases this extremely thin muscle takes origin by two fascicles from the malar bone, of which *one will form the inferior fascicle* of the palpebral part of *m. orbicularis oculi*. Usually this little muscle takes origin from the maxilla."* Thus an intimate connection exists between *m. zygomaticus minor* and the palpebral part of *m. orbicularis oculi*, and it is impossible for the first to be independent of the second. Then there are variations in the arrangement and direction of the nerves that supply these muscles, so that the current aimed at the superior part of *m. zygomaticus minor* may reenter the motor nerve that supplies the palpebral part of *m. orbicularis oculi*. It is impossible to say which of these

Traité d'Anatomie Descriptive, 3rd edition, vol. 11, p. 225.

anatomical variations is hindering the isolated electrization of *m. zygomaticus minor* in the woman shown in Plate 50.

Plate 46 shows the individual action of *m. zygomaticus minor* on the left side. The action of this muscle is oriented obliquely superolaterally, from the medial part of the upper lip and the nasolabial fold to its attachment on the lateral surface of the malar. At this degree of contraction, the free edge of the lip and the nasolabial fold corresponding to the excited muscle describe a delicate curve with an inferior concavity; and the tissues placed above the nasolabial fold are pushing back, in the same direction, producing a swelling of the cheek and an elevation of the lower eyelid.

On the left side of Plates 47 and 48, *m. zygomaticus minor* is a little less strongly excited and the curve described by the free border of the lips and by the nasolabial fold is a little less pronounced than in Plate 46. We see little superolateral oblique wrinkles on the skin of the upper lip of this old man and little transverse cutaneous folds on his lower eyelid.

These secondary wrinkles do not exist in the young; we can confirm this in Plate 50. In this young woman, the right *m. zygomaticus minor* has not only elevated the middle part of the right half of the upper lip, making it describe a curve with an inferior concavity, but at the same time it has turned up this half of the upper lip and revealed a greater area of the labial mucosa. The teeth have been equally covered, a fact that we cannot see from this photograph, because they are in shadow. The mechanism of this movement, is perfectly explained by the way *m. zygomaticus minor* inserts in the lip.

As this muscle terminates in the upper lip and the lateral side of *m. levator labii superioris*, its fleshy fibers become pale and *cease to be contractile for electrical excitation*. After crossing the fibers of *m. orbicularis oris*, which they cover, the fibers of *m. zygomaticus minor* continue with those of *m. levator labii superioris* nearly to the free border of the lips and terminate in the skin. The mobile attachment of *m. zygomaticus minor* takes place at the free border of the skin of the upper lip. This muscle, therefore, has a tendency to turn the lip out in elevating it. In order for this folding to occur, the lips cannot be thin, as in the old man shown in Plates 46, 47, 48, and 49. His lips, on the contrary, tend to turn inward, due to the absence of teeth. Infants' lips, which are thicker, evert themselves and curl up when they cry. Plate 50 gives a less than perfect idea of this lip movement and I regret not having been able to photograph it exactly.

The right side of Plate 47, where *m. levator labii superioris* is excited, shows that the action of this muscle is about the same as that of *m. zygomaticus minor*, except that its action on the upper lip and on the nasolabial fold is less oblique laterally and it elevates the side of the nostril slightly but without enlarging the opening.

In young subjects and those with thick lips, *m. levator labii superioris* also everts the upper lip. The mechanism of this action of this muscle is explained by its anatomical arrangement, which I dealt with above in discussing *m. zygomaticus minor*.

In the experiments shown in Plates 51, 52, and 53, the electrode has been applied to the superior portion of *m. levator labii superioris alaeque nasi* (see H, Plate 1), at about the point of entry of its motor nerve (see L, Plate 2a).

The ala of the nose is elevated and has dragged the superior extremity of the nasolabial fold with it. This fold is less oblique and therefore elongated and the lateral portion of the upper lip is pulled upward, following the direction of *m. levator labii superioris alaeque nasi*.

On the right side of Plate 51, the electrical stimulus is perfectly localized to this latter muscle. Thus, we do not see the cutaneous creases on the left side of the nose in Plates 52 and 53, where a stronger electrical current excited the motor nerve of both the transverse part of *m. nasalis* and *m. levator labii superioris alaeque nasi* at the same time.

B. Expression

These electrophysiological experiments all show that *m. zygomaticus minor*, which was previously thought to be an auxiliary to *m. zygomaticus major* for the expression of *joy* and *laughter*, is on the contrary the muscle of *weeping*.

In isolated contraction (the left side of Plate 46), this muscle portrays an emotion in which tears are produced; I have never seen tears flow from a moral cause without this muscle contracting. This expression of pity contrasts with the firmness of the features and the gaze of the opposite side. I gave him this air of resolution by fixing his gaze to the front and making him open his eyes wide. Yet we feel, from looking at the left side of this figure, that the tears produced by this emotion are not flowing with abandonment; they are only wetting the eyelids. Such is the expression of pity seen in the theater on the faces of spectators moved by a touching scene.

The same expression of pity increases gradually in the left half of Plates 46 and 47: tears, which in Plate 46 appear to be contained, flow with more and more abandonment in Plate 47. The subject is now frankly weeping. It is not that the contraction of *m. zygomaticus minor* is any stronger; I have already said on the contrary that it is less than in Plate 46. The emotion seems stronger because the contraction of the palpebral part of *m. orbicularis oculi* is linked with that of *m. zygomaticus minor*.

I have frequently followed this graduation of the expression of weeping in the same individual and in infants. Tears are always announced by the isolated action of *m. zygomaticus minor* and then open weeping as portrayed by the addition of the palpebral part of *m. orbicularis oculi*.

On the right side of Plate 47 *m. levator labii superioris* is contracting at the same time as the palpebral part of *m. orbicularis oculi,* and the subject seems more abandoned to his emotion, weeping more openly than on the left side. The expressive elements (the curve of the nasolabial fold, the movement of the upper lip, and the outline of the cheek) produced by these two muscles (*m. levator labii superioris* and *m. zygomaticus minor*) have much in common. But they do differ subtly, as I have said previously.

Finally, the left side of Plate 53 demonstrates the most unsightly kind of crying: *weeping with hot tears,* or *whimpering.* Such weeping is ridiculous in the adult and few dare abandon themselves to it entirely. It is the whimpering of infants, employed when they want us to show tenderness or give in to them.

The muscle that produces this type of weeping, the *whimpering muscle,* is *m. levator labii superioris alaeque nasi* (see H, Plate 1); but we only see this expression when it contracts synergistically with the palpebral part of *m. orbicularis oculi,* as in the left side of Plate 53.

Plates 51 and 52 prove that without the concordance of the palpebral part of *m. orbicularis oculi, m. levator labii superioris alaeque nasi* can no longer express *whimpering.* Instead we see then the signs of *discontent.* The right side of Plate 51, where this muscle is contracting alone, paints the expression of bad humor, representing a troublesome person who finds everything bad. The worst degree of this state of ill temper is best portrayed in Plate 52, where the action of *m. levator labii superioris alaeque nasi* is combined with that of *m. depressor labii inferioris* (see X, Plate 1), which pulls the lower lip inferiorly and laterally and everts it.

The different degrees or nuances of weeping, seen in Plates 46, 47, and 48, are an indication of sorrow or tribulation; but they equally portray an expression of pity, provoked by a moving scene: These tears are certainly not the tears of pain. Tears are even produced, of course, by pleasure. Really good news can make tears flow, and we say that we "weep for joy."

Ready tears show a great weakness of character. Sometimes this follows certain brain conditions: when tears and all degrees of weeping are excited indifferently by the slightest impression of pleasure or of pain, even when the patient's intelligence has remained intact.

Only recently I was caring for a man of great intelligence, the founder and director of a large factory. He had suffered a mild apoplexy. While his intellectual faculties remained intact, his character, formerly very strong, was so enfeebled that he wept at all times, as much when he experienced agreeable sensations as the opposite. At the sight of a friend or of someone who pleased him, his mouth and his eye initially smiled, but almost immediately the curvature of the nasolabial fold gave his face an expression of weeping, the contraction of *m. zygomaticus minor* having replaced that of *m. zygomaticus major*, and then his eyes filled with tears. He realized he was ridiculous, but, in spite of all his efforts, he ended up whimpering, as in the left side of Plate 53, having passed through all the degrees of weeping shown in Plates 46 and 47.

These expressions of weeping often provoke laughter, as they give a man an inane and ridiculous air.

Yet we feel compassion at the sight of the left side of Plate 49, because we sense that the subject must be tormented by a sharp and profound pain that wrenches the tears from him. Thus a man weeps for the loved one he has lost, a mother or a child: It is thus that the *Laocoön* (of Rome) is weeping. I have produced this expression of *painful weeping* in Plate 49, by the combination of *m. zygomaticus minor* with *m. corrugator super-cilii*, an expression that contrasts with the guarded appearance of the features of the opposite side.

14. The muscles complementary to surprise

(muscles that lower the mandible)

Plates 54, 55, 56, 57

Plate 54: To study the lines, the skin folds, and other changes produced by the muscles that lower the mandible, in an old man (also shown in Plates 3, 7, 8, 9, 12, 13, 14, 17, 18, 19, 20, 21, 22, 30, 31, 32, 33, 34, 37, 38, 39, 43, 44, 45, 46, 47, 48, 49, 51, 52, 53).
  Voluntary lowering of the lower jaw with the skin of the lower part of the face; inexpressive movement.

Plate 55: To show that it is not sufficient to open the mouth and elevate the eyebrows to portray astonishment. These movements may just produce a grimace, unless there is a perfect rapport between them.
  Maximal voluntary opening of the mouth, with voluntary, mild elevation of the eyebrows: *astonishment* badly rendered by the subject: a ridiculous and inane expression.

Plate 56: To study combined moderate contractions of *m. frontalis* and of *the muscles that lower the mandible*. Voluntary, moderate opening of the mouth and proportional electrical stimulation of *mm. frontalis: surprise*.

Plate 57: To study the combined maximal contraction of *mm. frontalis* and the muscles that lower the mandible. Voluntary maximal opening of the mouth and energetic electrical stimulation of *mm. frontalis: astonishment, stupefaction, amazement*.

Further notes on these plates

A.   Technical details

The muscles that lower the mandible and their motor nerves are covered by *m. platysma* and cannot be electrized without this latter muscle contracting at the same time; their independent excitation is only possible when *m. platysma* is atrophied or no longer excitable. Consequently, I asked the subjects for these experiments to open their mouths wide.
  In Plates 54 and 56, the features of the lower half of the face are pulled directly downward and are elongated at the time when the mouth is open. The lips describe two almost equal arcs with inverse curves inter-

87

secting at the labial commissures. These figures show the elongation of the features and curving of the lips that increase in proportion to the degree of opening of the mouth. We also see that a transverse fold develops on the skin beneath the mandible, and that this line is continued bilaterally by a furrow with a superior concavity, which rises 2½ cm behind the chin onto the cheeks, and through a second shallower furrow 1½ cm behind the first. The shape of the neck has not undergone the least modification, whatever the degree of opening of the mouth.

B.   *Expression*

Plate 55, where just the mouth is opened, certainly does not express any emotion. But we feel, when looking at Plate 56, that the subject has just received unexpected news or caught sight of something that surprises him. I obtained this expression of surprise by combining the voluntary opening of the mouth with the electrical stimulation of *m. frontalis*.

The same muscle combination is maximally contracted in Plate 57, portraying a similar emotion but at its highest level. The impression is stronger and the agitation is greater. This man gazes at something with the greatest surprise; he cannot believe his eyes and looks thunderstruck, astonished, and amazed; he in fact looks *stupid*.

To reproduce the expressions experimentally in Plates 56 and 57, a perfect rapport was needed between the degree of opening of the mouth and the elevation of the eyebrows.

My subject did not know how to imitate these expressions, because he never felt them. We know that his intelligence was limited. I made him express surprise and astonishment in the same way as in the photographic figures that I had produced artificially. He simply opened his mouth as if he were yawning (see Plate 55). Try as I might to make him open his jaws more widely and raise his eyebrows higher, I only achieved the silly expression shown in Plate 56. The mouth was open in an exaggerated manner, compared to the slackness of the eyebrows and eyelashes. So he rather has the air of singing than of being astonished!

15. The muscle of fright, of terror

(*m. platysma*, Y, Plate 1)

Plates 58, 59, 60, 61, 62, 63, 64, 65

Plates 58 & 59: To study the isolated action of *m. platysma* in an old man (also shown in Plates 3, 7, 8, 9, 12, 13, 14, 17, 18, 19, 20, 21, 22, 30, 31, 32, 33, 34, 37, 38, 39, 43, 44, 45, 46, 47, 48, 49, 51, 52, 53, 54, 55, 56, 57). In the first, electrical contraction of the left *m. platysma*: in the second, contraction of both *mm. platysma*: This contraction of *m. platysma* alone lacks expression.

Plate 60: To study the combined contraction of *mm. platysma* and *mm. frontalis*. Combined electrical contraction of *mm. platysma* and *mm. frontalis*: fright.

Plates 61 & 62: To study the combined electrical contraction of *mm. platysma* and *mm. frontalis*, associated with dropping of the lower jaw.
   Electrical contraction of *mm. platysma* and *mm. frontalis*, with voluntary dropping of the lower jaw: *terror* seen full face in Plate 61 and in semiprofile in Plate 62.

Plate 63: To show that the expression of *terror* can be rendered with truth and energy even though the eyelids are half closed. The same muscular combination as in Plates 61 and 62, with lowering of the upper eyelids and downward gaze: *expression of terror*.

Plates 64 & 65: To study the combined electrical contraction of *mm. platysma* and *mm. corrugator supercilii*, associated with opening the mouth.
   Combined contraction of *mm. platysma* and *mm. corrugator supercilii*, with voluntary dropping of the lower jaw: *terror mixed with pain, torture*. In Plate 64, the contraction of *m. platysma* is more energetic on the left than on the right: By looking at each side of this figure we see a gradation in pain and terror.

Further notes on these plates

A.   Technical details

The isolated contraction of one of the *m. platysma*, photographed in Plate 58, establishes that this muscle pulls the tissues of the lower part of the face obliquely inferolaterally. Yet the experiments shown in Plates 59, 60, 61, 62, 64, and 65 demonstrate that eversion of the lower lip does not happen when both *mm. platysma* are stimulated together.

These latter figures equally show the oblique action inferolaterally of the two *mm. platysma* on all the features of the face and teach us how these muscles lift and pull on the skin of the anterior half of the neck. It is like a curtain behind which the outlines of *mm. sternocleidomastoideus* disappear.

From Plate 60 we see that *mm. platysma* exert a very feeble action on the lower jaw. The subject's mouth was closed when I stimulated these muscles vigorously, and although I told him never to offer any resistance, the lower jaw is lowered barely 2 or 3 millimeters; the lower lip alone is separated from the upper lip by about 2 cm.

For the expressions in Plates 61, 62, 63, and 65, I needed to have the mouth open and then to electrize *mm. platysma;* when I did this, the form and modeling of the lips produced by simply dropping the lower jaw (see Plates 54, 55, 56, and 57) completely changed and showed the special features characteristic of the combined action of *mm. platysma* and the muscles that lower the mandible.

To understand properly the lines and reliefs produced by *m. platysma* and its importance in the play of facial expression, it is vital to remember the anatomical disposition of this muscle (see Y, Plate 1).

The *m. platysma* runs under the skin, from which it is difficult to separate with a scalpel, and in which it inserts superiorly at the inferior and lateral part of the cheek and inferiorly across the superior part of the thorax. It follows the curves of the face and the neck. The *m. platysma* pulls inferolaterally on the lower lip, the skin of the lower region of the cheeks, and the alae of the nose. Because it tends to straighten as it contracts, it lifts the skin that covers it over the anterior half of the neck. Finally, when maximally contracted, a great number of fibers of this muscle form very prominent cords across the anterior surface of the neck, showing their direction. This is well seen on most of the preceding plates, especially in Plate 63.

B.   Expression

The contraction of *m. platysma* alone is inexpressive, as we see in Plate 58. I have opened the subject's mouth while stimulating *mm. platysma,* but whatever the degree of lowering of the lower jaw, the result has been a grimace or a deformity analogous to that of burn scars in the cervical or thoracic region.

Plates 60, 61, 62, 63, 64, and 65 prove, however, that *m. platysma* can be eminently expressive when associated with certain other muscles. In fact, without it, several emotions that produce a spasmodic swelling of the neck and pull on the features cannot be portrayed on the face of man.

Plates 56 and 57 express surprise, astonishment, and amazement very accurately by the combined contraction of the muscles lowering the mandible and *mm. frontalis;* but this muscle combination cannot portray fear and terror. We can, however, make them appear by linking *m. platysma* with one of the muscles of the eyebrow. Here is the experimental proof.

Plate 60 is the image of fear, produced by combining *m. frontalis* with *m. platysma*. The subject's face was initially in repose, his gaze calm and indifferent, although it was directed laterally. First his *m. frontalis* was strongly stimulated and his eye became attentive, as we see in Plate 9. Then *mm. platysma* were stimulated and immediately the traits of fear were drawn on his face with an admirable accuracy. This occurred without the lower jaw dropping to any appreciable extent, but by all the features of his face being pulled down obliquely and by the elevation of the skin on the anterior part of his neck. His slightly oblique direction of gaze gives his eye an expression of restlessness, of dread, at the same time indicating the point from which he is being menaced.

In Figure 60, we feel that this man experiences the thrill of fear: His cutaneous muscles, *m. platysma* (of the neck) and *m. frontalis* ("platysma of the forehead") are tonically contracted by fear. It is the same as in quadrupeds; their *panniculus carnosus*, which is analogous to the cutaneous muscles of man, bristles up the hair under the influence of fear.

This distressing emotion is produced by the idea of danger, by the appearance of something, or by the play of a disturbed imagination. We do not see, at least in his face, that this individual is really in danger; we only sense that he dreads something.

But looking at Plates 61, 62, and 63, doubt is no longer possible; this man is frozen and stupefied by terror; his face shows a dreadful mixture of horror and fear, at the news of a danger that puts this life in peril or of inevitable torture. Before the introduction of chloroform, the anticipation of surgical operations induced this expression of terror and horror.

In all these figures, which portray terror so clearly, dropping the lower jaw is combined with other movements, which, in Plate 60, represented fear. The expression of terror only comes perfectly by associating *mm. platysma* and *m. frontalis* with the muscles lowering the mandible.

Plates 56 and 57 have already shown that the combined contraction of *mm. frontalis* and of the muscles lowering the mandible perfectly render astonishment and amazement, without being able to express fear and terror. We can use Plates 60, 61, 62, and 63, to study the distinctive characteristics of these different expressions; characteristics often misunderstood or confused in painting and sculpture.

The increased size of the palpebral fissure and the haggard look on most of these faces certainly add to their expression. In terror, the dread is such that the eyeball seems to be chased from its orbit. Plate 62 shows, however, that wide separation of the eyelids is not necessary for the expression of terror. We see that in spite of the lowering of the upper eyelid, the combined contraction of *mm. platysma*, of *mm. frontalis*, and of the muscles lowering the mandible, depict an expression of dread mixed with horror, of terror, with such accuracy as Plates 61 and 62. This gaze, terrified and *transfixed*, only shows the origin of the danger that menaces the man.

Plates 64 and 65 show that the combined contraction of *mm. platysma*, of the muscles lowering the mandible, and of *mm. corrugator supercilii* produces an expression of terror mixed with extreme pain. Plates 61, 62, and 63 show us a man terrified by the idea of near death, aware of torture to which he has been condemned; but in Plates 64 and 65, the horrible pain of torture has been added to the expression of this terrible emotion. This expression must be that of the damned.

16. A critical study of several antiquities from the point of view of *m. corrugator supercilii* and *m. frontalis*

Plates 66, 67, 68, 69, 70, 71, 72, 73

Plates 66 & 67: *Head of Arrotino* (the spy, the knife grinder, and so on), frontal view and profile. The transverse forehead lines, extending across the whole breadth of the brow, are not compatible with either the obliqueness or the curvature of the eyebrows due to the antagonism between *m. frontalis* and *m. corrugator supercilii*. The former muscle produces these transverse lines on the forehead and the latter this oblique and curved pattern of the eyebrow.

Plate 68: The same head as Plate 67 on which the curvature of the eyebrows has been adapted to the forehead lines, true to the action of *m. frontalis* (see Plates 7 and 8).

Plate 69: The same head as Plate 67 on which the forehead lines and the sculpting of the lateral portions of the brow have been adapted to the obliqueness and curvature of the eyebrow, true to the action of *m. corrugator supercilii* (see Plates 19, 20, 24, and 25).

Plate 70: Head of the *Laocoön* of Rome. The medial lines of the forehead are in perfect accord with the oblique and curved movements transmitted to the eyebrow by the contraction of *m. corrugator supercilii*, but the sculpting of the lateral portions of the forehead is impossible.

Plate 71: Same head as Plate 70 on which the lateral forehead is sculpted as it is in nature, and as it should be in Plate 70.

Plate 72: Head of the Laocoön of Brussels (property of the Prince of Aremberg), a copy of the Laocoön of Rome, on which the same faulty expression of physical pain and agonized convulsions as in the original (Plate 70) is seen.

Plate 73: Head of Niobe on which the smooth forehead and level eyebrows do not show the sculpting produced by the expression of pain.

Further notes on these plates

I anticipate that at first sight the captions to Plates 66, 67, 70, and 73 will offend general opinion. The corrections shown in Plates 68, 69, and 71 of works of art rightly admired by every age will perhaps be considered profane.

93

However, those readers well acquainted with the principles expounded in my study of the muscles of the eyebrow, will immediately recognize that my critical observations are well founded. It will, moreover, be easy for me to justify them.

A.   Technical details

Let us first of all inquire whether the lines, relief working, and sculpting on the forehead and eyebrows of these antique works can be explained by the mechanism of the muscles that move the eyebrows.

Obviously, the forehead lines of *Arrotino* (Plates 66, 67) and the form and direction of his eyebrows, are each well sculpted when examined separately; but observations of nature and electrophysiological experimentation show in the most irrefutable manner that they are mutually exclusive, that they cannot exist together on the same forehead.

After studying all the illustrations pertaining to the electrophysiological study of *m. frontalis* and *m. corrugator supercilii* (see Chapters 6 and 9), and after rereading the ideas in the notes on the plates, especially that part referring to the antagonism of these muscles, it will be seen that my assertion is substantiated by rigorous experiment.

Furthermore, the observation of nature happens to be in perfect agreement with the electrophysiological experiments; never, in fact, have I seen furrows extending across the whole breadth of the forehead, as in *Arrotino* (Plates 66, 67), without the eyebrow tracing a curve concentric to these furrows; and never have I seen a voluntary or induced contraction produce an oblique direction in the eyebrow, as in Plates 66 and 67 without the skin furrows being limited to the median section of the forehead and without the different planes of the face looking similar to those in Plates 23, 24, and 25. We know that these last plates show a young man voluntarily contracting his *mm. corrugator supercilii*.

How then can we reestablish the agreement that normally should exist between the forehead lines of *Arrotino* and the movement of his eyebrows and vice versa.

If the lines that transversely furrow the whole breadth of his forehead are retained, then the form and direction of his eyebrow must be changed; the eyebrow ought to trace a concentric curve to these forehead lines, as results from the vigorous contraction of *m. frontalis* in an adult. (See Chapter 6; the figures are devoted to the electrophysiological study of this muscle.)

If, on the other hand, we are to leave his eyebrows intact, the wrinkles should only exist on the central portion of the forehead, while the skin on the lateral parts of this region is taut and flat, just as we see when an adult vigorously contracts *m. corrugator supercilii*. (See Chapter 9; the figures are devoted to the study of *m. corrugator supercilii*.)

I have done just that. The Museum had the head of *Arrotino* cast from a beautiful bronze copy in the Tuileries, and on these plasters I tried to combine the movements of the eyebrows and the sculpting of the forehead by imitating the lines and relief marks and planes that are produced during energetic contraction of either *m. frontalis* or *m. corrugator supercilii*. Plates 68 and 69 are photographs of these plasters.

The profile view of the "*Arrotino* corrected" (pardon my term) forehead shows a plane similar to that in Plate 25.

I intend shortly to examine the modifying influence on the expression of the face produced by these corrections.

These same critical observations are for the most part applicable to the *Laocoön of Rome*. The sculpting of the lateral sections of its forehead is a fantasy of the artist Agasias; it is *impossible*, because no muscular contraction, isolated or combined, would ever produce it. The furrows and the relief marks on his forehead should, in order to be natural, be continuous with those of the central part, as in Plate 33, where we see *m. frontalis* in action, as well as in many other figures where this muscle has been activated. Here too, however, as in *Arrotino* (Plates 66 and 67), they could not exist with the curving movement of the eyebrow.

In Plate 71 I have tried to combine the sculpting of the *Laocoön's* forehead with the form of his eyebrow, using the rules established by my electrophysiological experiments.

These corrections would certainly have been more proficient if executed by an artist. But I thought that only a profane hand could be permitted such boldness. Nevertheless, I am convinced that the expressive lines on Plates 68, 69, and 71 are those of nature; whereas the foreheads of *Arrotino* and of *Laocoön*, as they are in the original and that we see photographed in Plates 66, 67, and 70, are physiologically impossible given the sculpting and shape of the eyebrow.

B. Expression

The discordance between the appearance of the forehead and the eyebrow of *Arrotino* makes it difficult to ascertain his facial expression, because the lines and relief marks produced by these movements belong to several expressions and are mutually exclusive.

The forehead and eyebrows of this face cannot be combined without profoundly confusing the expression.

When *m. corrugator supercilii* produces a line parallel to the forehead lines, as in Plate 68, the facial expression of *Arrotino* expresses *attention, curiosity*. If the eyebrow remains oblique (and the natural relation between eyebrow and forehead is restored) by shaping the forehead as in Plate 69, then his eye expresses *pain*, or appears to be troubled by a bright light, thus apparently producing a spasm of *m. corrugator supercilii*.

Which of these diverse expressions should be attributed to *Arrotino*? In order to resolve this question, we would have to be certain of the history of this antique figure. However, knowledge of this field is limited.

To quote M. Viardot: "The Italians call him *Arrotino;* but we have given him several names: *The Knife Grinder* and also *The Spy,* because his turned head and distant gaze seem to demonstrate that his attention is focused on anything but his manual action. Some have taken this face to be that of Cincinnatus, others Manlius Capitolinus, others Milicus or Accius Navius; the opinion of the latter group considers him to be the slave who exposed the Catiline conspiracy. Evidence has, however, proved those suppositions false. Among the Prussian kings' collection of engraved stones there is one described by Winckelmann, which represents the torture of Marsyas. The victim is tied to the tree and in front of him is the figure (exactly the same as *Arrotino*), of the Scythian whose job it was to flay Apollo's unhappy rival. The same figure in the same position is found in every representation of the Marsyas story; as a low-relief in the Borghese gallery and on the back of several antique medallions. It is certain, as the antiquarian Zannoni confirms in his *Illustrazioni* of the Florence Gallery, that the Grinder, the Spy, the Cincinnatus, the spy exposing the plots are all the Scythian who flayed Marsyas.*

If *Arrotino* is actually a slave exposing secret plotting, then that expression of close attention, of curiosity, in this man who is listening to what is happening around him, all the while seeming to sharpen a knife on a stone in front of which he is crouching, which I photographed on my corrected plaster cast of the original in Plate 68, renders perfectly the state of the subject.

Zannoni affirms with M. Viardot that had the artist wished to represent the Scythian ordered by Apollo to flay Marsyas, then the expression of pain produced by the contraction of *m. corrugator supercilii* (in Plate 69) is perhaps more accurate. Perhaps the sculptor wished to present us with the Scythian struck with fear and compassion at the sight of the

---

*Musées d'Italie, Paris 1852, p. 150.

unfortunate victim whom he was charged to torture so cruelly and for such a petty and frivolous motive. We do know that it was for having dared to defy Apollo in a music contest that this latter jealous rival had Marsyas flayed alive.* But could the heart of this man, vulgar-faced and with a low forehead, be accessible to such sentiments? Did the sculptor simply want to show this barbarian interrupting his torture in order to examine his victim, who had just been bound and tied to a tree? In this case the Scythian, peering up is troubled by the light and contracts his eyebrow in spasm as in Plates 22 and 25, where the contraction of *m. corrugator supercilii* is maximal.

Of all these hypotheses is one alone absolutely true?

The group of *Laocoön* is certainly one of the most beautiful legacies of antiquity. Winckelmann ascribes it to Alexander's epoch; but the expert Lessing has shown that it is a product of the more decadent era of sculptors.

The great priest of Apollo† frightened by two enormous snakes during his sacrifice, retreats with his two children to the altar, the sanctity of which he hopes will provide protection. Nevertheless, vengeful Minerva attacks them, wrapping them in the coils of these monsters. Laocoön's flank is already horribly torn by a deep bite; wracked with convulsions, his body and limbs alone demonstrate his physical pain.

His face does not show a single convulsion or spasmodic move to express the pain that the monster's bite must cause him.

The curve of the nasolabial folds and the everted lips (movements produced by *m. zygomaticus minor* and by the outer fibers of *m. orbicularis oris*) indicate that Laocoön is crying. The obliqueness, the sinuosity of his eyebrows, and the puckering of the heads of his eyebrows give his crying a character of extreme pain. Finally, his half-open mouth and his upturned eyes reveal that in his despair he is invoking the help of the gods.

This expression, which is the ideal of paternal love, is not to be found on the Prince of Aremberg's bust of *Laocoön* in Brussels.

The sculpting of the forehead and eyebrows in the *Brussels Laocoön*

---

*It is said that the nymphs cried so much that a Phrygian river, swollen with their tears, was named after the satyr, Marsyas.

†If I may be permitted to recall the legend of the *Laocoön* group. The day preceding the destruction of Troy, Laocoön, son of Priam and Hecuba, objected to the Greek's wooden horse being admitted inside the walls; he even hit it with a javelin. The same day, while performing a sacrifice, he and his two children were strangled by two enormous snakes. This tragic end was the revenge of Minerva, to whom the wooden horse was consecrated – the dreadful death of Laocoön furnished Virgil with one of the most beautiful passages in the *Aeneid* (Bk. II, pp. 201–227).

(see Plate 72) is exactly the same as that of the *Roman Laocoön;* with the exceptions that the former's eyes are turned convulsively inward, the mouth is wider open and, finally, the lower lip and corners of the mouth are pulled obliquely down and out.

Certainly there are signs of pain on the face of the *Brussels Laocoön;* but the convulsive movement of his mouth and lips limit him to the expression of physical pain, and the convergence of his eyes show him succumbing to a violent and horribly painful death.

This expression is striking and has a startling reality; some people thus maintain that this is the original *Laocoön* bust.

This opinion, for which there is a complete lack of historical documentation, is, in my view, untenable for the following reasons.

The head of the *Brussels Laocoön* just cannot be matched with the *Laocoön* group of Rome. His face shows agony and it is incomprehensible how, in this state of asphyxiation and near death, a man could still battle with snakes and keep himself seated on the edge of the altar, in a position in which it would seem difficult to maintain balance. The sculptor would have, in this case, shown him collapsing or overwhelmed by the snakes.

More than likely, the bust of the *Brussels Laocoön* is a copy of the *Roman Laocoön,* on which the artist has taken the liberty of modifying the original expression. This agony, these convulsions with the mouth gaping open to emit the death rattle can scarcely be compared to the nobility of the *Roman Laocoön,* to this ideal of paternal love admired by all and particularly the enthusiasm of Winckelmann.

"The *Laocoön,*" says Winckelmann, "presents us with the interesting spectacle of human nature suffering its greatest pain, a man summoning all the strength of his spirit against this pain. While his muscles distend under the force of his extreme suffering and his nerves are tautened, from his bulging forehead shines his serenity of mind, and his chest, held by the cruel grip, rises painfully to confine its torment. Not daring to exhale his sighs, his abdomen is compressed and his sides sunken so that we can study the action of his internal organs. His own suffering, however, seems to affect him less than that of his children, whose eyes are riveted imploringly on their father. *Laocoön's languishing look reveals his paternal tenderness and compassion clouds his eyes. His face expresses his groans and not his cries; his upturned eyes implore divine assistance.*"*

I am sorry to disturb this general admiration – with which I agree – by criticism of *Laocoön* regarding the physiologically impossible fore-

---

* *Histoire de l'art chez les Anciens,* Paris, 1802, vol. II, book vi, ch. 3, p. 293.

head. This criticism, as I have demonstrated, arises from electrophysiological experimentation; and it is confirmed by rigorous observation of
nature.

I nevertheless hasten to say that this fault in no way detracts from the
expression of *Laocoön*'s mental pain, because the movement of the eyebrow is wonderfully sculpted, and it alone is responsible for the fundamental line of this expression. I have already dealt adequately with the
subject of the differential value of the fundamental expressive lines and
the secondary expressive lines of *m. corrugator supercillii* – I will simply
recall here the important fact that explains how *Laocoön*'s forehead could
have been sculpted so incorrectly without the fundamental expression
being profoundly altered.

Nevertheless this fault mars the work and contrasts with the perfection and accuracy of the complex and expressive lines of the *Laocoön's*
facial expression.

In Plate 71 I have tried to restore the natural relation of the central
lines and the lateral planes of the forehead with the obliqueness and
sinuosity of the eyebrow and we can see how much more beautiful the
expression would have been if Agésandre had sculpted *Laocoön*'s forehead in accordance with the immutable laws of nature.

Up to this point my comments have dealt only with works of art from
the period of late antiquity. *Arrotino* and even *Laocoön* date from a period
when for a long time Greek art had been banned from temples by the
Roman conquest; the only remaining artists had by then been taken to
Rome in chains or had been forced into exile.

But who has ever dared to adversely criticize *Niobe*?

I too want to pay her homage as one of the most noble and sublime
beauties of antique art.

She is among the most noble because she dates from the moment
when statuary art was at its zenith: She is the work of Praxiteles; some
writers even claim Phidias helped create her.

Sculpted beauty for the Greeks was the highest artistic criterion, the
cult of form being elevated to the extent that the expressive signs of the
spirit's emotions were usually sacrificed. For fear of damaging the serene perfection of the lines, artists subordinated the emotions in favor
of portraying the face in absolute repose. Thus most of their statues can
only be admired for their physical beauty, that which appeals to the
senses alone. Do not expect more of innumerable Venuses; they have
neither heart nor spirit.

Niobe is not in this category. In this work Praxiteles knew how to wed
perfection of form with beauty of expression – these two elements to-

gether compose the ideal of beauty. For this reason I claimed *Niobe* as the most sublime of the antique beauties.

But alas! My admiration is here again reduced by several "desiderata" or flaws revealed through my electrophysiological research and confirmed by a more accurate observation of nature.

The artist's task was to depict the despair of a mother seeing her children massacred.

Praxiteles shows us this weeping mother frenziedly clutching to her breast the last daughter whom Diana's vengeance has just struck dead. So dramatic is this scene that the spectator is struck with both admiration and painful distress. This is at least the impression I experienced on entering the Niobe room in the Florence Gallery.

However, on looking more closely at Niobe's facial expression, I was soon amazed at the serenity of her features, a serenity that contrasted with the extraordinary movement of her gestures and stance, which express the turmoil of her soul.

In order to express the pain caused by this spiritual turmoil on this mother's face, Praxiteles has obliquely moved her eyebrows superomedially – he has ennobled this painful expression by raising her eyes skyward.

Such a fairly large curve of the eyebrow is certainly present in the expression of pain; but it alone does not suffice to express this emotion. In fact, in many people this is the natural shape of the eyebrow in repose, when they are feeling no spiritual emotion.

The eyebrow's movement of pain – in other words, the action of the muscle producing this movement (of *m. corrugator supercilii*) – is characterized by a group of inseparable lines and relief marks, namely: curvature of the eyebrow, bulging of the medial end of the eyebrow, and the central forehead furrows.

Would such an important fact – demonstrated by electrophysiological experimentation (see the figures devoted to the study of *m. corrugator supercilii*) – have escaped the genius of Praxiteles' observation? Or did he rather hesitate to disturb, by a too servile imitation of nature, the harmony of his Niobe's beautiful lines?

But would Niobe have been less beautiful if the dreadful emotion of her spirit had bulged the head of her oblique eyebrow as nature does, and if a few lines of sorrow had furrowed the median section of her forehead? On the contrary, nothing is more moving and appealing than such an expression of pain on a young forehead, which is usually so serene.

C. AESTHETIC SECTION
Foreword

My Scientific Section could be considered to have completed my appointed task. The faces in that section demonstrate the principal facts of the grammar and orthography of human facial expression with the most complete empiricism. The six subjects were of differing ages, both male and female. Some of them had an attractive facial expression. However, some readers must have disapproved of the unpleasantness of some of the faces.

The old man photographed in most of my electrophysiological experiments did have common, ugly features. To a sophisticated man such a choice may seem strange. Some artists and eminent amateurs, believing that this part of my album had been assembled from an aesthetic point of view, asked me: Why use such an ugly face for an artistic subject? I would certainly like to present only young and beautiful faces but, above all, I had scientifically to demonstrate the *workings* of the lines of the face; for this, an electrophysiological study of Adonis would have been much less fitting than my old and ugly subject.

I would remind the reader of the motives governing my choice of subjects – "I have preferred this coarse face to one of noble, beautiful features, not because in order to be true to nature one must show her imperfections; I simply wanted to prove that, despite defects of shape and lack of plastic beauty, every human face can become spiritually beautiful through the accurate rendering of his or her emotions."*

Of course, I did have other reasons for preferring this subject, which I shall explain briefly. His face was insensitive, which allowed me to study the individual action of the muscles with as much effectiveness as on a corpse; due to the aging process he had developed all the lines produced by the expressive muscles, lines that I have divided into principal lines constituting the expression, and secondary lines indicating the age of the subject and the different degree of expressive movement.

*This text, p. 42.

101

Although he was relatively unintelligent, his facial expression underwent numerous transformations: Under the influence of my electrodes his facial expression was disguised by the manifestations of thought (attention, reflection) or animated by differing passions.

It is true that instead of this man I could have used a corpse, which I often did in our hospitals, in front of numerous witnesses. I could animate the face by localized electrical stimulation to each one of the muscles, and the emotions rendered on the corpse were as genuine as those of the living person. But there is no more hideous or revolting spectacle! Although I have long been accustomed to the sight of death, it has always deeply affected me, and I would have been loath to submit the public to such an experience. My old man was thus a fitting subject for the demonstration of these physiological facts I needed to establish.

Nevertheless, I agree that this common character does not comply with all the demands of aesthetics. I did manage, with the help of my electrodes, to mark the lines of the highest sentiments and the most profound thoughts on the mundane surface of this dull forehead. However, I do not want such a character to be the vehicle for great and noble actions. Thus, while admiring Caravaggio's science of chiaroscuro, I cannot admire the famous master's practice of always finding the models for his most sublime religious scenes in gambling dens and cabarets.

In addition, I did write earlier: "I reproduced some expressions on other individuals; thus I used this opportunity to assemble as far as is possible, the set of conditions that constitute beauty from the aesthetic point of view."

At this point, therefore, I am going to fulfill that commitment, and reply to the *desiderata* of art.

In an attempt to placate those who possess "a sense of beauty," and wishing to please while at the same time teaching, I performed some new electrophysiological studies in which I hope the principal aesthetic conditions are fulfilled: beauty of form, associated with exactness of the facial expression, pose, and gesture.

The aesthetic studies could be multiplied and diversified indefinitely; but the already considerable additions to the scientific section of the album oblige me to limit the number of faces included in the aesthetic section. Moreover, by publishing these aesthetic studies, I only wanted to show a sample of what could be obtained in the realm of art and beauty, using my electrophysiological experiments on human facial expression.

The faces in the Aesthetic Section were photographed by myself.* The

---

*I have explained (see this text, Scientific Section, p. 39) that these faces cannot be photographed well by the person conducting the experiments. This is how one can simulta-

creation of these faces is much more difficult than those of the Scientific Section, where I sacrificed everything to the demonstration of expressive lines and to the truth of expression; as long as the expressive lines of these faces were perfectly in focus and outlined in relief, the rest was secondary.

The same does not apply to the "aesthetic faces," in which the gesture and the pose together contribute to the expression; the trunk and the limbs must be photographed with as much care as the face so as to form an harmonious whole.

Unfortunately, the badly photographed head of the experimenter sometimes impairs the scenes that these figures are portraying. A word of explanation on this matter. Sometimes I could not stand far enough from my subject to avoid being caught in the field of the photographic plate, or so that I could not be focused by the camera. In one face only (Plate 75) was I perfectly in focus.

Nevertheless, despite my difficulties in executing these aesthetic photographs, I am sure they will be found to be infinitely superior to those of the scientific section, most of which were produced in 1856. Since that time the apparatus has been perfected and the *art* of photography has made great progress.

neously perform an electrophysiological experiment and photograph it. After having arranged the pose of the subject corresponding to the desired scene, and having positioned the head, with the aid of a head rest, the experimenter illuminates the head so as to highlight the expressive lines that he wants to depict by electrical stimulation; then he proceeds to focus. During this stage of the operation, which demands considerable *artistic feeling*, the photographic plate is colloidonized and sensitized by an assistant. Before placing the plate in the camera, the assistant focuses the experimental artist in the position he must hold, without disturbing the subject. This involves the experimenter first moving the hand holding the electrodes forward, and then his head and body to avoid placing himself in the area of the photographic plate. Finally, he signals the assistant to open and shut the objective lens; then the experimenter himself proceeds with the development of the plate.

17. Aesthetic electrophysiological studies on the mechanism of human facial expression

Plates 74, 75, 76, 77, 78

The faces of the aesthetic section will at first sight seem like mere grimaces to those without the key to my experiments. Thus I repeat that the isolated electrical contraction of the muscles that produce the different expressions on each side of a face can in fact only display a grimace, if we look at both sides of the face simultaneously. Therefore, as I indicate in the captions, care will be taken to cover this or that part of each of these faces, while we look at the opposite side; in this way we will see the expression of the face depicted completely, often becoming quite beautiful.

Plate 74: Portrait of a young woman in repose, following which the various expressions in Plates 75, 76, 77, and 78 were photographed.

Plate 75: General view: nun saying her prayers, with resigned suffering at left, and with only sadness at right.* A sorrowful prayer, but with resignation by covering the eye, eyebrow, and forehead of the right side; a somewhat sad prayer, by covering the same parts of the left side.
   The head alone: a painful or sorrowful memory, by covering the eye and forehead of the left side; a somewhat sad memory, by covering the same parts of the opposite side. Electrization of the muscle of pain and sorrow (of *m. corrugator supercillii*, see O, Plate 1) at the left: upturned look and slight lowering of the angles of the mouth.

Plate 76: General view: same nun, with deep sorrow on the left, and with divine ecstatic joy on the right. An extremely sorrowful prayer, by covering the eye, the eyebrow, and the forehead of the left side; ecstatic prayer with saintly transports of virginal purity, by covering the eye, eyebrows, and forehead of the right side. The head alone: extreme sorrow, without any religious character, by covering the left side as above; ecstatic admiration, by covering the opposite side in the same manner. Electrization of the muscle of pain and sorrow (*m. corrugator supercilii*) at left; upturned look and half-opened mouth.

Plate 77: Earthly love at right and celestial love at left. Ecstasy of human love, by covering the left half of the face; gentle rapture of divine love (ecstasy of St. Teresa), by covering

*The convention in all the captions is that I am indicating the side of the subject's face, not the side of the photograph as seen by the reader.

104

the opposite side. Moderate electrization of the muscle of lasciviousness (transverse part of *m. nasalis,* see Q, Plate 1), on the right side; with eye movement obliquely upward and a little laterally.

Plate 78: Scene of coquetry, with different expressions on left and right. Offended look, by covering the parts of the face below the nose; haughty look, by covering the left side of the lower half of the face; mocking smile, by covering the right side of the lower half of the face. On the right, electrization of *m. depressor anguli oris* (see X, Plate 1); on the left, electrization of *m. zygomaticus major* (see I, Plate 1); eyelids slightly drawn together and gaze directed slightly laterally; a mannered pose and exaggeratedly naked chest.

Further notes on these plates

I. The person represented in Plate 74, and whom I have chosen as model for this electrophysiological and aesthetic study of facial expression, is neither pretty nor ugly but rather has regular features; her face is not very expressive; however, we shall see in the following figures that she is completely transformed under the influence of various expressions that I have given her, and that she even gains in beauty.

This girl is almost blind (for several years she has been afflicted with a bilateral optic nerve atrophy). I am trying to improve her condition by means of electrization and she has become accustomed to the unpleasant sensation of this treatment so that she is well suited to my electrophysiological experiments.

She is large, fairly well built, suitable for the external study of the shape of the body; but she cannot understand the gestures or the poses that I show her, so that I am obliged to position her and dress her as if she were a mannequin.

I have provided an explanation of the different scenes in which this girl is featured in the following plates, so that the expressive and aesthetic value of these studies can be better appreciated. Of course, these same expressions could certainly apply to other scenes or situations that the sight of these faces may evoke.

In most of these studies we shall see two different expressions, one on each side of the same face. Hereby I wished to demonstrate the general modifying effect of one expressive muscle on all the other facial features. Thus I often put a voluntary expression on one side of the face, comparing it to the expression on the other side, which was artificially produced by electrical excitation.

For the benefit of those who would repeat or continue these studies in electrophysiological aesthetics I shall outline the procedure. I pose my subject, with the gestures in harmony with the facial expression I intend to produce; I then set her voluntarily to execute the facial movements suitable to these expressions. Being familiar with the muscular combinations or movements suitable to each expression, I am careful, in these circumstances, not to involve my subject's feelings; I rely only on my judgement and on my artistic feeling. Thus I arrange her head in a particular direction, open or shut the eyes and mouth, ask her to smile or laugh, and so on. In this way I obtain the expression that I want, as I feel it. Not every expression can be produced in this way because there are muscles that are not controlled in isolation by the will and that only contract as a result of reflex excitation of the emotions, or under the influence of localized electrization. At the moment when the expression produced by the voluntary movements is forthcoming and its characteristic lines stand out on the whole face, I provoke, on one or both sides, an electrical contraction of one or several muscles whose specific expressive action modifies or completely changes the voluntary expression.

You can imagine the difficulties I encounter in such experiments. Their perfect execution demands besides great precision, a well developed artistic sense, which I have not attained adequately for such an important task, being prevented by my normal work. Armed with my electrodes, it is not enough for me to only excite those exact muscles whose individual action produces the lines and characteristics of the emotion or intellectual state that I am trying to render. I must, in addition, convey the different degrees and accentuate an infinite variety of nuances, without sinking into exaggeration or grimace.

These artifically produced expressions are not completely perfect. They cannot be because in my procedure I would not presume to translate the expressions as exactly as does the spirit.

When I experiment, I do not uncover the lens until the moment when the electrized muscle has reached just that correct degree of contraction necessary for the perfect expression that I wish to paint. However, this contraction does not always remain long enough at this degree because the galvanic current that runs the induction machine is not perfectly constant. What is more, when the pose is held a little too long, the sensitivity of the excited muscle weakens because of the continued passage of the current. Altogether, as I have said, the photography of these aesthetic studies in electrophysiology presents quite considerable difficulties.

II. In Plate 75, the expressive facial movement is similar to that on the old man in Plate 21 (see my Scientific Section). In both cases I directed the gaze upward (a movement produced by the synergistic action of the superior rectus extraocular muscles and *m. frontalis*). In each the curve of the eyebrow had increased as it rose and the forehead was, in the old man's case, furrowed by transverse wrinkles parallel to the curve of the eyebrows, as is seen in old age (see the left side of Plate 21), whereas the young woman's forehead stayed smooth (see right side of Plate 75). At the same moment I electrized the left *m. corrugator supercilii*; the lines and shape resulting from the action of this muscle stood out in features that distinguish the age difference of the two subjects (see chapter 5, scientific section, for the design of the expressive lines of the muscle of pain or sorrow).

If we look only at the face of the young girl, that is, by covering everything below the neck, we can ascertain that her expression is approximately the same as that of the old man (Plate 21). In both we can recognize on one side (the right Plate 75, the left Plate 21) the expression of remembrance, which on the other side (left Plate 74, right Plate 21) becomes sorrowful. It must, however, be noted that the young woman's slight lowering of the angles of the mouth and her lateral inclination of the head add despondency to her sorrow. The old man shows more firmness in his sorrow.

Look, however, at Plate 76 as a whole: The scene enlarges and changes completely. This upturned look, instead of evoking remembrance, tells us that the young woman's spirit is being exalted by her ardent faith. In addition, does not her white veil and homespun dress signify that she is doing something great, that she is going to renounce this world? If you cover the eye and forehead of the left side, the sadness of her features (due to the slight lowering of the angle of her mouth) makes you feel that she is not leaving her dearest loved ones without some regrets. And if you cover the eye and forehead of the other side, you see that her sacrifice is sorrowful; you feel that the heart of the nun, who is perhaps leaving her dear mother and family, has not yet been withered through the exaltation of religious feelings.

III. Plate 76, seen as a whole, represents the same scene as the preceding plate: the taking of the veil; but the emotion of the young woman is so great that her facial expression has become even more moving and beautiful.

She is seated, hands joined, the trunk bending forward, the back a little arched, head tipped backward and upward: This very moving pose already shows that she is praying ardently. If then we cover her right eye and forehead, we see the face illuminated by a saintly exaltation, and her spirit unites with God's in adoration: This is religious exaltation.

But as soon as the left side is uncovered, after having covered the forehead of the right side, all the features of this girl, which a little while ago radiated divine joy, seem to be painfully or sorrowfully affected; her half-open mouth now only emits moans; her appearance – just recently ecstatic – is now painted in an expression of deepest sorrow. Is she perhaps the victim of some violence? Has she perhaps been torn from her lover? Overcome with despair, is she imploring the aid of God? Such thoughts spring to mind on looking at this figure as a whole.

The top of this figure seen alone (cover the parts below the neck) inspires similar feelings. The saintly ecstasy expressed on the right half of the face is pure, virginal, and most beautiful – a Madonna. The other half could represent a *mater dolorosa.*

I have proved abundantly and experimentally, in a sufficiently large number of faces, that each movement of the eyebrow, especially those of *m. corrugator supercilii* (see Plates 19, 20, 21, 27, 28, 29), greatly modifies the expression of every facial feature; Plate 76 is a new and even more startling demonstration of this important proposition. In fact it is only necessary to alter the direction and the shape of the eyebrow, as can be seen on the left eyebrow of Plate 76, that is, to make it curving and oblique from medial to lateral and from superiorly to inferiorly, and to bulge the head of the eyebrow, to imbue all the features with sorrow. [These were the very features that together had previously portrayed the height of the purest most saintly happiness, a divine ecstasy.]

Comparing Plates 75 and 76, it is interesting to examine how I managed to make them express two nuances or degrees of the same passion, of sorrow. The first expresses a resigned sorrow; the second shows a deeper affliction. In both of them, however, the eyebrow has the same curvature, and its head the same bulge, the forehead lines are similar,* and finally the gaze is upturned. It is the shape of the mouth and lips that establishes a difference between the expressions of these two faces. In Plate 75, in fact, the mouth, the nasolabial fold, and the labial commissure are at rest, which adds sorrow and peacefulness to the expression as well as a resignation and an air of suffering similar to Plate 20 and 21. The slight lowering of the angle of the mouth, which is natural in my model (see her portrait, Plate 74), adds only a little sadness to this expression. The half-open mouth, combined with the contraction of *m. corrugator supercilii*, in Plate 76, adds a note of sharp sorrow to the nun's expression. Seeing her in this pose I can almost hear her weeping.

Plate 76 proves that in the expression of sorrow nothing could ever replace the shape that the eyebrow assumes under the influence of *m. corrugator supercilii*. Some people have, however, tried to paint this expression by keeping and even increasing the curve of the eyebrow.

*The central lines of Plate 76 are less visible than in Plate 75, as the thrown back head obscures them.

I cite as an example Guido's *Cleopatra* in the Florence Museum. This undone queen is represented at the moment when, out of despair, she commits suicide by an asp bite. Seeing this beautiful picture, which everyone knows, we feel that Cleopatra must be suffering an intense physical and spiritual sorrow; but far from finding signs of this on her face, we find instead an ecstatic happiness, similar to that expressed on the right half of Plate 76. (To better recognize the truth of this remark it would be better to look at Cleopatra's head alone.)

I noticed in the Capitol Museum (in Rome) a sketch of the same picture, where the eyebrows, drawn obliquely, give Cleopatra a beautiful expression of sorrow. Why then did Guido, to whom this sketch is attributed, not reproduce this same expression in the *Cleopatra* of Florence? Had he lost it irretrievably once his picture was finished, as happened to him in his *Ecce Homo* that I so admired in the Colona Gallery in Rome? Examining each half of the beautiful face separately we do in fact notice an expression of deep sorrow on the right and an ecstatic look on the other side.

Still one more critical comment occurs to me on looking at Plate 76. I have said that the sorrowful expression is incomplete in *Niobe*, and that the head of the eyebrow should be puckered. Such is the action of the muscle of sorrow, of *m. corrugator supercilii,* at every age (see every plate devoted to its study), and this fact is even more evident in the left eyebrow of Plates 75 and 76. I have written earlier, "Would Niobe have been less beautiful if the dreadful emotion of her spirit had bulged the head of her oblique eyebrow as nature does, and if a few lines of sorrow had furrowed the median section of her forehead?"* The answer is in Plates 75 and 76, where we see that this raised eyebrow and these forehead lines delineated by the action of the muscle of sorrow on a forehead much younger than Niobe's, do not the slightest harm to the facial beauty, while still making it more precise, natural, and attractive.†

---

*This text, Scientific Section, p. 100.

†I permit myself here to reiterate my declaration of principles, in reply to the objections addressed to me on the occasion of a critical essay on several pieces of antiquity, which I included in the scientific section of this work. As a critical essay it is merely a practical deduction from my electrophysiological studies.

The scientific press judge my work very favorably; they consider it as a new victory in physiology and a welcome intervention into the domain of psychology and the plastic arts. Nevertheless, one of the most eminent and authoritative voices of the medical publishing service, Mr. A. Latour, did, in a flattering and well written article, have some reservations as to the practical use of my aesthetic research: "Mr. Duchenne will be accused," he says, "of stripping art of its ideal of beauty and reducing it to anatomical realism along the lines of a certain modern school of art. The essays he attempted on three famous works of antiquity – *Arrotino, Laocoön* and *Niobe,* whose orthographic faults

IV. Several figures in the Scientific Section have already been devoted to the study of the muscle of lasciviousness, which is activated by amorous excitation. In men's faces (see Plates 39 and 42, in the Scientific Section) the expression is crude and even cynical, as is seen on the faces of the satyrs or fauns.

This transverse muscle of the nose lends a lascivious expression to the female face. Therefore, I have performed a metamorphosis by changing the purest, most angelic smile and the most saintly ecstasy of Plate 76 into the most provocative and licentious by means of combining a strong contraction of this muscle to the other features; in so doing I transformed virgins into bacchantes.

But, when the contraction is modified, this muscle paints a charming expression of pleasure on the female face. The experiment photographed in Plate 77 is a good example of this. In fact, I managed to photograph the pleasure of a pure spirit, devoted to God, owing to the general effect of her appearance: with her eye slightly obscured and obliquely upturned to the side, and with her smile and half-opened

he claims to have corrected, will appear to the worshipers of ideal beauty as rather brutal . . .''

I present a résumé of my reply to my friend Mr. Latour's objections (see *l'Union Médicale*, 26th August, 2nd September and 2nd October, 1862): "If this should be the result of my research, those men of taste who follow the traditions of art, would be right to ostracize me. But be reassured; I am far from arriving at this modern realism that only shows us nature with her imperfections and even deformities, and that seems to prefer the ugly, the vulgar, or the trivial. On the contrary, the principles arising from my experimental research allow art to attain the ideal of facial expression, by teaching how to render correctly and with perfect exactitude, like nature herself, the language of passions, and even certain operations of intelligence.

"In the same way, the art of antiquity revealed plastic beauty, physical beauty, by copying nature exactly. But contrary to modern realism, it imitated nature in her most beautiful, noble, and perfect aspects.

"I have also proved, by a study of history, that in antiquity Greek statues were universally admired, primarily because, as Galen said, they were faithful imitators of nature.

"Briefly then, the intense physiological study of our heritage of masterpieces has revealed that if the Greek sculptors managed to attain the ideal of beauty in the fields of symmetry and body shape, it was primarily through imitation of beautiful nature; in other words, they produce an *idealized naturalism* – two words whose combination may shock initially: but which perfectly convey my thought.

I believe that I have also demonstrated that the Greek sculptors had no fear of repressing their freedom and spontaneity by submitting to the severe rules instituted by their masters, either in the sphere of body proportions or relating to the muscle reliefs produced by movements and by poses.

It should not be concluded, from the above, that it is sufficient to copy nature exactly, even in her most perfect work, in order to attain *beauty in art*. It need hardly be said that the artist also needs *creative genius*. I would not agree with Boileau when he said: "Nothing but the truth is beautiful, truth alone is to be admired." Modifying this great poet's thought I would write: "Nothing is beautiful without truth."

mouth, with her head and body leaning slightly backward, with her hands crossed on her breast, and with her little cross around her neck. This expression of devotion can be seen by covering the right side of Plate 77, to the midpoint of the space between the eyebrows and the mouth. The left side thus displays a delightful expression of rapture reminiscent of the ecstasies of St. Teresa. At this point I made the muscle of lasciviousness (the transverse part of *m. nasalis*) on the right contract slightly, and then the expression on this side alone assumed a charming character of sensual pleasure, more evident after the left side of Plate 77 is covered. This rapturous state no longer has an element of mysticism; we sense that it is not only the result of the delights of divine love but that the memory of her loved one exalts her imagination and her senses. This is the ideal poetry of human love.

There is only a very slight difference between the ecstatic expression of celestial love and that of terrestrial love. This is what I wished to show in Plates 76 and 77, especially in the latter; and this is something that artists have seldom appreciated. Their saints and even their virgins, painted in states of beatitude and sweet rapture, whose features should always exude innocence and purity, too often have the expression of sensual pleasure. Bernini's group representing the ecstasy of St. Teresa in the basilica of St. Peter, in Rome, is a striking example. A beautiful angel armed with a spear appears to her and everything in St. Teresa's expression breathes *the most voluptuous* beatitude.

Just as the rapture of human love, as shown on the right side of Plate 77, adds beauty to the face, to the same degree licentious ecstasy disfigures it. In order to render this cynical expression on Plate 77, I had only to make the muscle of lasciviousness (the transverse part of *m. nasalis*) contract more energetically. We all know that such an expression should not be part of the composition of a work of art. It would, however, be useful for the artist to know of it. He must know, besides, that there exist several intermediate degrees between the maximum cynical ecstasy and the charming expression of human love photographed in Plate 77.

V. In Plate 78 I wanted to show a little comedy, a scene of coquetry, a gentleman surprises a young lady while she is dressing. On seeing him, her stance and her look become disapproving (cover the bottom half of her face). Nevertheless, we note her nudity, which instead of covering she seems to reveal with a certain affectation. It is the mannered pose of her hand, which supports a rather overly revealed bosom. All this betrays her coquetry. The young man was becoming more audacious, but the words "Get out!" pronounced in a scornful way by the girl, stops him in his enterprise (see only the left side of the lower half of the face).

The mocking laughter that accompanies the amorous rejection (see the right side of the lower half of the face), we believe to mean "Conceited ass!" Perhaps she says also, much lower: "the fool, if he had dared . . ." At least we are permitted to suppose this from her slightly irritated air.

I have described before (Plate 36, Scientific Section) a physiological study analogous with that of Plate 78. Here are the differences that distinguish these two figures.

1. The first (Plate 36) had a gentle spasm of his eyelids, because they were hit by the light of the studio; at my request, the second (Plate 78) had closed her eyes voluntarily a little and had adopted the given pose. This closing of the eyelids indicated that the second subject was offended; whereas, in the first, who was seated and in repose, this same approximation of the eyelids never had any expressive significance.

2. The contraction of *m. depressor anguli oris* of Plate 36 is very strong and can appear exaggerated for the expression of scorn; yet I have seen it act thus in common people who, when injured, can express a profound scorn almost bordering on disgust. But then the expression is vulgar. In Plate 78, on the contrary, where the contraction of *m. depressor anguli oris* is less, we are struck by the distinction and the truth of the expression of disdain. Perhaps we will also find here that the lowering of the corner of the mouth is a little strong and that this expression could be more natural if it were a little less. But I intended to exaggerate slightly the contraction of *m. depressor anguli oris*, wishing to indicate that this coquette is feigning indignation, and that at heart, on the contrary, she was flattered by the enterprise of her audacious lover. It would have been easy for me to diminish the degree of electrical excitation of *m. depressor anguli oris* elsewhere.

3. In these two women, the expression of mocking laughter is very subtle but no less true; they distinguish themselves by a slight nuance: One (Plate 36) smiles, and the other, without laughing out loud, has more mocking gaiety.

4. Everyone notices that Plate 78 prevails over Plate 36 by the beauty and the distinction of the features.

5. Finally, these two figures show the considerable influence of attitude, of gesture, of action, and in a word, of expression. Why this disdainful air on one side and this mocking laugh on the other? To this question, Plate 36 doesn't reply at all; but it is not so for the beautiful coquette represented by Plate 78. It seems to tell of the

little scene that I have recounted above. Actually her nightdress and her rumpled hair show fairly clearly that she is dressing; her head is a little turned to the left, her expression wounded, directed to the same side, indicating clearly the presence of an unexpected indiscreet witness, but the small amount of clothing that she uses to cover her charms contrast with her semblance of prudish alarm. All of which betrays a coquette who acts indignant with a lover at whom she laughs.

18. Further aesthetic electrophysiological studies

Plates 79, 80, 81, 82, 83, and 84

Plate 79: *Maternal happiness mixed with pain*, from a psychological and aesthetic study of the expression resulting from the *conflict* of *joy* and of *crying*.

By covering the left eye, joy of a mother who sees her infant recovering from a serious illness; covering the right eye, the same maternal joy, united with pain produced by the death of another child. Electrical stimulation of *m. corrugator supercilii*, associated with the natural expression of joy.

Plate 80: *Compassionate smile of charity. Benevolent smile*, in covering the right side of the face; *smile of pity*, in covering the left side of the face. Light electrical contraction of *m. zygomaticus minor*, associated with natural laughter.

Plate 81: Lady Macbeth: Had he not resembled
　　　　　My father as he slept, I had done't.*
　　Moderate expression of cruelty. Feeble electrical contraction of *m. procerus* (P, Plate 1).

Plate 82: Lady Macbeth: Come, you spirits
　　　　　That tend on mortal thoughts, unsex me here,
　　　　　And fill me, from crown to the toe, top-full
　　　　　Of direst cruelty.†
　　Strong expression of cruelty. Electrical contraction of *m. procerus.*

Plate 83: Lady Macbeth – about to assassinate King Duncan. Expression of *ferocious cruelty.* Maximal electrical contraction of *m. procerus.*

Plate 84: Lady Macbeth – receiving King Duncan with a perfidious smile. False smile on the left, by covering the right side of the mouth; frigid air of discontent on the right, by covering the left side of the mouth.

Feeble electrical contraction of the left *m. zygomaticus major* at the time when the face expressed malcontentment.

Further notes on these plates

I. Here is the scene that I wanted to portray in Plate 79. A mother comes to lose one of her infants. Another infant – the only one that remains –

Macbeth, act II, scene II.
†*Macbeth*, act I, scene V.

114

is equally gripped by a mortal illness; he is on the point of succumbing. Sitting at the foot of his cradle, she abandons herself to the greatest sorrow. Yet a last hope can save him: A crisis may deliver him! Clinging to the life of her poor child, she anxiously follows the progress of the disease and discovers in these features the first signs of this happy crisis; she cries: "He is saved!"

Such are the emotions of maternal pain and joy that I have tried to express, on the left side, of the young woman photographed in Plate 79.

Certainly nothing would be easier to portray than maternal joy, as a mother who senses that her child is coming back to life. We confirm that this expression is fairly well rendered in Plate 79, if we cover the left eye.

But in the scene comprising the principal subject of Plate 79, the expression is complex. Actually, the happiness of this mother when the second infant just escaped his death could not have made her forget so soon the one who had died. Her maternal heart is therefore seized at the same time by two contrary emotions: joy and pain. It is this that is expressed in the left half of Plate 79, when the right eye is masked.

I managed to obtain this expression in the following manner. One day my model was very sad and could only laugh with her lips. In order to evoke in her face the real signs of joy, I had to make her gay. After having made her open her mouth slightly, I evoked her natural joy. As soon as the expression of real joy mixed with a little surprise was reached to a degree that agreed with the emotion that I had to portray, I produced, on the left, the expressive lines of pain, by stimulating *m. corrugator supercilii* of this side, and then, by combining these two primordial and contrary expressions, I produced, on this side, this touching expression of *joy mixed with pain*.

In order to complete it, I had to render her eye moist and make the tears flow, for a mother who loses her son cries with great abandonment. But we understand that I could not do this with electricity. It will be easy for the reader to fill in for this *missing detail*.

I have already dealt with this type of expression, composed of contrary muscular contractions. I recall here the terms in which I have spoken.*

"One should not conclude from the preceding facts that there is always absolute antagonism between contrary primordial expressions.

"I have seen the lines of *joy* associated marvelously with those of *pain*, provided that the contraction was moderate; the image being that of a *melancholy smile*. It was a flash of contentment, of joy, where the subject

*This text, p. 18.

was unable to dissipate the traces of a recent pain or the signs of habitual sadness. I thought to myself of a mother smiling down at her child, at the same time mourning the loss of a dear one, of her husband.

"These composite contractions by opposite expressions, and that portray what one might call a forced sentiment, I call *combined expressive contractions* that are discordant.

When I wrote these lines, I had forgotten that the greatest poet of antiquity, Homer, had created an analogous situation, and that to portray this emotion of the soul, he composed a most harmonious expression: "δακρυόεν γελάσασα," an expression which I tentatively translate as "smiling through her tears." Here is a translation of a passage from the *Iliad* by Homer that describes the parting of Hector and Andromache:

"Having thus spoken, Hector handed the boy to his wife, who took him to her perfumed breast. *She was smiling through her tears . . .*"* I will show, that this translation does not exactly reproduce the situation created by Homer.

This conflict between pain and joy, producing the combination of expressive discordant contractions, is portrayed on the human face on countless occasions! Why then are there so few examples of it in art?

I can only cite a very small number: *The Resurrection of a Young Japanese Girl*, by Poussin (Louvre, no. 434); *Israelites Collecting Manna* (Louvre, no. 420); *The Birth of Louis XIII*, by Rubens (Louvre, no. 441); *The Martyrdom of St. Agnes*, by Dominican (in Boulogne). There also exist rare examples among modern works, but I will exclude them.

Poussin, in his work, no. 434 in the Louvre, makes us attend the resurrection, by Saint Francis Xavier, of a young girl stretched out on her death bed. At the moment when the prayers of the saint start to recall the breath of life to the lips of the dead, we see her mother detach herself from a group of other Japanese, fall on her and stretch out her arms with an expression of *great joy mixed with pain*.

This mixture of joy and pain, a combination that constitutes a *discordant* expression, cannot be borne for long without wounding the emotions. This discordant expression must rapidly resolve itself and accord with all the expressive lines of good humor. It differs essentially from Plate 79, which, we recall, represents a mother in whom the joy at seeing her last child escape the danger of death cannot efface the profound pain produced by the recent death of her other child. In the Japanese woman, the happiness is so complete that at its first appearance on the face, the

*Verse VI of the *Iliad*.

lines of pain must have been largely dispersed to make way for maternal joy. In the same way, after the thunderstorm, the sun appears in all its splendor chasing away the clouds to the horizon.

Poussin, it seems to me, has not sensed this nuance or this form of expression of joy mixed with pain. In fact, he has painted the eyebrow at its maximum of painful contraction, which contrasts in an offensive way with the expression of extreme joy that he has given his subject.*

I have experimentally produced, in Plate 34 of the Scientific Section, a grimacing expression the same as I have just criticized in Poussin, by maximally stimulating the muscle of pain *(m. corrugator supercilii)* and the muscle of joy *(m. zygomaticus major)*.

Joy mixed with pain shows itself in diverse degrees on the face. In the two variations that I have just analyzed in Plate 79 of the album and in the picture by Poussin, no. 434, joy was pushed almost to ecstasy.

For example, we see this discordant expression portrayed in a touching manner and to its lightest possible degree on the face of the mother who has just given birth to a child.

The pain of childbirth ceases, in general, soon after the birth of the child. This unexpected transition from the most atrocious pain to perfect calm is a moment of unutterable well-being. Shattered with fatigue, she would abandon herself to a restoring sleep if she were not tormented by the overwhelming need to embrace her baby. We can imagine the happiness with which she smiles at the baby, when we present it to her; her face all at once both caressing and languishing. This sweet expression of maternal happiness is well rendered by Jeanne d'Albret in the picture by Devéria: *The Birth of Henry IV* (Luxembourg gallery, no. 43).

But sometimes, above all after a long labor, the pain doesn't go away entirely; the mother has an expression both of prostration and of pain. She must force herself to give a first kiss to the child, even though she has hardly the strength. She smiles at him and becomes tender; her happiness is so great that she hardly shows the traces of her physical pain. Marie de Medici, in the *Birth of Louis the XIII*, by Rubens (Louvre, no.

---

*I once again observe that in the painful expression portrayed by this master painter, there is no rapport between the modeling of the eyebrow and that of the forehead; the skin of the forehead needs some wrinkles on the middle part, and to be modeled in a particular way in the lateral parts, as I have shown in all my experiments on this muscle (see all the figures in chapter 10, Scientific Section). Now, in the Japanese by Poussin, who is skinny and rather old, the forehead remains smooth, in spite of the energetic painful contraction of *m. corrugator supercilii*. Poussin has committed the same fault in another woman that we see in the middle of a group of Japanese, who cries at the same time as painfully contracting her eyebrow. Everywhere he has wanted to paint pain energetically, we notice the same absence of modeling of the forehead.

441), offers an admirable example of this discordant expression of both sweet maternal joy and feeble physical pain. The curve of her eyebrow is interrupted, near its inner end, by a slight elevation of the head of the eyebrow. The modeling of her mouth and of her lower eyelid shows the profound emotion of maternal joy, an emotion that is close to tears, as shown by the concavity below the nasolabial fold.

On the whole this combination of very lightly accentuated lines, which is produced at the same time by joy, by pity, and by physical pain, results in an harmonious ensemble – a discordant expression at its most gentle, of smiling mixed with physical pain, a most gracious and most touching expression.*

II. I have previously written, "Smiling does not just indicate an inner contentment, it also shows kindliness, that happy disposition of the soul that makes one sympathetic to the trials of others, sometimes even to the point of pity. We link, for example, a smile with moderate crying, or even better with the slight contraction of the muscle of suffering, and obtain an admirable expression of compassion, a most sympathetic emotion."†

Plate 80 is designed to portray an analogous scene. The young woman photographed in this figure is visiting a poor family; we recognize, from her tender laughter (cover the left side of the face), or from her kind smile (cover the right side of the face) that she is touched by the misery and the suffering of this unhappy family, and that this sentiment has inspired an act of charity.

The expression of compassion is the object of this study; it is important to understand the mechanism here.

I have demonstrated before that the contraction of *m. zygomaticus ma-*

---

*This expression excited general admiration. Yet I have to signal a correction that prejudices the whole. The modeling that gives the gaze of Marie de Medici a light nuance of physical pain does not exist on the left side. In fact, the left eyebrow describes a curved line; its head does not show the relief that, on the opposite side, gives its internal portion a slightly sinuous form. The result is that in covering the right eye, the expression is one of pure maternal joy, with no admixture of pain, a sweet expression that recalls that of Jeanne d'Albret, in the *Birth of Henry the IV* by Devéria, which has been referred to above. The head of Marie de Medici has then a double expression, which throws a little indecision on her physical pain. This double expression is analogous to what which I have produced experimentally in Plates 26 and 27, where the right *m. corrugator supercilii* is electrized in isolation (see the study of this, on p. 61 of the Scientific Section). The mistake committed by Rubens escapes notice at first, because the painful contraction of the right eyebrow is very feeble and contrasts little with the opposite eyebrow, which is not pained, and because the head in three-quarter view is turned from right to left, the left side of the face is less seen. Guido has committed the same mistake in his *Ecce Homo* in the Colona Museum in Rome. I have made this critical observation in the Scientific Section of the Album.
†This text, p. 18.

jor causes the labial commissure to move obliquely superolaterally, the nasolabial fold to form a curve with an inferior convexity, and the cheek to pucker. This is shown in all the figures in the Scientific Section of the Album, where the muscle of joy is shown in a state of electrical contraction (see Plates 30, 31, 32, 33, 34, 35, 36, and 37). We established also that, on the left side of Plate 80, natural laughter has acted in the same way on the labial commissure and on the nasolabial fold. Such are, for all ages, the fundamental expressive lines of joy.

We might now wish to recall the fundamental lines developed by the muscle of crying (*m. zygomaticus minor*), when localized electrization is applied to this muscle: The nasolabial fold, as I have said, describes a curve with an inferior concavity.

Well then! When the fundamental lines of smiling were developed, by the electrization of *m. zygomatcus major,* and I activated *m. zygomaticus minor* (muscle of crying), I had always seen the nasolabial fold become concave below and to deepen a little. At the same time the margin of the upper lip on this side was slightly raised or curled up at the level of the interior attachment of *m. zygomaticus minor.*

In order to obtain a just and harmonious expression by the combination of the muscle of crying with the muscle of joy, it is necessary, as with smiling mixed with pain, that the contraction of these muscles does not exceed certain limits; otherwise it becomes a grimace.

This experiment has sometimes been a complete success. It is very difficult, and I have never been able to maintain the contraction at just the right degree for long enough to reproduce it by photography. The procedure I employed in Plate 80 was more simple. I produced a spontaneous kind smile on the face of my model (see the left half of Plate 80), and then I gently stimulated the muscle of crying, on the opposite side (see the right half of Plate 80). Then the nasolabial fold and the form of the upper lip were altered on the right, as I had described above, although the lower lip maintained the form that it had affected in the smile. We can assure ourselves of this by covering the parts of this figure immediately below the lower lip. It results in a *smile both kind and sad,* or in other words, *a smile of pity.*

No one would confuse this kind of tearful smile with the smile mixed with pain shown on the left side of Plate 79. Nor is it the same smile that Homer has so admirably described in the parting of Andromache and Hector. The tears that the great poet made flow from this princess who was being separated from her husband with such dark forebodings, are the tears of pain. By translating the expression "δαχρυόεν γελάσασα," by which Homer wanted to depict this emotion of the spirit, too literally by the words *laughter with tears (lacrymabundum ridens),* authors have not exactly rendered the thoughts of Homer, since compassion made these tears flow, distinct from when we cry from happiness.

III. Plates 81, 82, and 83 reproduce my experiments on the muscle of aggression (*m. procerus*, P, Plate 1), from the aesthetic point of view.

This muscle was so well developed in my young female subject that on her face, on which I had just shown the sweetest and the most touching emotions, I was able to make a head of Medusa, one of the furies, and so forth. I have also recalled on her face the features of women in history who were renowned for their cruelty.

Thus, inspired by the tragedy of Macbeth, one of Shakespeare's most marvelous plays, I tried to represent the expression that Lady Macbeth must have had, when, after assuring herself that Duncan and the guards, whom she had drugged, were soundly asleep, and after having given Macbeth the murder signal, she waited while he cut the throat of the king, his host and benefactor (in Plate 81).

Lady Macbeth: That which hath made them drunk hath made me bold;
What hath quench'd them hath given me fire. Hark! Peace!
It was the owl that shriek'd, the fatal bellman,
Which gives the stern'st good night. He is about it:
The doors are open and the surfeited grooms
Do mock their charge with snores: I have drugg'd their possets,
That death and nature do contend about them,
Whether they live or die.
Macbeth (within): Who's there? What, ho!
Lady Macbeth: Alack I am afraid they have awaked
And 'tis not done: the attempt and not the deed
Confounds us. Hark! I laid their daggers ready;
He could not miss 'em. *Had he not resembled
My father as he slept, I had done't.**

It is at the moment where Lady Macbeth expresses this last thought that I wanted to portray her expression in Plate 81. We don't notice on her face the terrible air that I gave to her soon after, when I showed her letting herself be carried away by her furious jealousy and homicide. Here the resemblance of her royal victim to her sleeping father has caused her such emotion that her strength has abandoned her. So I have represented her falling onto a seat and restraining the violent beating of her heart. But her heart is made of bronze, we know from the hard gaze and the wicked attitude that she still retains. She wants to be queen, even at the price of her king's life! The courage that had been wanting she had left to her husband, of whom she is the evil genius and to whom she has communicated the cruel instincts of her ambitious rage, the responsibility for this murder, and she waits, armed with a dagger, to see that

*Macbeth, act II, scene II.

he has finished his work, ready to come to his aid again if he should falter.

Shakespeare's *Macbeth* has impressed me quite differently from M. Guizot's interpretation. According to this master of English tragedy translation, the foundation of her nature is not cruelty; Lady Macbeth is only ambitious. She sees only the pleasure of ruling in the death of Duncan. But must not the woman be cruel whom Shakespeare has made to say:

I have given suck, and know
How tender 'tis to love the babe that milks me:
I would, while it was smiling in my face,
Have plucked the nipple from its boneless gums,
And dash'd the brains out, had so I sworn as you
Have done to this.*

Maternal love does not exclude cruelty, she loves her children as a she-wolf loves her young.

In another electrophysiological study on the same scene (Plate 82), I have tried more strongly to mark the forehead of Lady Macbeth with the seal of cruelty. Her appearance here is terrible; this cannot be a woman in whom any filial piety came to be mingled with her thoughts of murder to lessen their heat.

This expression of cruelty (Plate 82) well portrays the Lady Macbeth who has just received with sinister joy the news of the arrival of King Duncan to Inverness and who, when learning that he wished to pass the night in her castle, hatched the plot of assassination. It fits more with the scene where she makes a call to her ferocious instincts, in this savage invocation:

Come you spirits
That tend on mortal thoughts, unsex me here,
And fill me, from the crown to the toe, top-full
Of direst cruelty! Make thick my blood,
Stop up the access and passage to remorse,
That no compunctious visitings of nature
Shake my fell purpose. . . .†

A muscle that displays the worst emotions (*m. procerus*) certainly does not beautify the face. The features that accentuate this action are no more sympathetic.

Yet the terrible Lady Macbeth that we see in Plate 81, dominated by

---

*Macbeth, act I, scene VII.

†*Macbeth*, act I, scene V. If Plate 82 had originally been designed to represent this scene, I would have liked to put my model in a costume suiting the circumstances. We know that, in this scene, Lady Macbeth needs to be ready to receive the visit of King Duncan, who has announced his imminent arrival.

the wish to kill the king, has not lost any of her beauty! Here *m. procerus* has been very lightly stimulated. (We recall that I have done this to show that the homicidal fury of Lady Macbeth was moderated by the sentiment of filial piety that came over her when she found a resemblance between Duncan and her sleeping father.)

Beyond this degree of excitation, *m. procerus* has, in Plate 82, altered the beauty of my model, although this muscle has been only moderately stimulated.

The facial expression of this young girl was made more terrible and more disfigured than even in Plate 82 by the maximal contraction of this little muscle, and we need to consider it as the principal and true agent of the aggressive and wicked passions, of hatred, of jealousy, of cruel instincts.

Plate 83, where *m. procerus* has been maximally contracted, is a striking proof of this. Who would recognize the young person in this figure whose face is transfigured in such a stunning way by divine or human love? I imagine Lady Macbeth to myself, coming down on Duncan, dagger in hand, with the ferocious air that I have photographed in Plate 83. We see that these darkened features are singularly ugly. I have imagined that Lady Macbeth, in recognizing a resemblance between King Duncan and her sleeping father, lost her courage to strike and collapsed onto a seat. (This scene is not in Shakespeare.)

Thus the unfavorable effect on the beauty of the face of a fairly strong contraction of *m. procerus* is seen when we compare Plates 81, 82, and 83.

All subjects are not equally suited to an electrophysiological study of aggressive emotions; in other words, the principal expressive muscle that is put in action by such feelings does not always exert the same power on the eyebrow.

This fact has been shown experimentally in the Scientific Section of the Album. We recall that after having portrayed on the face of a good-natured old man (see his portrait, Plate 3) an expression of wickedness and also of cruelty (see Plate 18), by the contraction of *m. procerus*, I have found this muscle so feeble or so little developed in a young man (see his portrait, Plate 4), that I have been hardly able, in spite of strong stimulation of this muscle, to lower the head of his eyebrow (see Plate 16). It is true; the face of this latter subject took on then an expression of hardness, but it would have been impossible for me to produce the cruel features of an assassin.

This does not apply to the eyebrow muscles of the young girl I chose to model in the aesthetic part of the Album. The muscles that lower the eyebrow (*m. procerus* and the superior part of *m. orbicularis oculi,* P & B, Plate 1) are stronger than the elevators, *m. frontalis* and *m. corrugator supercilii* (A & O, Plate 1). This latter muscle is so feeble that to put it into action in Plates 75 and 76 I had to use an intense current, whereas a much more gentle excitation of *m. procerus* has been able to give this girl the features of a fury.

In order to complete the expression of aggressive emotions, we need to combine the lowering of the head of the eyebrow with the lowering of the angle of the mouth. These movements are obtained electrophysiologically by the combined contraction of *m. procerus* and *m. depressor anguli oris.* Now, as in my model, the corners of the mouth may be lowered naturally (see her portrait, Plate 74). It has sufficed for me to make her *m. procerus* contract, to produce the photographic results in Plates 81, 82, and 83. (We know already in these figures the reciprocal role of the mouth and the eye, by alternately covering one or the other of these parts of the face.)

In every instance, the fundamental facial signs of wickedness and cruel instincts have been perfectly expressed (the oblique direction of the eyebrow lateral to medial and superiorly to inferiorly, by lowering the head of the eyebrow). It is with this obliquity of the eyebrow, and by exaggerating it, that we have represented the spirit of evil, the demon.

This sign of wickedness can also be recognized on the face of men who instinctively do evil for evil's sake, whether they are armed with the pen or a dagger: These are the tyrants for whom life has been just a long list of atrocities and who show generally a permanent stigma. See, for example, the portrait of Nero: His face is in repose; the signs of wickedness or cruelty that distinguish it are due to the increased tonic force of *m. procerus,* developed by the frequent exercise of these bad passions.

The expression of aggression or cruel passions in movement has nearly always been equally well portrayed. I have admired a remarkable example of it in the *Conspiracy of Catilina* by Salvator Rosa (Florence, Pitti Palace). The plotters, whether their faces are in repose or moving, have an expression of wickedness and of ferocity perfectly characterized by the lowering and puckering of the head of the eyebrow, by the transverse cutaneous creasing of the root of the nose, and finally by the oblique inferomedial direction of the eyebrow. Salvator Rosa had, without any doubt, chosen his models from the bandits whom he made his habitual companions. He has shown, in his picture, the types that we find in great numbers in our prisons.

It has happened, however, that, diverging from nature, some artists have committed errors of detail, upsetting the expression, errors that they could certainly have avoided if they had known the mechanism of action of *m. procerus.*

Although this mechanism has already been discussed in the Scientific Section, it seems useful to recapitulate here. I have shown that the fixed point of this muscle is always below and consequently that its upper end is mobile in the skin, in the space between the eyebrows at the level of the head of the eyebrows. Its contraction necessarily pulls the skin inferiorly, in such a way that it folds at the root of the nose, *whereas it stretches the central part of the forehead.* These facts emerge from the experiments shown in Figures 81, 82, and 83, as they have been demonstrated in the Scientific Section (see Plates 19, 20, 21, 22, 23, 24, and 25).

Long and careful observation convinced me that, in all these actions, nature is in perfect accord with experimentation; yet too often they have been misunderstood in the practice of art. I regret that one of the most illustrious masters of contemporary art, Paul Delaroche, has committed a grave fault in his picture *The Assassination of President Duranti,* and that it is clear that he has departed from the principles that I have just outlined. Before demonstrating this, I will relate the story behind this great picture.

Duranti, President of the Parliament of Toulouse, was opposed to the League, and tried uselessly to calm the people secretly agitating on the occasion of the death of the Duke of Guise. Forced to hide in a convent with his wife and their two children, Duranti was discovered by the populace, who, despite the opposition of some monks, priests, and his family, seized him from the convent and assassinated him.

The artist has chosen the moment when the populace discovered Duranti and his family in their hiding place. We see the leader of the mob menacing President Duranti with his fist, while the President's noble face remains calm. The hair of this man is ruffled; his hands and gross features inspire revulsion. Delaroche has given him an expression of ferocious hatred by obliquely lowering his thick eyebrows inferolaterally, and by transversely creasing the skin of the root of his nose. This expressive movement demonstrates to the physiologist that *m. procerus* is strongly contracted, and that the *skin of the central part of the forehead* must be pulled down and necessarily stretched. Delaroche, on the contrary, has transversely creased the skin of this region of the forehead, such as we see produced by *m. corrugator supercilii,* the muscle of pain (see all the plates dealing with this muscle), which, as an antagonist of *m. procerus,* normally would elevate the eyebrow. It is, therefore, incontestable that mechanically the modeling of the forehead of this man cannot coexist with the movement shown of his eyebrow. It is more than an orthographic fault; for although the fundamental expressive lines of hatred and of cruelty (the obliquity of the eyebrow, the outline and the transverse wrinkles of the root of the nose) are exactly rendered, the presence of median transverse wrinkles, which constitute the secondary lines of pain, always a sympathetic expression, considerably diminish the effect of the expression of wickedness that Delaroche has wanted to give to the chief of the band.

As *m. procerus* is the only muscle that lowers the head of the eyebrow to portray cruel instincts, just as *m. corrugator supercilii* raises it to express pain, we are not surprised that each contracts separately under the influence of certain emotions. Normally, therefore, it contracts with the superior part of *m. orbicularis oculi* (O, Plate 1), and the whole eyebrow is lowered still, conserving its inferolateral obliquity, if the individual is carried away by wicked or cruel instincts.

In calling *m. procerus* the muscle of aggressive passions, I wanted to imply that it was not only in the service of bad emotions, such as wickedness and cruelty. They may be legitimate and even praiseworthy sentiments that we display in becoming aggressive toward our enemies. Offended honor excites anger and demands vengeance; man arms himself for freedom against his oppressors. In all these situations, man can become aggressive; the expression of this is transmitted by the wrinkling of the eyebrows and by their lowering en masse (under the influence of the combined action of *m. procerus* and of the superior part of *m. orbicularis oculi*). Then we know if in the heat of emotion, the instinct of cruelty does not predominate, the lowering of the heads of the eyebrows will not be very pronounced; this lowering may not even be noticeable if the muscle which represents this passion is poorly developed as in the subject shown in Plates 4 and 16.

These diverse nuances of aggressive expression have been generally well rendered in painting. In order to make this better understood, I can show an example in the picture by Prudhon, titled: *Justice and Vengeance Pursuing Crime* (Louvre, no. 459).

I wish to recall the legend behind this beautiful composition.

"On the left, in a desert place, bristling with rocks, lighted by the moon, a man, a dagger in his hand, dressed in a tunic and a coat, is retiring quickly. On the right, stretched out on the ground is the body of a young assassinated man. Above the victim, floating in the air, Vengeance carrying a torch, prepares to seize the murderer, and Justice is personified by the balances and the sword."*

The wild figure of Vengeance, whose clenched fist is going to grasp

---

*Commentary on the pictures of the Louvre, F. Villot.

the murderer, has an expression of indignation and of anger; his gaze is menacing and terrible, but without being cruel; his *puckered eyebrows have a horizontal direction.* Cain, pursued by Justice and divine Vengeance, flees terrified, but the eye of the brother-killer is cruel and ferocious. *This expression is produced by the lowering of the head of the eyebrow (whose direction is consequently coming down from outside inward) and by the swelling of the space between the eyebrows.* The gross features of Cain and his stocky limbs only add to the energy of this ferocious expression and the repulsion that it inspires.

The young girl, in whom the muscle of aggression is strong enough for isolated electrical stimulation to produce the signs of wickedness and the cruelest instincts, cannot voluntarily express these same emotions. I have confirmed this same phenomenon on a great number of subjects. Might we not conclude that the aggressive muscle, of wickedness, and so on, is one of those that are less under the control of the will, and that usually it is put into play only by instinct or by that emotion for which it is the sole expressive agent.

We notice that a muscle that expresses a sentiment contrary to the muscle of aggression, the muscle of kindness (the inferior part of *m. orbicularis oculi*, E, Plate 1), is equally resistant to the will. It only obeys the sweet movement of the soul, which inspires a sympathetic gaze, as in the left half of Plate 80. This is one of nature's preventative measures, which has not permitted us to easily dissimulate or feign expressive lines, so that a man can distinguish his friends from his enemies.

IV. "But it will be simple for me to show that there are some emotions that man cannot simulate or portray artificially on his face; the attentive observer is always able to recognize a false smile."* I have previously formulated this proposition in protesting against the assertion by the great philosopher Descartes, who claimed that we can just as easily use these actions of the face and eyes to distort the passions as to declare them.† My proposition again emerges from the facts given in chapter 6 of the Scientific Section.

The emotion of frank joy is expressed on the face by the combined contraction of *m. zygomaticus major* (I, Plate 1) and the inferior part of *m. orbicularis oculi* (E, Plate 1). The first obeys the will but the second (the muscle of kindness, of love, and of agreeable impressions) is only put in play by the sweet emotions of the soul. Finally, fake joy, the deceitful laugh, cannot provoke the contraction of this latter muscle.

We have seen, in Plates 31 and 32 (Scientific Section) the differential signs of false and real joy. These are characterized in Plate 32 by a hori-

*This text, p. 30.
†*Les passions de l'âme*, 2nd partie, art. 14.

zontal depression situated beneath the lower eyelid (which represents natural laughter) and in Plate 31 by the absence of this depression (see also Plate 30, where *m. zygomaticus major* is stimulated in isolation, on the right side). People cannot confuse these two sorts of laughter, because they are at their maximum. The false laugh of the right side of Plate 30 contrasts in fact with its impassive gaze. Who could take this kind of convulsive laughter, which is disagreeable, for that of gaiety?

The false smile, produced by the isolated action of *m. zygomaticus major*, at a weaker degree of contraction, is at first sight more deceptive than the preceding one, although an attentive observer would be difficult to deceive.

The experimental study of this expression is represented in Plate 48. Lady Macbeth has provided the subject for me. Hearing of the arrival of King Duncan, she has conceived the project to assassinate him. She has roused her cruel instincts and has called on infernal spirits to help her; and yet in her welcome, the smile is on her lips, protesting her affection! It is at this moment that I wanted to represent Lady Macbeth in Plate 84 – when she has pronounced her affection, pledging that "All our service,

In every point twice done, and then done double,
Were poor and single business to contend
Against those honors deep and broad wherewith
Your majesty loads our house, . . .*

We have seen, in Plate 82, the expression of cruelty that I have given her, under the impression of her horrible invocation. But quite at home in the art of dissimulation, Lady Macbeth, in going to receive her king, has already been able to dissipate the last traces of her furious transport of anger, and her mouth composes itself into a false smile, as she knows how to reinforce the affectionate and lying remarks.

Here, happily, the control of her face ceases. She cannot impose on her gaze a sympathetic expression in harmony with her smile.

The attitude and the gesture that I have given to my model are well in keeping with the welcome extended to the king by Lady Macbeth. Her mouth is smiling in saying "Your servants ever." But what a smile (cover the right side of the mouth and of the cheek)! See how the eye is cold and freezes the smile! It is a smile that kills, and Duncan, who, when remembering the treason of Cawdor, might have cried sadly: "If we could have only seen it on his face," certainly would not have let himself be fooled by this false expression, if he were not blinded by the kindness in his heart.

You cannot always exaggerate the significance of this kind of smile,

Macbeth, act I, scene vi.

which is often only a simple smile of politeness, just as it can cover a treason. In the case of Lady Macbeth, it needed to excite the defiance of Duncan, because it was in discord with her protestations of love. We, in other circumstances and in normal intercourse with society, politely smile with our lips at the same time as being malcontented or when the soul is sad. When I did the experiment that is the subject of Plate 84, my model was in a very bad mood; her gaze was cold and the corners of her mouth a little lowered (cover on the left side the half of the mouth and the lower part of the cheek). As soon as I had produced the slight contraction of *m. zygomaticus major* on the left (cover the same parts on the opposite side), the false smile of Lady Macbeth in the above described scene, is portrayed on the face.

The electrical stimulation, in this experiment, was strictly limited to the right *m. zygomaticus major*, so the eyelids of this side stayed immobile, as on the opposite side. I will add that maximal electrical excitation can be equally well localized in *m. zygomaticus major* of this young girl. Her eyelids don't undergo any movement, and we don't see, in her, wrinkles radiating from the lateral canthus of the eye, as in the old man in Plates 31 and 32, because these wrinkles are secondary expressive lines, which do not appear until after a certain age, or in very thin people.

This precise electrization of *m. zygomaticus major* allows me to discuss the reciprocal expressive influences of the eyelids at rest and of the moderate movement of the labial commissures belonging to the smile. This study has already been mentioned, in the Scientific Section, dealing with the maximal contraction of *m. zygomaticus major* (see Plates 30 and 32). If the part of the face situated beneath the nose is covered, the gaze of Plate 84 seems cold and dry; but as soon as the right side of the lip is uncovered, the eyes seem to brighten up and the features open out a little, although the contraction of *m. zygomaticus major* is very light. This illusion, however feeble it may be, is evident at first glance, without always provoking sympathy.

But when the smile of the lips is joined by the sweet look that we have seen on the left side of Plate 80, in an instant we are irresistibly drawn by sympathy. Here the lower eyelid has been transversely creased, a certain distance from its free border, by the muscle of kindness (the inferior part of *m. orbicularis oculi*), the study of which has been shown in chapter 10.

I close this section by recalling what I have said of this muscle on page 72 of the Scientific Section of this text: "The muscle that produces this depression on the lower eyelid does not obey the will; it is only brought into play by a genuine feeling, by an agreeable emotion. Its inertia in smiling unmasks a false friend."

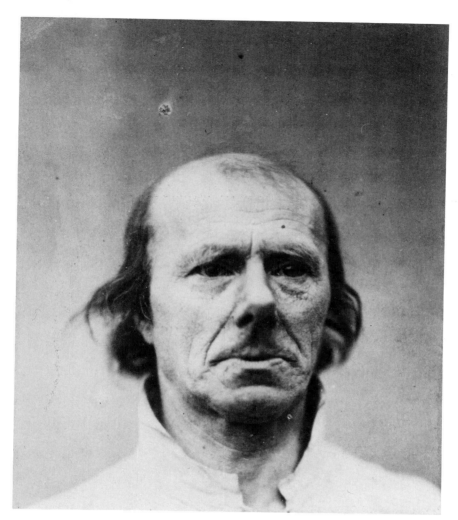

Plate 3

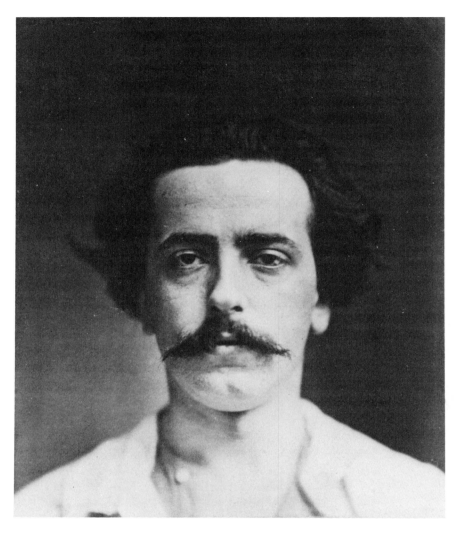

Plate 4

Plate 5

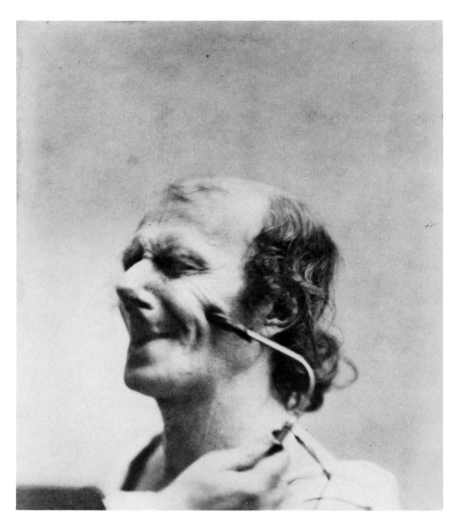

Plate 6

132

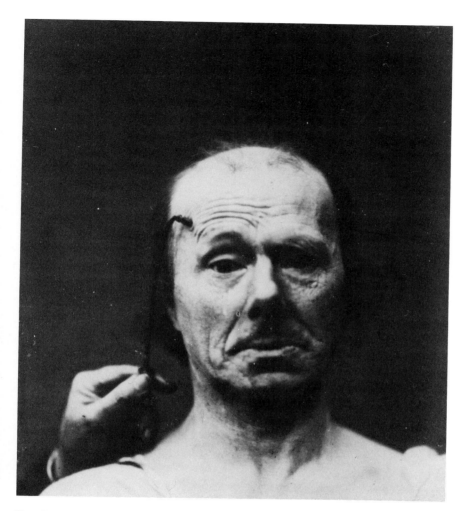

Plate 7

133

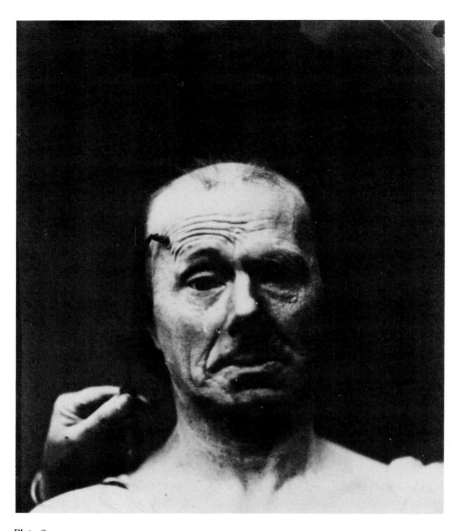

Plate 8

134

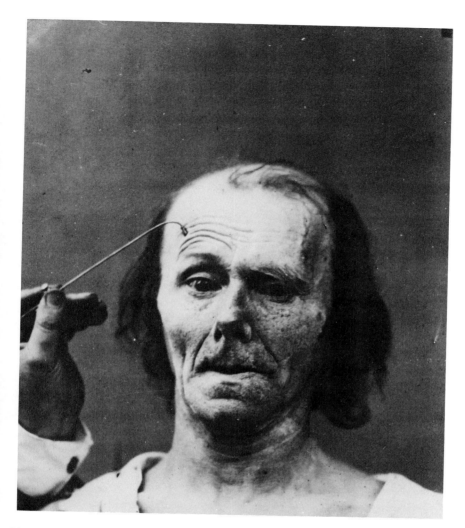

Plate 9

135

Plate 10

Plate 11

137

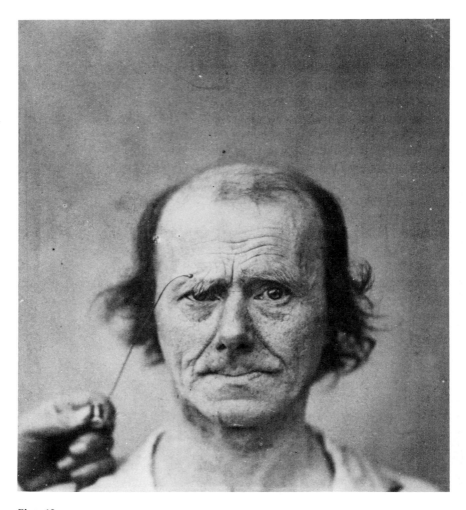

Plate 12

138

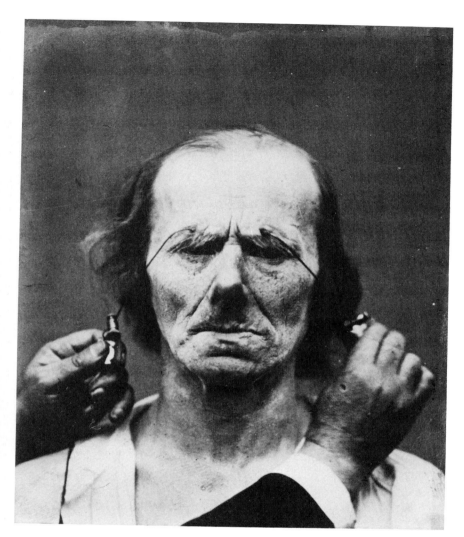

Plate 13

139

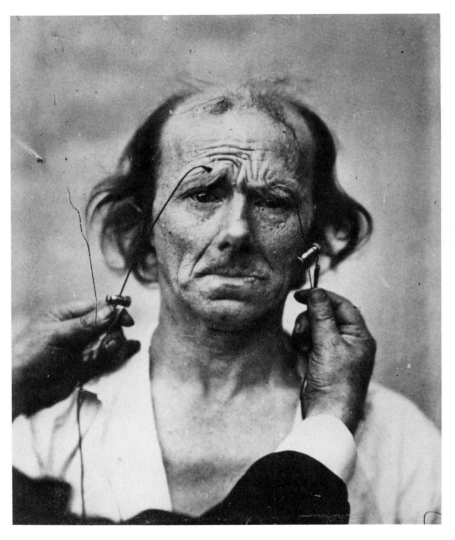

Plate 14

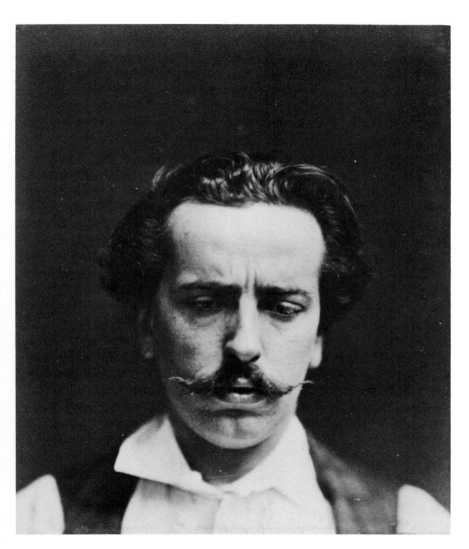

Plate 15

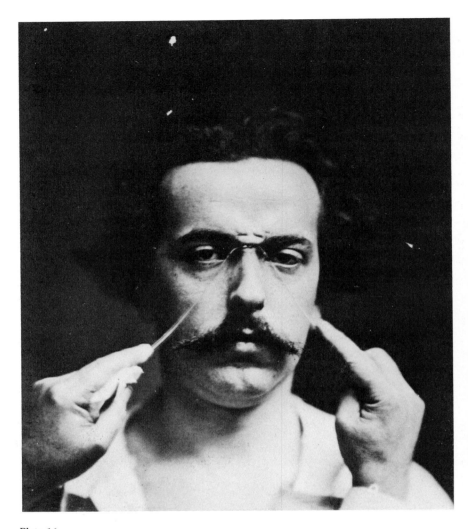

Plate 16

142

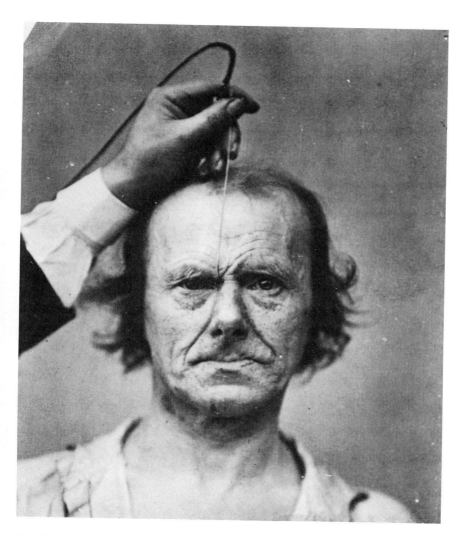

Plate 17

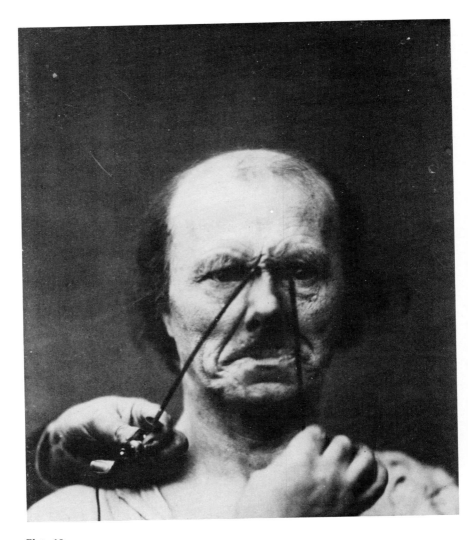

Plate 18

144

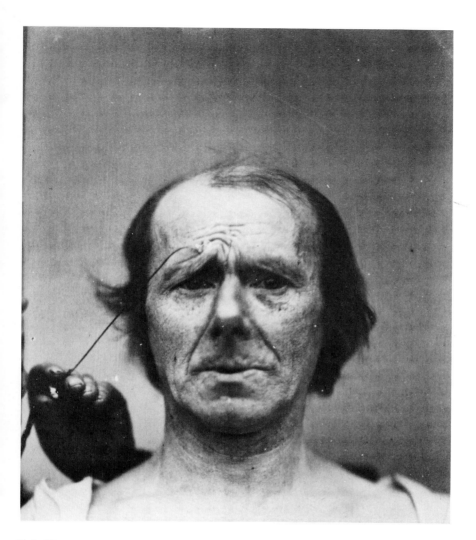

Plate 19

145

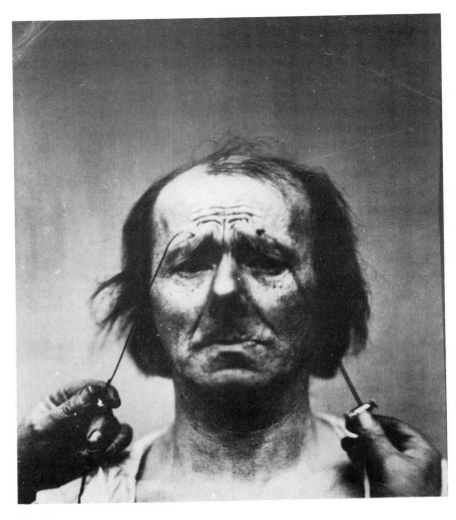

Plate 20

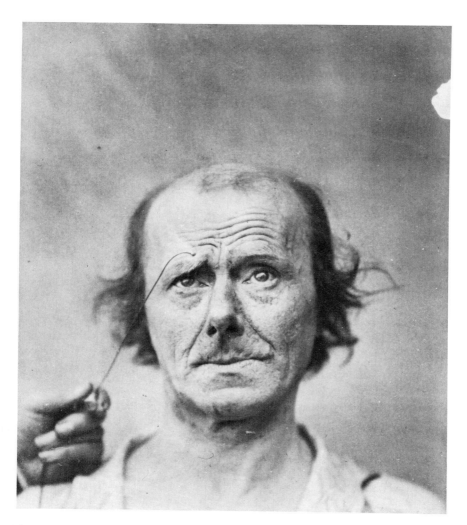

Plate 21

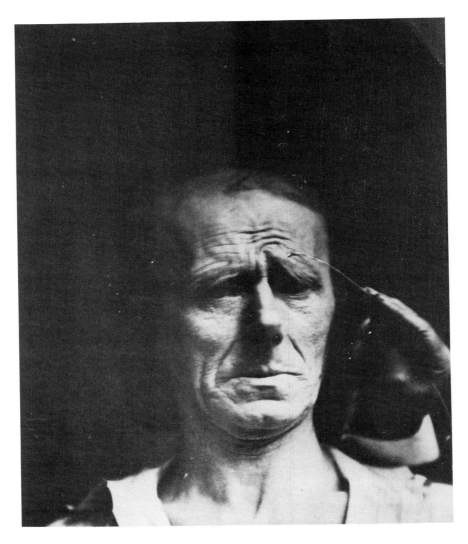

Plate 22

148

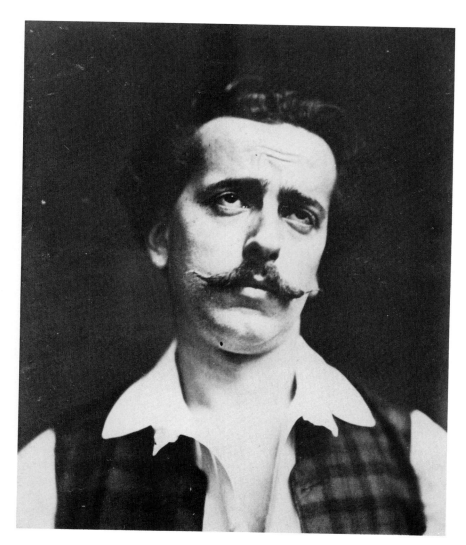

Plate 23

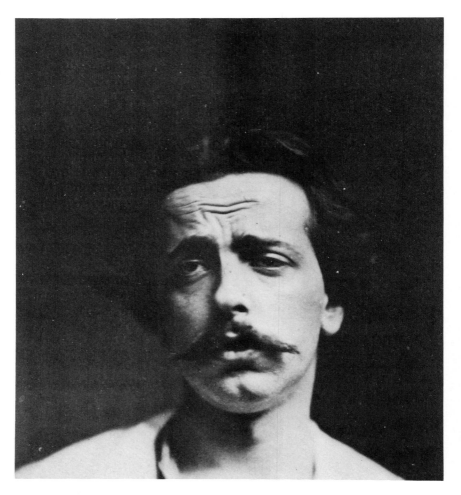

Plate 24

150

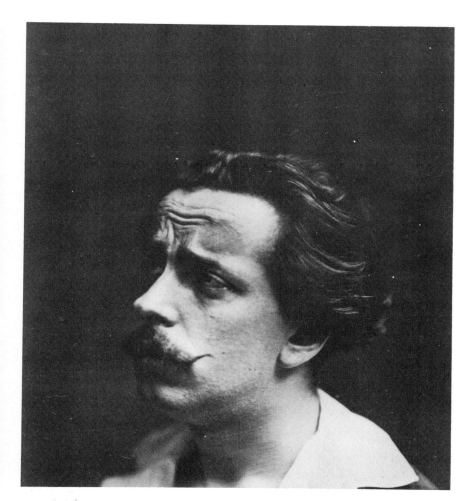

Plate 25

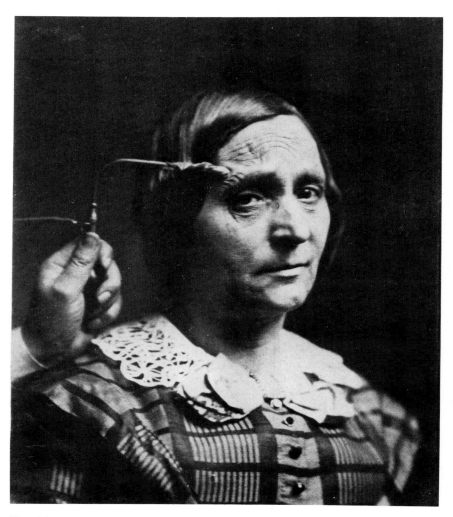

Plate 26

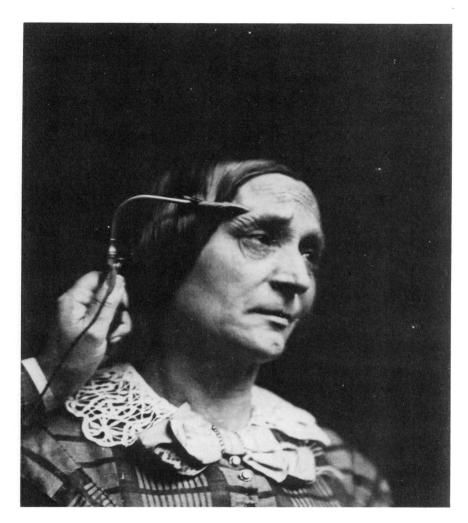

Plate 27

Plate 28

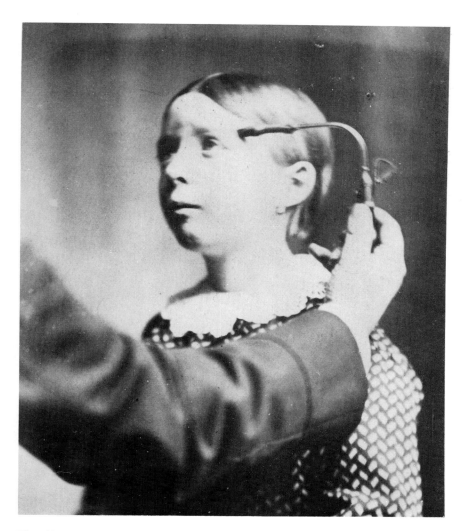

Plate 29

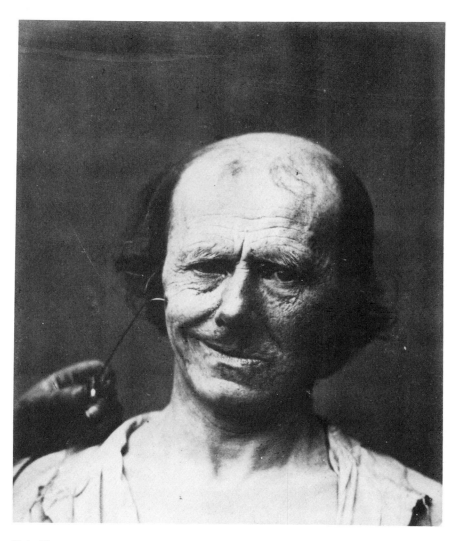

Plate 30

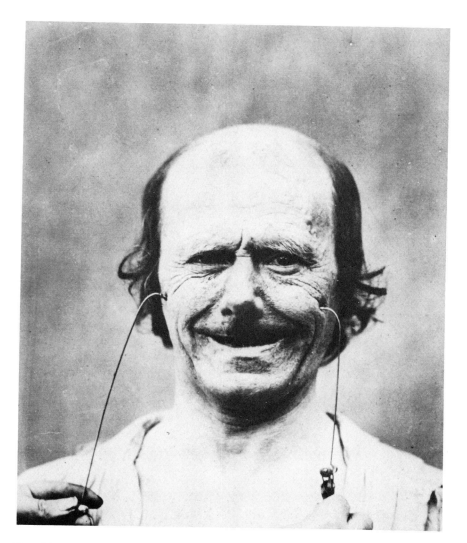

Plate 31

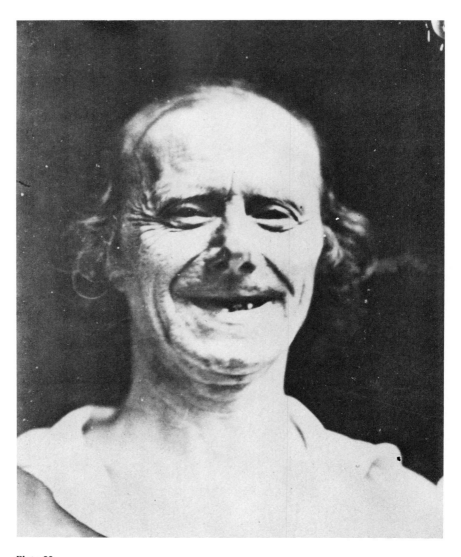

Plate 32

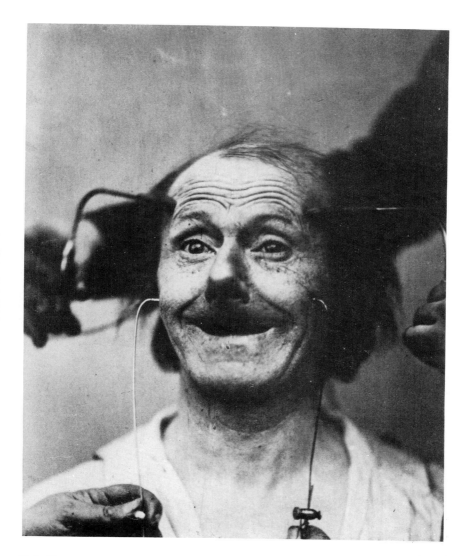

Plate 33

159

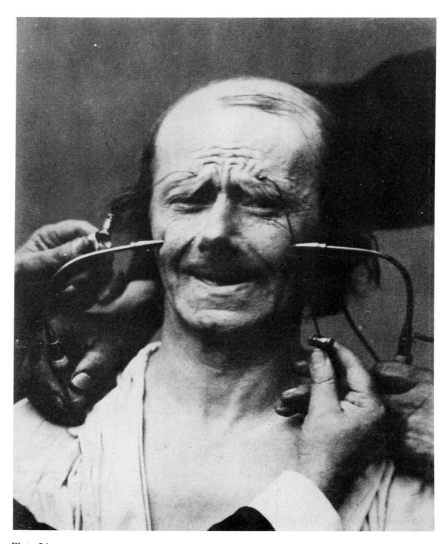

Plate 34

160

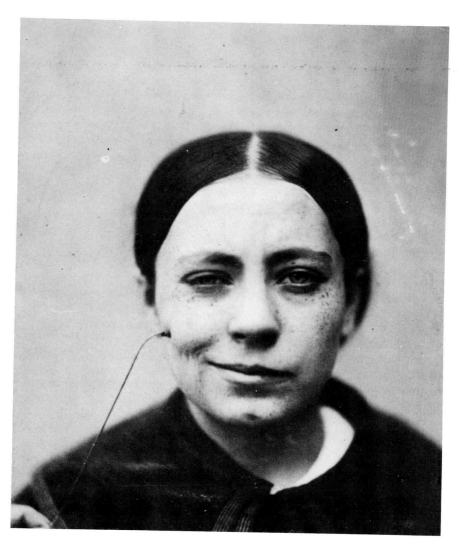

Plate 35

161

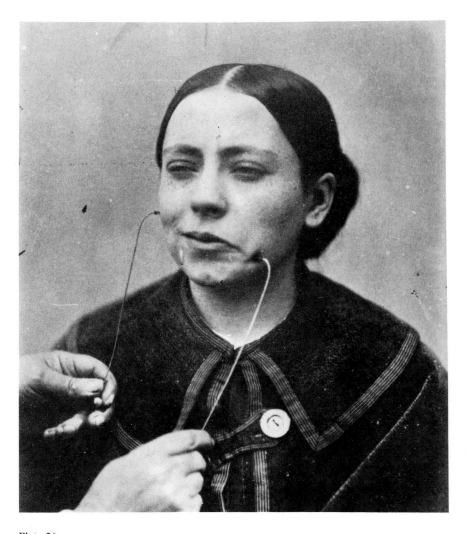

Plate 36

162

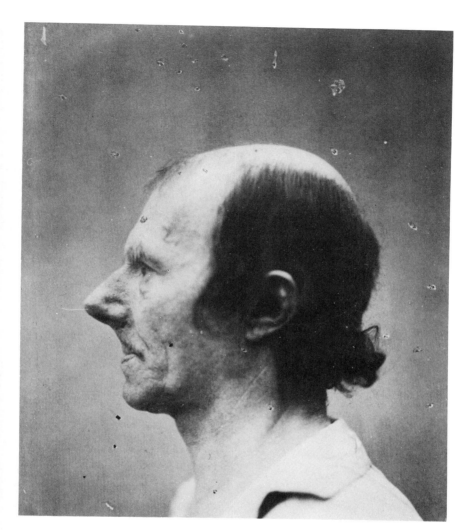

Plate 37

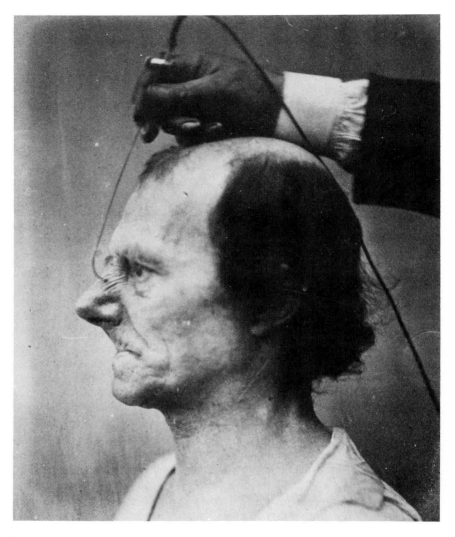

Plate 38

164

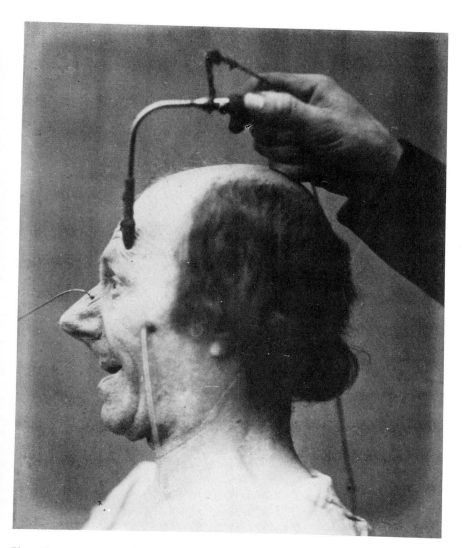

Plate 39

165

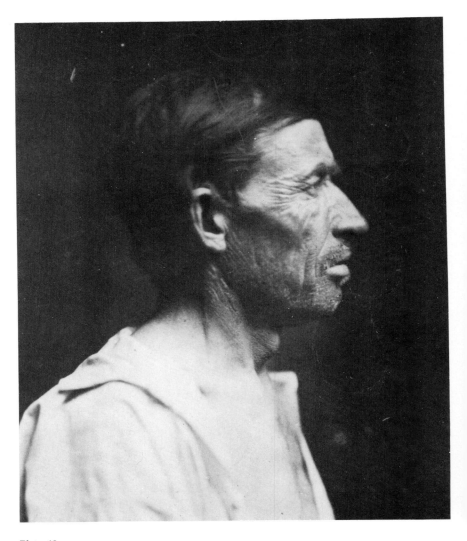

Plate 40

166

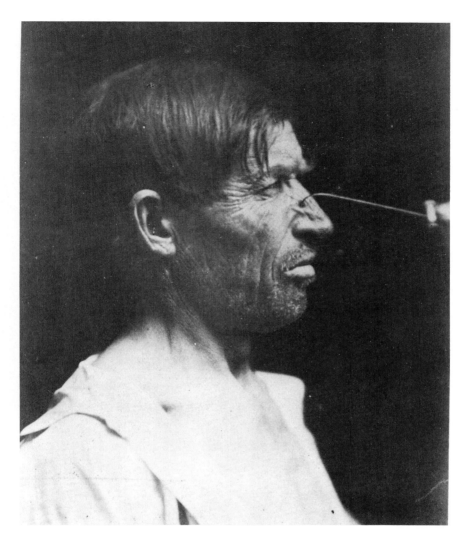

Plate 41

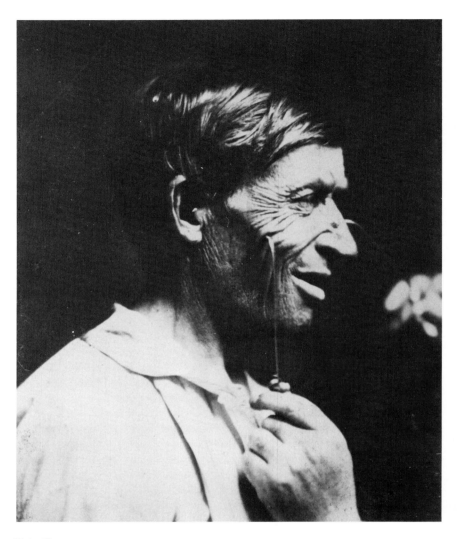

Plate 42

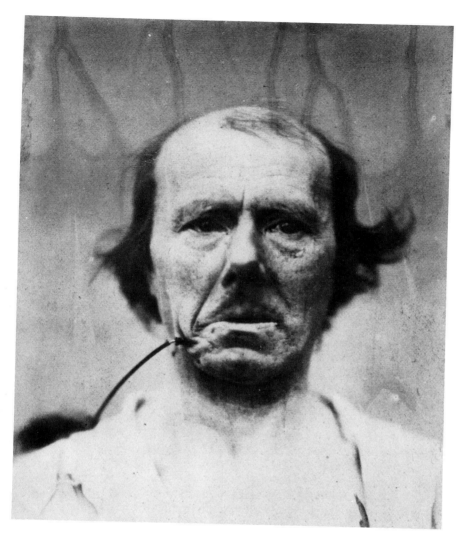

Plate 43

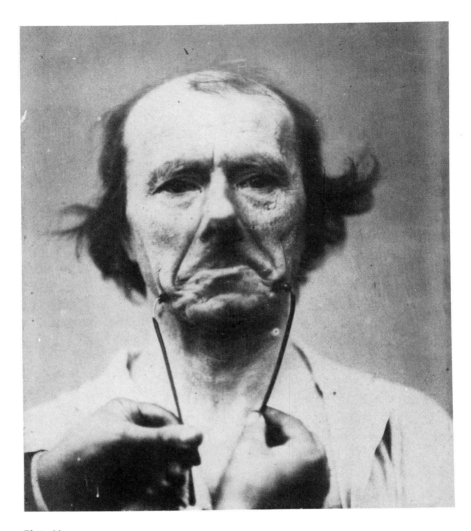

Plate 44

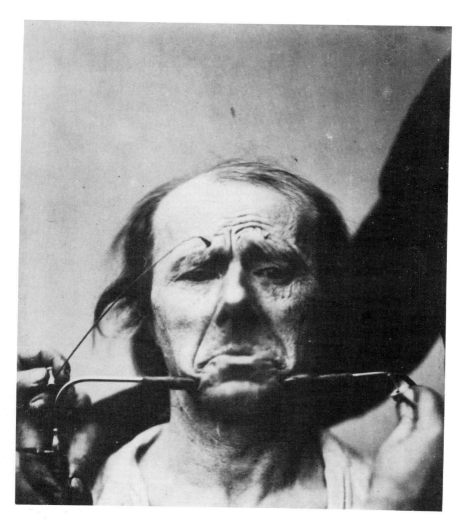

Plate 45

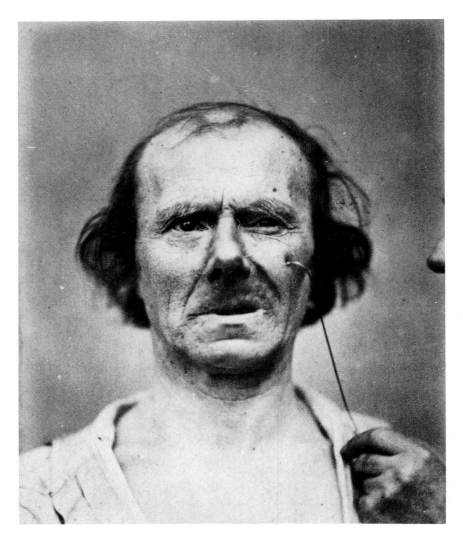

Plate 46

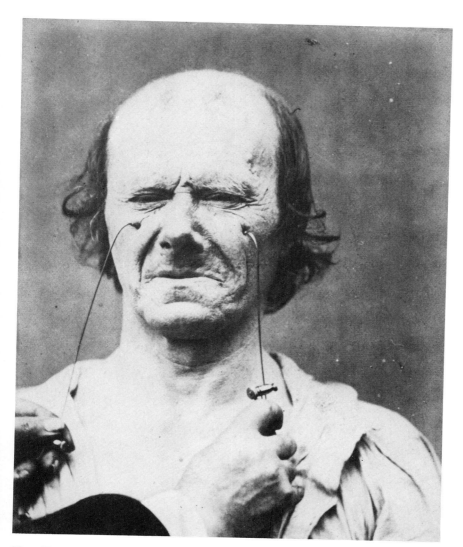

Plate 47

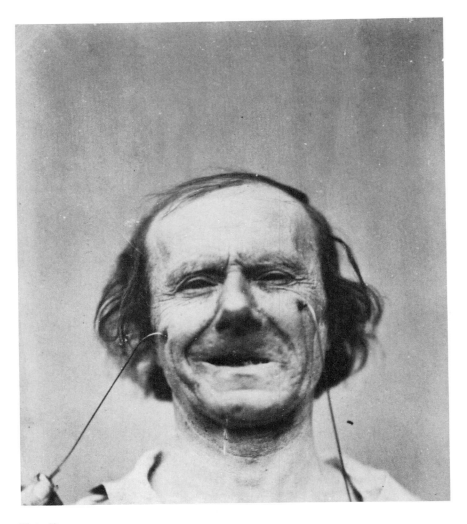

Plate 48

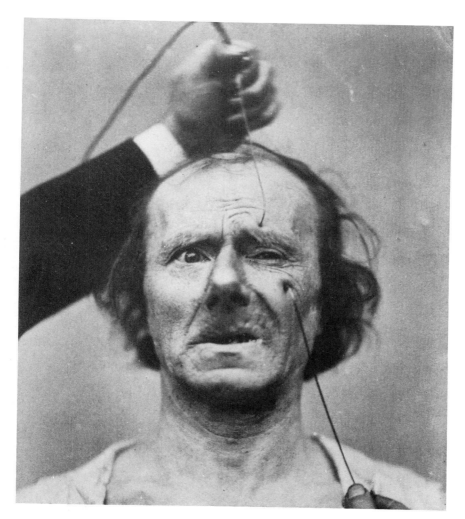

Plate 49

175

Plate 50

176

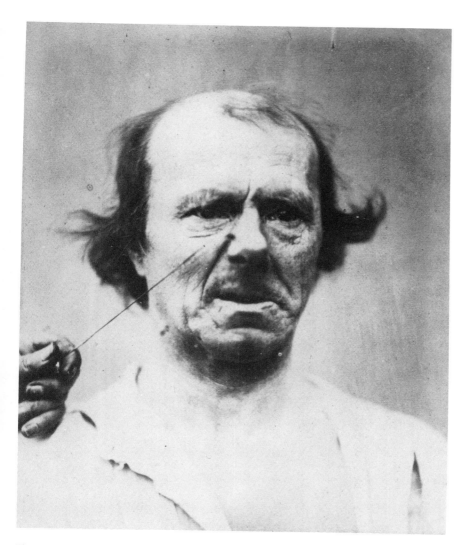

Plate 51

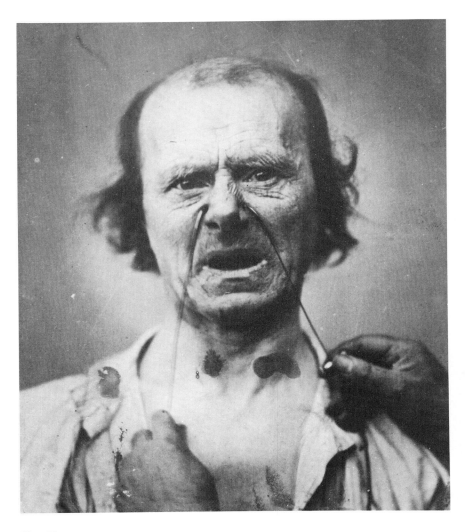

Plate 52

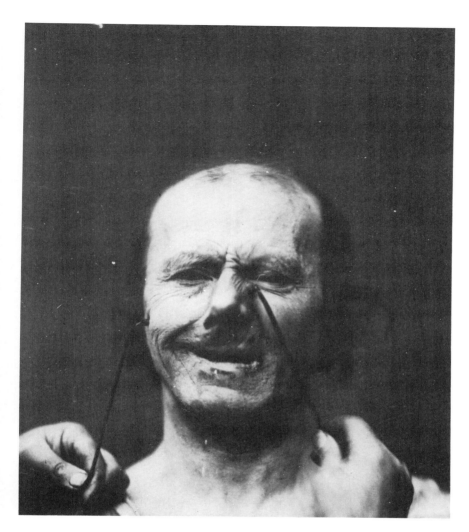

Plate 53

Plate 54

180

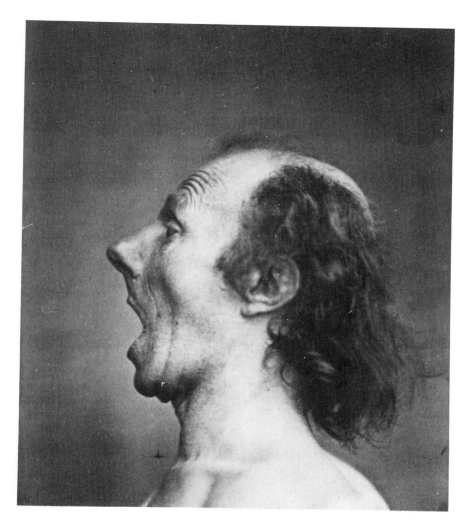

Plate 55

181

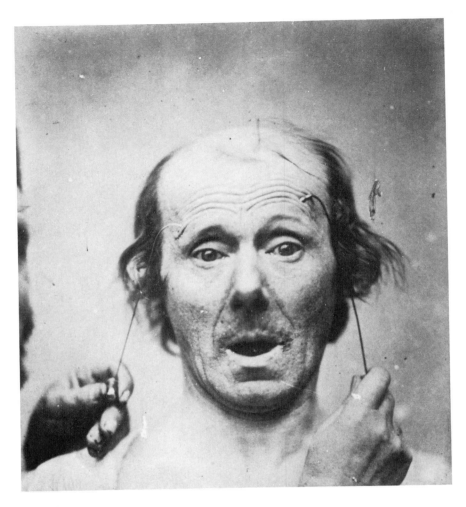

Plate 56

182

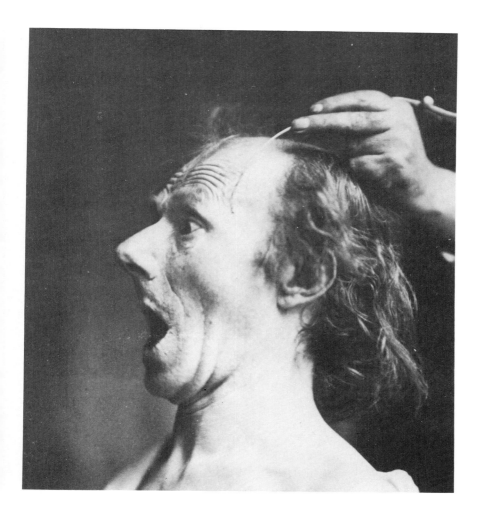

Plate 57

183

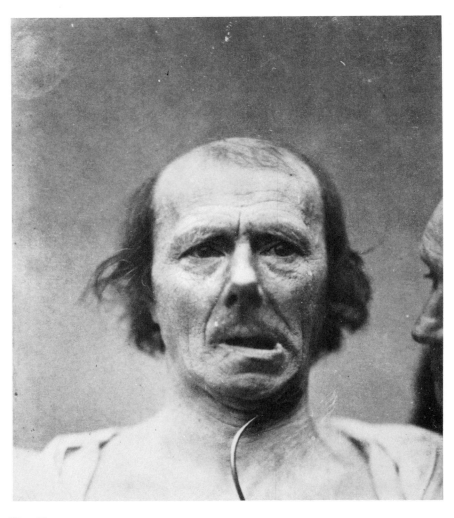

Plate 58

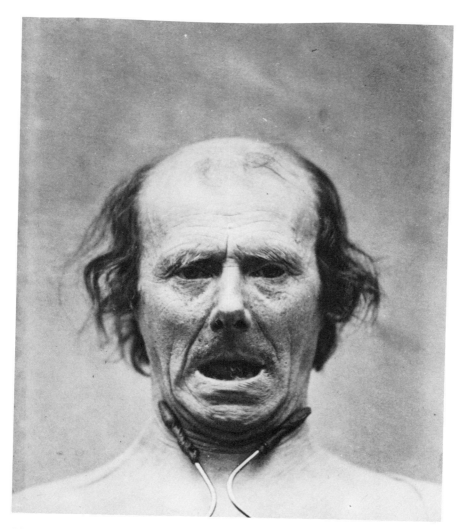

Plate 59

Plate 60

186

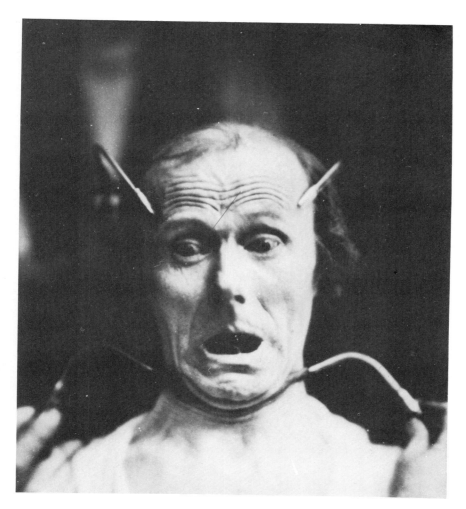

Plate 61

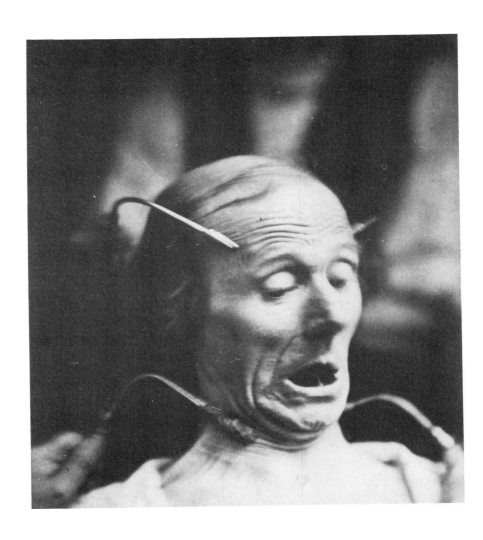

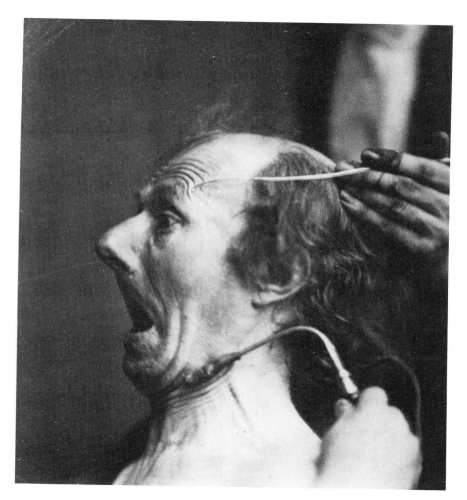

Plate 63

189

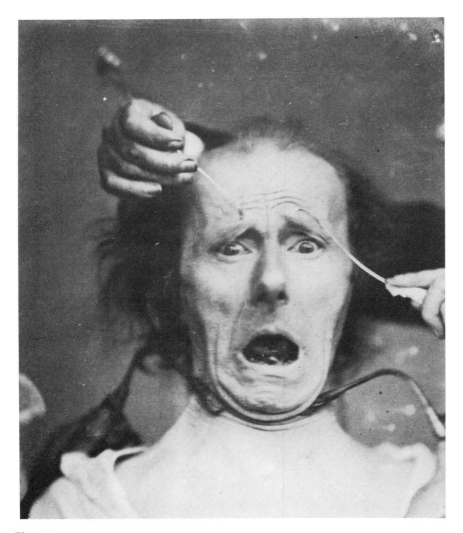

Plate 64

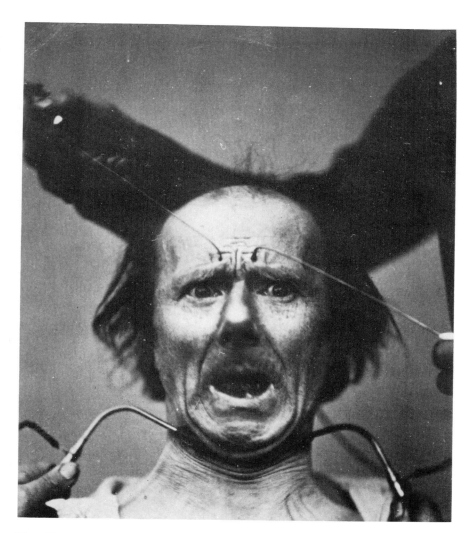

Plate 65

Plate 66

Plate 67

193

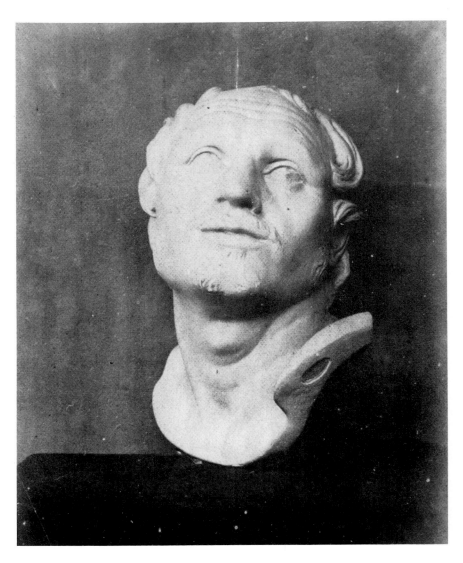

Plate 68

194

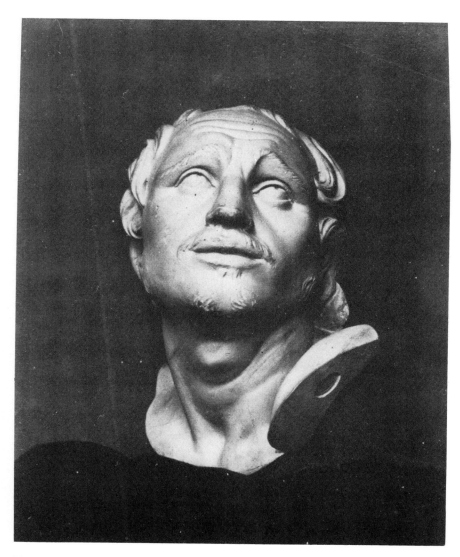

Plate 69

195

Plate 70

196

Plate 71

197

Plate 72

Plate 73

Plate 74

200

Plate 75

201

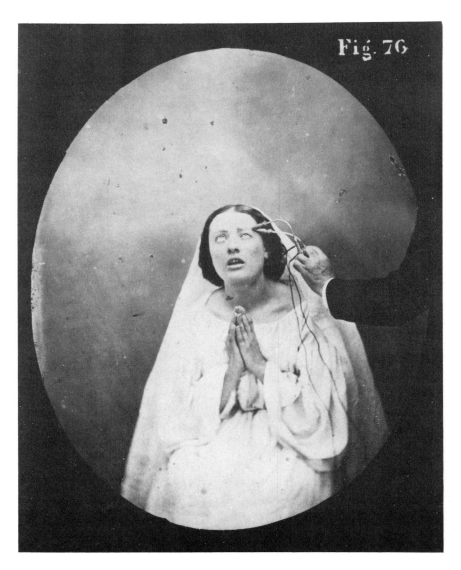

Plate 76

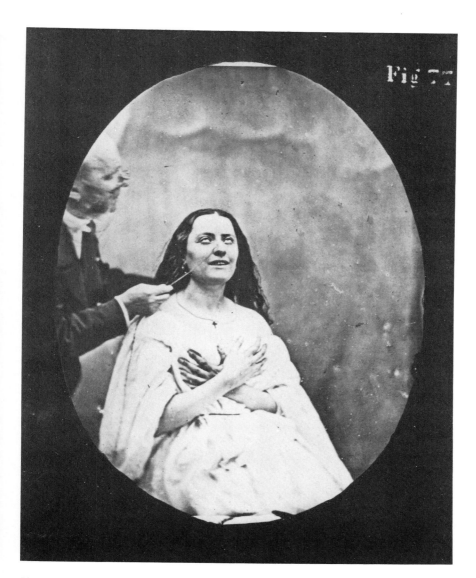

Plate 77

Plate 78

Plate 79

205

Plate 80

206

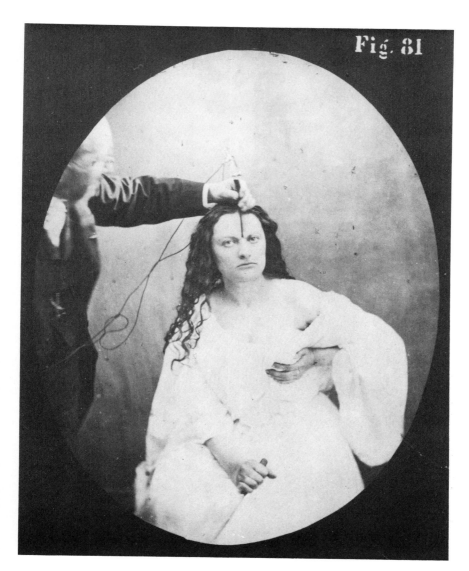

Plate 81

207

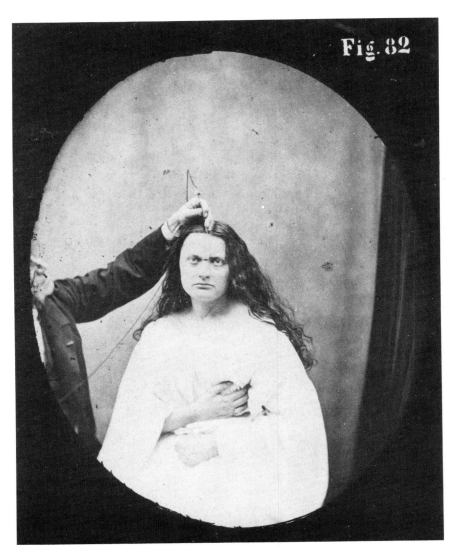

Plate 82

Plate 83

Plate 84

19. Synoptic table on the plates of the Album

I have gathered the heads of the 82 plates, in the form of little medallions, that make up the Scientific Section and the Aesthetic Section of the Album of *The Mechanism of Human Facial Expression* in nine synoptic tables. Some of the figures are repeated, where, for example, I have produced a different expression on each side of the face. The result is that this synoptic table is made up of 102 heads.

1. I have indicated in the captions to these plates that we can alternatively cover the diverse features of these photographs, which have a double expression, in order to make a comparative study. The synoptic tables show these experiments already done, and make the analysis of the expressive lines of the human face even easier and clearer. They suffice, at a pinch, for understanding the developments detailed in the text of this work.
2. The modifying influence of certain expressive lines on the other features of the face is assuredly, from the point of view of the practice of painting and sculpture, one of the most important facts to come from the electrophysiological experiments performed in my work on the mechanism of human facial expression. The synoptic tables facilitate the study of this phenomenon that I call *simultaneous contrasting of the expressive lines of the face.**

    When we looked alternately, and employed the procedure set out in the captions, we could well recognize the differences between the two sides of the face in those figures that had a double expression. Yet the time that we take to cover one of the sides spoils slightly the recall of the features with which we want to compare those that we see. It is preferable to have both sides of the face constantly before us; then their distinctive characteristics be-

---

*This phenomenon seems to me to be well-named, because of its analogy, as I have already observed (this text, p. 14), with the illusion produced in color vision by different color traits put next to one another; that which M. Chevreul has called *simultaneous contrast of colors*. (See his book, *On the law of simultaneous contrast of colors, and of the arrangement of colored objects*.)

211

come more striking and the demonstration of the problem to be resolved is easier.

Let us take only, for example, the four figures 78 of Table 8. The first of these figures (i-78) shows the experiment done on both sides at once; seen in its entirety, it is only a grimacing expression, for, on each side of the face, a different muscle is put into action in isolation. Two other figures (iii-78 and iv-78) let us see only one side of the mouth in such a way that comparison becomes easy and more conclusive. Thus the eye seems cold and disdainful in figure iv-78, whereas it is gay and mocking in figure iii-78. Yet, in reality, there does not exist any difference between these eyes; for the palpebral part of *m. orbicularis oculi* contracts in exactly the same manner on each side; this is quite convincing when we cover the parts situated beneath the eyes, as in figure ii-78.

This apparent modification of the gaze results from the influence exercised on the eye by the form of the mouth. This illusion is much more powerful when we compare the experiments in figures iii-78 and iv-78 than when we alternately cover one of the sides of figure i-78.

These points, applicable to all the figures with double expressions in the Scientific Section and the Aesthetic Section, demonstrate the usefulness of the synoptic tables for studying the contrasting expressive lines of the face.

3. I have also included the heads where the expression is not double in these synoptic tables, so that in presenting the ensemble of all the figures that make up the album we can better compare them.

The heads in the Scientific Section have been reduced two-thirds to be part of the synoptic tables, each one composed of 16 figures. Consequently, the expressive lines are less apparent and less easy to study in all their details. Also, these synoptic tables do not present the attitude and the gesture that come to the aid of facial expression and give it a greater and sometimes special significance in the whole figures of the aesthetic section.

In summary, even if the synoptic tables are only supplementing the large-scale figures of the album, they have the advantage of showing reunited what we have already seen separately. We can comprehend in one sweep of the eye things that may not be apparent in isolation. They form the résumé of the experimental results and the synthesis of the principles that constitute the grammar and the orthography of human facial expression.

Synoptic Plate 1

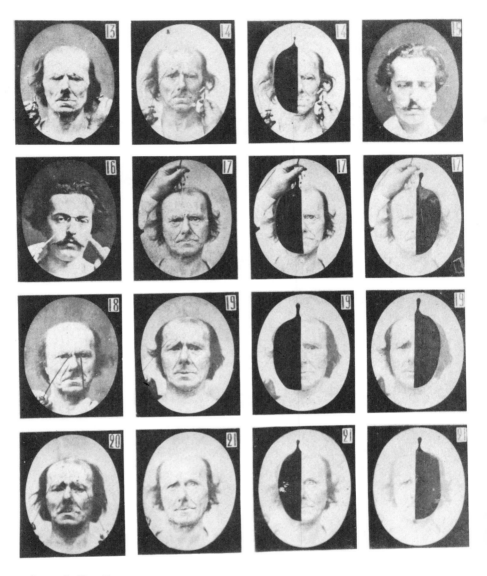

Synoptic Plate 2

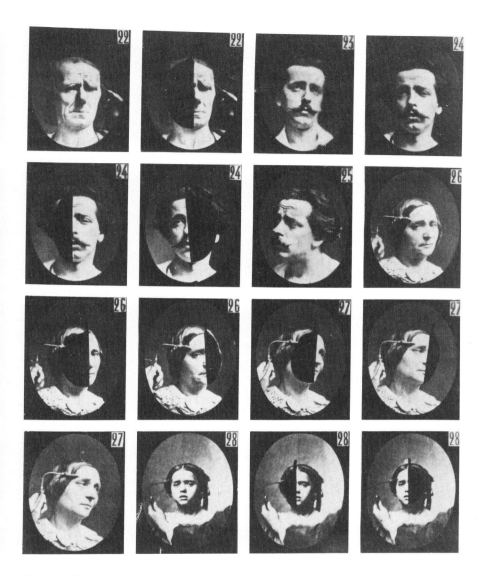

Synoptic Plate 3

215

Synoptic Plate 4

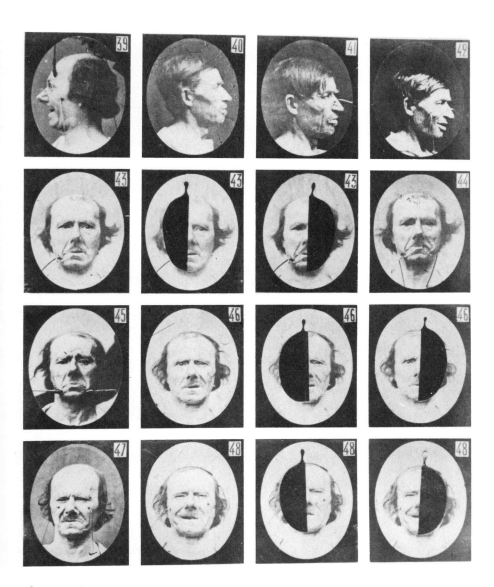

Synoptic Plate 5

Synoptic Plate 6

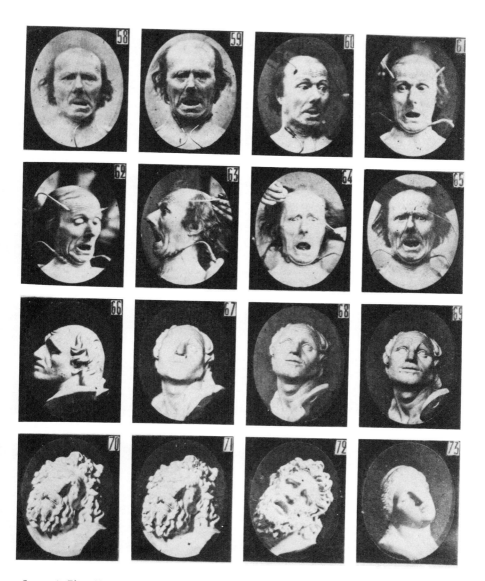

Synoptic Plate 7

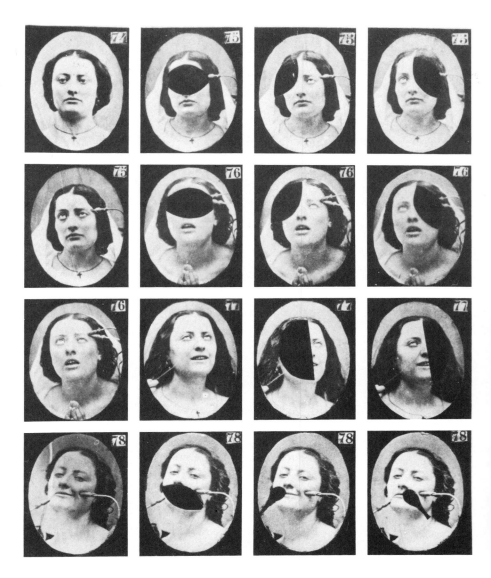

Synoptic Plate 8

Synoptic Plate 9

PART 2

Commentary chapters

1. The highly original Dr. Duchenne

R. ANDREW CUTHBERTSON

Duchenne de Boulogne was an eccentric man with a passion for order. Disregarding his conventional professional training, he systematically catalogued the myriad manifestations of human neurological disease, using novel techniques such as electrical stimulation and photography to perform and document his experiments. When *Mécanisme de la Physionomie Humaine* was published by Renouard in Paris in 1862, Duchenne was already renowned for his work in neurology, experimental physiology, and medicine. This book extends his earlier investigation of skeletal muscle action into the study of the facial muscles and the mechanism of human expression. He also departs from his earlier descriptive science and enters an important contemporary debate on aesthetics: the nature of what he calls "idealized naturalism" in art.[1] Most of what we know of Duchenne's life has been gleaned from obituaries and tributes.[2,3,4,5,6,7,8] His publications and membership in national and international societies provide evidence of a professional success, but his private ambitions were aesthetic. Published records fail to explain his personality, his eccentricity, and his drive. It is the uneasy coexistence of the professional scientist with the amateur aesthetician that will be explored in this chapter.

[1] Duchenne, G.B.A. (1862): *Mechanism of Human Facial Expression*, p. 110, this volume.
[2] Brissaud, E. (1899): L'Oeuvre scientifique de Duchenne de Boulogne. *Rev Internat d'Electrothérapie*, 3.
[3] De Courmelles, F. (1896): La statue de Duchenne de Boulogne. *Chron Méd*, 3:71.
[4] Guillain, G. (1925): L'Oeuvre de G.B. Duchenne (de Boulogne). *Presse Méd*, 97:1601.
[5] Guilly, P. (1936): *Duchenne de Boulogne*. Paris: Baillière et fils. Reproduced by Laffitte Reprints, Marseille, 1977.
[6] Houzel, P. (1903): Notice sur la vie de Duchenne de Boulogne. *Mém Soc Acad de Boulogne-sur-Mer*, xix, 2ᵉ fascic., p. 139.
[7] Lasegue, C., and Straus, J. (1884): Duchenne de Boulogne: sa vie scientifique et ses oeuvres. In *Études Médicales de Lasegue*, Paris: Asselin, p. 178.
[8] Lhermitte, J. (1946): Duchenne de Boulogne et son temps. *Prog Méd*, 24:596.

A family doctor turned experimental physiologist

Duchenne's early life was conventional. Born in 1806, the son of a corsair,[9] he attended medical school in Paris and then returned to marriage and a provincial practice on the English Channel coast in Boulogne-sur-Mer. With the exception of his required thesis, an uninspired *Essai sur le Brûlure*,[10] probably based on Dupuytren's burns classification, he published nothing until he was 40 years old. In 1842 this pattern began to change. He left his country practice and returned to Paris as an unpaid 36-year-old student. Duchenne's wife had died of puerperal sepsis after he delivered their first child and it has been suggested that this tragedy was the reason for Duchenne's departure from Boulogne. His wife, however, died in 1833, but Duchenne did not leave Boulogne until 9 years later.

Further clues to the conversion of this country practitioner into a roving student of clinical neurology may lie in Duchenne's family background. His relationship with his son, Émile, was always difficult. There was a long period of estrangement following the death of the boy's mother. But in 1862, Émile joined Duchenne as an apprentice in Paris. This seemingly happy working arrangement ended with the official announcement of the son's death, of typhoid fever in 1870, during the siege of Paris by the Prussians.[11] A letter, written by a neighbor of the Duchenne family in 1899 as a contemporary account of the time and kept in the archives of the city of Boulogne-sur-Mer,[12] can only be given a certain amount of credence. The letter states that Duchenne's son was seen alive after 1870 and that he had been committed to an asylum.

"Then (and this is confidential) . . . , I *saw* him after 1870: He was interred at St. Anne [a local hospital for the insane] . . . he was an unbalanced person all his life." This memoir goes on, "it was said that four sisters of the celebrated physician [Duchenne himself] died following *nervous accidents* before reaching adulthood. We heard them in the neighborhood screeching, so much so that they frightened the passers by. I don't know whether they ever identified this disease, but as to the facts of these incidents, and the deaths that followed them, each has remained burned in my memory."

[9] The Corsairs were part-time French privateers who attacked English shipping in the Channel and enjoyed the approval of the French government (See Lord Russell: *The corsairs*. London: Robert Hale & Co.).

[10] Vol. 240, no. 82, Paris, 1831, 35 pp.

[11] From September 1870 to January 1871.

[12] Courtesy of Dr. P.-A. Wimet, Vice-Président de la Commission Départementale des Monuments Historiques du Pas-de-Calais, who allowed me personally to examine the text.

A history of neurological disease in Duchenne's family could perhaps explain his motivation to investigate clinical neurology. It is interesting to speculate on the influence that Duchenne's family background may have had on his most famous pupil, Jean Martin Charcot,[13] who sat by his death bed, and in turn on Charcot's pupil Sigmund Freud.

The birth of neurology

It must be emphasized that, before Duchenne, French neurology did not exist.[14] Duchenne's original contributions to this new science may be found in his numerous scientific articles and summarized in two key texts: *Localized Electrization*[15] and *Physiology of Motion*.[16] In Paris he had no specific hospital appointment and was free to seek out or to be consulted in cases in any of the hospitals across the city. Many of the cases cited in these highly original publications were seen at the Salpêtrière Hospital in Paris, on the lower left bank of the Seine. The Salpêtrière of the 1840s and 1850s was fertile ground for Duchenne's prodigious skill in recognizing patterns of previously unidentified neurological disorders. The old and rambling hospital had for 200 years cared for women – whether ill, insane, or merely indigent. Under Louis XIII a small arsenal had been built on this site, where gunpowder was made from saltpeter, and in 1656 Louis XIV – the Sun King – constructed La Salpêtrière as the General Hospital for the Poor People of Paris, with the object of ridding the streets of beggars. Within 6 years it held 6,000 outcasts and within a decade nearly 20,000. Even in the 17th century it was anything but an ordinary hospital: "It was a city within a city, consisting of about forty-five buildings with streets, squares, gardens and a beautiful old church."[17] A feature of the hospital was the number of "incurable" cases with unidentified paralysis or atrophy. It was by studying, sorting, and classifying these rejected people – the mad, the epileptic, spastic, and paralytic – using physical examination aided by electrical stimulation, that Duchenne began to catalogue neurological disorders. In 1847, he presented his first paper on his new method of localized

[13] 1825–1893. Charcot called Duchenne his "master in neurology." See McHenry, L. C. (1969): *Garrison's history of neurology*, Springfield, IL: Charles C Thomas, p. 282.

[14] McHenry, *op. cit.*, p. 278.

[15] *De l'électrisation localiseé, et son application à la pathologie et à la thérapeutique.* 1st edition, xix, 926 pp., 108 figs., 1855; 2nd edition, 1046 pp., 179 figs., 1861; 3rd edition, 1120 pp., 155 figs., 1872. Paris: J. B. Baillière et fils.

[16] *Physiologie des mouvements, demontrée à l'aide de l'expérimentation électrique et de l'observation clinique et applicable à l'étude des paralysies et des deformations*, xvi, 872 pp., 101 figs. J. B. Baillière et fils, Paris, 1867.

[17] McHenry, *op. cit.*, p. 284.

electrical stimultion by which he could stimulate an individual muscle without having to cut or pierce the skin.[18]

Duchenne had made himself a master of the anatomy, physiology, and pathology of the skeletal muscles. Knowing that skeletal muscles acted in groups and that these synergistic movements masked the actions of individual muscles, Duchenne used localized electrical stimulation to map individual muscle actions and then reassembled these isolated actions into physiological movements. This great study of the kinesiology of the entire muscular system was first published in 1867 as the *Physiologie des Mouvements*.[19]

Among Duchenne's other original contributions were his descriptions of the now eponymic Duchenne-Aran type of motor neuron disease (1849);[20] Duchenne's pseudohypertrophic muscular dystrophy (1852);[21] locomotor ataxia (1858);[22] the Duchenne-Erb palsy caused by upper brachial plexus injury during childbirth;[23] and his description of glossolabiolaryngeal paralysis (1860), brilliantly predicting that the lesion would be found in the bulbar nuclei.[24] Another novel application of medical electricity was his resuscitation of a 15-year-old baker's apprentice who had asphyxiated after crawling into an oven when drunk. Duchenne applied a type of artificial respiration by stimulating the boy's phrenic nerves electrically until he recovered (1855).[25] This resuscitation technique was also used by Duchenne to treat chloroform intoxication. And he was the first to use photography to illustrate neurological disease, in

[18] De l'art de limiter l'excitation électrique dans les organes sans piquer ni inciser la peau, nouvelle méthode de l'électrisation appellée électrisation localisée. *Compte Rendu de l'Acad des Sciences*, Paris, 1847.

[19] Translated by Emanuel B. Kaplan, M.D. (1959) and published as *Physiology of motion*, Philadelphia: W.B. Saunders & Co.

[20] *Recherches électro-physiologiques, pathologiques et thérapeutiques*, a series of papers addressed to the Academie des Sciences, Paris, 21 May, 1849. Duchenne's cases of progressive muscular atrophy were subsequently published by François Amilcar Aran (1850), who acknowledged Duchenne's primary contribution. See McHenry, *op. cit.*, p. 279.

[21] First mentioned in a communication: De la valeur de l'électricité dans le traitement de maladies, to the Société Médico-Chirurgicale de Paris, 11 March and 6 April, 1852; formalized in a series of reports: De la paralysie musculaire pseudo-hypertrophique ou paralysie myo-sclerotique, *Arch Gén de Méd*, January–May, 1868. In this latter work Duchenne described the use of muscle biopsy to study this condition.

[22] Recherches sur l'ataxie locomotrice, maladie caractérisée spécialement par des troubles généraux de la co-ordination des mouvements, *Bull de l'Acad de Méd*, xxiv, p. 210, 1858–59 and *Arch Gén de Méd*, December 1858 and January, February and April, 1859.

[23] *De l'électrisation localisée*, 3rd edition, 1872, pp. 354–364.

[24] Paralysie musculaire progressive de la langue, du voile du palais et des lèvres non encore décrite. *Arch Gén de Méd*, September and October, 1860.

[25] Mentioned in: Note sur l'influence de la respiration artificielle par la faradisation des nerfs phréniques dans l'intoxication par la chloroforme. *Union Méd*, 29 and 31 March, 1855.

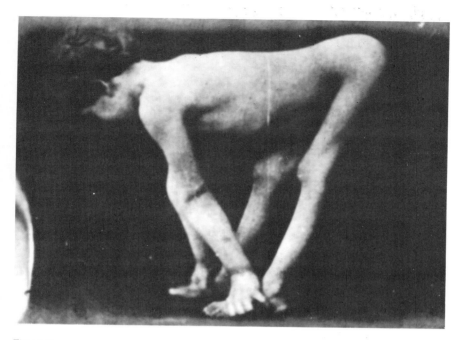

Figure 1
This very early photograph, probably taken in the mid-1850s, shows a boy with obvious lower limb wasting making use of his intact ligaments to "lock" his joints and so to stand up.

1862. These first published clinical photographs included a most evocative portrait of "a young boy, affected from the age of 6 years with a progressive atrophic paralysis that destroyed the muscles of locomotion of his lower limbs" executing "Gowers' Maneuver" by climbing up his own legs[26] [Figure 1].

Facial expression: Duchenne and Darwin

Duchenne maintained that ". . . the laws that govern the expressions of the human face can be discovered by studying muscle action."[27] He felt that the "language" of facial expression was created by God and, once

[26] *Album des photographies pathologiques.* This booklet, made up of 17 photographic plates and 20 pages of explanatory text, was probably the first example of published medical photographs. It appeared in 1862, prior to the release of *Mécanisme de la physionomie humaine,* as a supplement to the second edition of *L'électrisation localisée,* published in 1861. See Cuthbertson, R.A. and Hueston, J.T. (1979): Duchenne de Boulogne and clinical photography. *Ann Plastic Surg* 2: 332.
[27] Duchenne, G.B.A. (1862): *Mechanism of human facial expression,* p. 1, this volume.

in place, rendered this language "universal and immutable" by giving all human beings the instinctive faculty of always expressing the same sentiments by contracting the same muscles.[28] Mapping the emotions through the actions of the facial muscles was henceforth a special part of his life's work on skeletal muscle kinesiology.

Charles Darwin's *The Expression of the Emotions in Man and Animals*[29] was likewise a special pleading of the case for the evolution of behavior rather than of morphological characteristics, following from *On the Origin of Species by Means of Natural Selection*[30] and *The Descent of Man*.[31] Darwin clearly relied on *Mécanisme de la Physionomie Humaine* when writing his *Expression of the Emotions in Man and Animals:* He emphasized his debt to Duchenne, quoted Duchenne's theories, and used several of Duchenne's illustrations in his book.[32] Duchenne gave Darwin permission to use some of his photographs in his *Expression of the Emotions* without asking for remuneration, stating that "questions of money should not arise between men of science. . . ."[33]

Photography and electricity

The use of increasingly sophisticated technical equipment that extends our senses is part of the history of science. Photography could be used to record the fleeting effect of electricity on the facial muscles, which, Duchenne claimed, was so transient that it had not always been possible for "even the greatest masters to grasp the sum total of all their distinctive features."[34] By "activating" with electricity and then "fixing" with photography Duchenne could manipulate and record the facial muscle mask at will, introducing photography as a means of documenting these electrophysiological experiments.[35]

[28] *Ibid.*, p. 19.
[29] London: John Murray, 1872.
[30] London: John Murray, 1859.
[31] London: John Murray, 1870, 1871.
[32] The care with which Darwin examined Duchenne's text can be seen by the detailed annotations in Darwin's copy of *Mécanisme de la physionomie humaine* in the Darwin Collection of the Cambridge University Library.
[33] Letter from Duchenne in the Darwin Collection, Cambridge University Library. It appears that Duchenne sent Darwin plates from his own copy of "Mécanisme . . . ," from some of which Darwin had engravings made. These particular photographs are still missing from the collection of plates donated by Duchenne to the *École Nationale Supérieure des Beaux Arts* on his death.
[34] Duchenne, G.B.A. (1862): *op. cit.*, p. 34, this volume.
[35] Duchenne was assisted by Adrienne Tournachon, "Nadar jeune," the younger brother of the celebrated Nadar whose portraits recorded the famous people of his day and who

The success of *Mécanisme de la Physionomie Humaine* also rested on the noninvasive technique of electrical stimulation developed by Duchenne. Direct current or "galvanic" stimulation had been used by Sarlandières[36] and Magendie[37] but required the skin to be punctured with sharp electrodes, often resulting in abscesses. Using an alternating "faradic" current and small moist electrodes, Duchenne identified "motor points" at which percutaneous surface stimulation gave isolated muscle contractions. Duchenne published the evolution of the technical details used in his electrophysiological experiments in the three editions of *De l'Électrisation Localisée*.[38]

Duchenne's interests were quite different from those of the physiognomists such as della Porta[39] and Lavater,[40] who had predicted nuances of character from the morphology of the human face. Duchenne was concerned not with facial morphology, but with the semiotic meaning of individual and groups of facial muscles as they portrayed particular emotions. Using his new technology, Duchenne explored this central theme: that each emotion was portrayed by either specific individual facial muscles or by small groups of these muscles. While his *Mécanisme de la Physionomie Humaine* added a dimension of complexity to previous studies, it did not encompass the sequential nature of facial expression. By stimulating facial muscles in a static way he captured a single frame from the moving picture. Lacking the later technology of a Muybridge[41] to record the temporal dimension, Duchenne captured only a moment. While Duchenne broke the facial mask into its individual constituent facial muscle actions, Muybridge fragmented movements of the whole body into a temporal serial sequence.

Duchenne produced the facial markings of "faked" emotions in an experimental setting. The experimental physiologist drew the lines he wanted on the passive faces of his models with his localized electrical current. The criterion for a successful experiment was whether these faces looked "real" to Duchenne. We admire successful mimicry; and the successful mimicking of something real can rely on the blatant use

first photographed Paris from a balloon (See Jammes, A. (1978): Duchenne de Boulogne, la grimace provoquée et Nadar, *Gaz des Beaux-Arts*, 92:215).

[36] Sarlandières, J.B. (1825): *Mémoires sur l'électropuncture considerée comme moyen nouveau, de traiter efficacement la quotte, les rhumatismes et les affections nerveuses, et sur l'emploi du "Moxa japonaia" en France*, iv, 150 pp., Paris: Mlle Delaunay, 1825.

[37] Magendie, F. (1839): *Leçons sur les fonctions et les maladies du système nerveux*. Paris: Ebrard.

[38] Paris: Baillière et fils, 1855, 1861, and 1872.

[39] Giovanni Baptista della Porta (1623): *Coelestis physiognomiae*, Padua.

[40] John Caspar Lavater (1789): *Essays on physiognomy*, London: John Murray.

[41] Haas, R.B. (1976): *Muybridge: Man in motion*. Berkeley: University of California Press.

of technology. Recently Umberto Eco described the contemporary "completely real" as being represented by the "completely fake" in the creation of holograms by photorealists using lasers.[42]

Duchenne the scientist was intrigued by the utility and passivity of the photographic record. "Photographs furnish evidence . . . something seems proven when we're shown a photograph."[43] But apart from providing scientific evidence, photography helped him perform his "aesthetic" experiments, and documented a fundamental contradiction in his aesthetic philosophy.

His models

Although the Scientific Section of *Mécanisme de la Physionomie Humaine* is an objective study in human physiology, this objectivity cannot hide the human drama of his models. Their faces peer out as vulnerable individuals from the plates of the Album, anticipating Diane Arbus's work on freaks: the innocent young girl [Figure 2], the narcissistic actor [Figure 3], the old simpleton [Figure 4], the seductive wanton [Figure 5], and finally the opium addict [Figure 6] – who died two days after the photograph was taken. There is a certain voyeurism in Duchenne's Album that seems at times to be only thinly veiled by the scientific enquiry.

There is also something sinister about Duchenne and his assistant creating the appearance of torture on the face of an inoffensive old man [Figure 7] and this epitomizes the reservations that some people have about experimental medical science. In the late twentieth century we fear the indignity of control being in the hands of powerful technocrats. Reassuringly, however, the old man *felt* no pain. He was not really being harmed. His breathing remained regular, slow, and normal, and on the cessation of the electrical stimulus his features resumed their calm, quiet, and relaxed state.

Duchenne recognized the infinite anatomical variety of human features: the background of the different contours of the face and the varying permanence of lines arising from the habitual sentiments of the subjects.[44] He repeated some experiments, stimulating the same groups of muscles in old and young, male and female, the privileged and the degraded, and showed that the effect of a common isolated muscle contraction was influenced by its setting. But the fact that contraction of a

[42] Eco, U. (1987): *Travels in hyperreality*. London: Picador, p. 3.
[43] Sontag, S. (1978): In "Plato's Cave." *On photography*. London: A. Lane, p. 5.
[44] Duchenne, G.B.A. (1862): *op. cit.*, p. 42, this volume.

Figure 2
The young girl, photographed in the strong light of an open window. (From the École Nationale Supérieure des Beaux Arts collection.)

Figure 3
The actor, who taught himself to control his own facial muscles. (From the École Nationale Supérieure des Beaux Arts collection.)

Figure 4
The simple old man, who suffered from facial anaesthesia and was thus an ideal subject for Duchenne's experiments. (From the École Nationale Supérieure des Beaux Arts collection.)

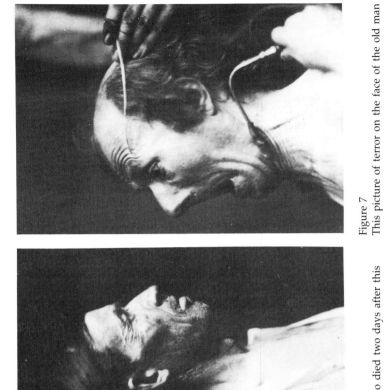

Figure 5
Mixed signals: the seductive wanton.

Figure 6
The opium addict: who died two days after this
photograph was taken.

Figure 7
This picture of terror on the face of the old man
was not accompanied by any other physiological
signs of distress.

particular muscle, whether performed on the face of a young girl or an old man, still gave the impression of a particular emotion was powerful evidence for the universality and simple truth of Duchenne's principles. He was interested in the plasticity of the mask itself and not the character behind the mask.

He dressed and posed one of his models (who could not understand his instructions) like a mannequin,[45] allowing her to "gain in beauty" by electricity! He never evoked his subjects' feelings, but rather relied on his own judgment and what he termed his own "artistic feeling" to reproduce an emotion.[46]

It is in the choice of his models that we first appreciate the conflict between Duchenne's scientific mind and his aesthetic prejudices. Duchenne did not use the idealized facial subjects often chosen in the early decades of photography. While the old man was certainly not classically beautiful, his worn, insensitive skin was a perfect experimental surface on which to explore the movements of human facial expression.

"Idealized naturalism"

Duchenne extended his experimental findings to ". . . their happy or fortunate applications to the study of the fine arts."[47]

The Scientific Section of the book describes his remodeling of antique sculpture as well as his electrophysiological results. The Aesthetic Section is more theatrical, adding costume and gesture to supplement facial expression. The Aesthetic Section was published separately some months after the Scientific Section, allowing Duchenne to answer some of his critics.[48,49] On his death, Duchenne donated all his original photographs and remodeled plaster casts to the École Nationale Supérieure des Beaux Arts in Paris to allow the widest recognition of the practical usefulness of his physiological and photographic research.[50]

[45] *Ibid.*, p. 105.

[46] *Ibid.*, p. 106.

[47] *Ibid.*, p. 22.

[48] For example, Latour, A. (1862): "Critique sur le *Mécanisme de la physionomie humaine.*" *Union Méd*, 26 August and 2 September.

[49] Duchenne's book was reviewed not only in medical journals but also in contemporary political and popular newspapers. While the overall response was laudatory, some writers were less enthusiastic. Verneuil, for example, in his "Critique sur le *Mécanisme de la physionomie humaine*" in the *Gazette Hebdomadaire de Médecine et de Chirurgie*, no. 28, 11 July, 1862, noted that he found "the combination of artist, scientist, and worst of all photographer, abhorrent!"

[50] Some of the remodeled casts are shown in the original Plates of *Mécanisme de la physionomie humaine*, and in Figure 6 in the chapter by J.-F. Debord in this volume.

Unlike his other contributions to neurology, skeletal muscle action, and the mechanism of human facial expression, Duchenne's contribution to the fine arts was flawed. Not only did Duchenne want to *know* the individual actions of the facial muscles, but he wanted to "formulate rules to guide the artist in the true and complete portrayal of the movements of the soul . . ."[51] His aim was to bolster traditional figurative painting and sculpture against contemporary trends toward "realism," yet the techniques he used were "realistic."

The facts he demonstrated on the isolated action of individual facial muscles and their synergism in the mechanism of human facial expression are beyond reproach. His description and proof of "the illusion"[52] are particularly illuminating and useful. Duchenne, however, wanted to alter the course of artistic fashion and philosophy, while remaining "scientifically" detached. He saw himself as an extension of nature. He denied that his rules would "menace the liberty of art," or "suffocate the inspirations of genius," declaring that they provided "no more shackles than the rules of perspective."[53] Paradoxically, his efforts may have produced the very opposite effect from his aim.

Although Duchenne cites well-known paintings in his Aesthetic Section, it was his remodeling of famous antique works of sculpture that gave him some contemporary notoriety. He remodeled the *Arrotino*,[54] the *Laocoön* of Rome,[55] the *Laocoön* of Brussels, and the *Niobe*.[56] Repro-

[51] Duchenne, G.B.A. (1862): *op. cit.*, p. 35, this volume.

[52] Duchenne showed that an observer given a cue from, for example, a muscle contraction moving the corner of the mouth, can "fill in" the rest of the face in an appropriate way. Thus eyes that appear neutral when viewed in isolation seem to "smile" with an upturned mouth or "frown" when the mouth is downturned. See Plate 78 and *Mechanism of Human Facial Expression*, p. 13, this volume.

[53] Duchenne, G.B.A. (1862): *op. cit.*, p. 13, this volume.

[54] This sculpture had many aliases (the spy, the knife-sharpener, the listening slave, and so on). It was discovered in sixteenth century Rome and was generally acclaimed (but not by Winckelmann). Some considered it to be a Scythian slave (Arrotino) who had been ordered by Apollo to flay his rival (Marsyas) alive. Mansuelli, G.A (1958–61): *Galleria degli Uffizi: Le Scultura*, vol. 1, 84–87, Rome, (see Plates 66–69 in the Album of *Mechanism of Human Facial Expression*, this volume).

[55] Discovered near S. Maria Maggiore in Rome in 1506, this archetypal antique sculpture was known well enough in popular imagination for Dickens to feature it in *A christmas tale* (1843) as Scrooge struggling with his stockings. Many bronze and marble copies of the original find were made. The original is now regarded as a late Hellenistic group more recent in date than the mid-1st century A.D. (Helbig, W., 1963–72): *Führer durch die öffentlichen sammlungen klassischer altertümer in Rom*, pp. 162–166, 4th edition, 4 volumes, Tübingen, (see Fronticepiece B and Plates 70–72 in the Album of *Mechanism of Human Facial Expression*, this volume). Often a cast of *Laocoön* alone, or even a copy of *Laocoön's* head, sufficed for academic copying purposes. *Laocoön* was admired for the realism of its physiognomy (Haskell and Penny, *op. cit.*, pp. 243–247). The variety of expressions

ductions of these famous works were jealously collected by the aristoc-
racy, and drawing from plaster casts of antique sculptures formed the
initial part of the long apprenticeship for artists in the École des Beaux
Arts. "The Academy itself encouraged this fetishistic view of the copy.
The goal was to wrest from Genius its secret."[57]

The *Laocoön*, accorded the highest praise by Pliny the Elder in ancient
Rome and admired by Michaelangelo when the sculpture was rediscovered in 1506, was almost a cult object for antiquarians of the 18th and
19th centuries.[58] It was regarded by Winckelmann[59] as the greatest
sculpture of antiquity, and therefore of all time, and discussed at length
by Lessing, Goethe, Schiller, Hegel, and others. Thus the *Laocoön* was
almost a household object to an educated Frenchman in the mid-
nineteenth century; Duchenne had read and quoted from at least the
works of Winckelmann and Lessing. The choice of the *Laocoön* as his
first sculpture to be remodeled was therefore most significant.

Duchenne was aware of the controversy likely to follow the work of
his "profane hand",[60] a boldness he justified by his "strict scientific

---

in the group: from suffering, to dying, to compassion were often noted. Many felt that
the artist emphasized restraint and dignity, in spite of the awful death described by
Virgil in the *Aeneid* (e.g. Richardson, Jonathan (Senior and Junior) (1722): *An account of
some of the statues, bas-reliefs, drawings and pictures in Italy, etc. with remarks*, London, p.
277).

[56] The *Niobe Group*, now in the Uffizi Museum in Florence, was discovered near Porta S.
Giovanni in Rome in 1583. Several copies were made of the group, and very often only
one figure was cast or copied as a statuette or bust (Haskell and Penny, *op. cit.*, pp. 274–
279). The passions expressed by the faces of the statues in the group were particularly
admired (Evelyn, J. (1955): *The Diary*, vol. II, p. 232, (E.S. de Beer, Ed.), Oxford), especially the ability to express these emotions, of grief, dread, and supplication, without
detracting from their beauty (Moore, J. (1790): *A view of society and manners in Italy*, 5th
edition, vol. I, p. 502, London). The Florentine *Niobe Group* is now thought to be an
antique copy (Mansuelli, G.A. (1958–61): *Galleria degli Uffizi: Le Sculture*. vol. I, pp. 104–
109, Rome). See Plate 73 in the Album of *Mechanism of Human Facial Expression*, this
volume.

[57] Boime, A. (1971): *The Academy and French painting in the nineteenth century*. London: Phaidon, p. 124.

[58] Nisbet, H.B., Editor (1985): *German aesthetic and literary criticism: Winckelmann, Lessing,
Hammann, Herder, Schiller and Goethe*. Cambridge: Cambridge University Press.

[59] Irwin, D., Editor (1972): *Winckelmann: Writings on art*. London: Phaidon. Johann Joachim
Winckelmann was one of the principal writers to influence the development of Neoclas-
sicism in the eighteenth century. His books were widely read and affected the way several subsequent generations saw antiquity. He emphasized the ideals of "noble simplicity" and "quiet grandeur," but not necessarily accuracy of portrayal.

[60] Many other modifications had occurred to the *Laocoön* group from just after its discovery
until as recently as 1942 (Haskell, F., and Penny, N. (1981): *Taste and the antique: The lure
of classical sculpture*. New Haven and London: Yale University Press, p. 246). These changes
were restricted to replacing or remodeling missing limbs (*Laocoön* lacked his right arm

analysis."[61] Furthermore, Duchenne's citing of Winckelmann and Lessing[62] shows that he was an educated adherent of that tradition that glorified Greece and Rome. Although his attribution of the *Laocoön* to Agasias,[63] and the Niobe to Praxiteles[64] is disputed by more recent scholarship,[65] Duchenne had seen some of these original works in Italy[66] and knew their key place in the teaching of traditional sculpture and painting. Duchenne therefore understood the enormity of his stating that the fault in the forehead of the Roman *Laocoön* "mars the work," because he believed that it was not sculpted according to "the immutable laws of nature" displayed by his research.[67]

He argued that artists did not need a detailed knowledge of anatomy. Rather, they needed to understand "the laws of expressive movement."[68] Duchenne wanted to enlighten the artist, "without shackling the freedom of his genius."[69] His rules were to "prevent or modify errors of the imagination."[70] Citing the Greeks, who studied the living nude, but had little anatomical knowledge, Duchenne asked rhetorically: Was not "the exaggeration of morbid anatomical science one of the principal causes of the decline in art?"[71] He knew that anatomy was even less useful in the face, where few of the muscles leave a contour under the skin, as they do in the limbs.

Duchenne criticized a number of artists (Le Brun,[72] for instance) for having "followed their own inspirations, rather than exactly observing nature."[73] He suggested that the masters usually got the fundamental lines right, but were incorrect with their portrayal of secondary lines, producing combinations that were "mechanically impossible."[74]

Duchenne's artistic sympathies lay with the traditions of Winckelmann, Lessing, and the École des Beaux Arts, but his methods placed him firmly with the iconoclastic practitioners of the new realistic photography. His principal aesthetic considerations were "beauty of form, as-

on discovery). Duchenne's facial changes were seen as representing "the positivism of the second half of the nineteenth century prompting a more peculiar modification than the sentimentality of the late eighteenth" (Haskell and Penny, *op. cit.*, p. 246).

[61] Duchenne, G.B.A. (1862): *op. cit.*, p. 34, this volume.
[62] *Ibid.*, pp. 97 & 98, this volume.
[63] *Ibid.*, p. 95, this volume.
[64] *Ibid.*, p. 99, this volume.   [65] Haskell and Penny, *op. cit.*, pp. 243, 274.
[66] Duchenne, G.B.A. (1862): *op. cit.*, p. 109, this volume.
[67] *Ibid.*, p. 99, this volume.   [68] *Ibid.*, p. 32, this volume.
[69] *Ibid.*, p. 35, this volume.   [70] *Ibid.*, p. 36, this volume.
[71] *Ibid.*, p. 33, this volume.
[72] Charles Le Brun or Lebrun (1619–1690).
[73] Duchenne, G.B.A. (1862): *op. cit.*, p. 34, this volume.
[74] *Ibid.*, p. 35, this volume.

sociated with exactness of facial expression, pose, and gesture."[75] Duchenne was attacked for "stripping art of its ideal beauty and reducing it to anatomical realism along the lines of a certain modern school."[76] While this debate within the Realist School centered on landscape painting rather than portraiture, Duchenne was linked closely to it through his use of photography.[77]

Duchenne denied any allegiance to "realism." He felt he was allowing art to attain the ideal of facial expression "like nature herself." He noted that while antiquity copied nature, it was copied in its "most beautiful, noble, and perfect aspects," resulting in an "idealized naturalism."[78] Finally, he felt that while it was necessary to copy nature exactly in order to obtain beauty in art, this alone was not sufficient. To achieve beauty also required creative genius.[79]

There was a spectrum of opinions on photography in the mid-nineteenth century from those who saw it as "art's mortal enemy" and the "triumph of materialism," to others who hailed photography as a "welcome destroyer of the mechanical, insensitive and mediocre artist."[80] Duchenne, it seemed, hoped that photography might be "established as the standard against which all naturalistic painting would be measured."[81] He was portraying the natural world, and at the same time distorting the world of nature with electricity. Duchenne's *Mécanisme de la Physionomie Humaine* came at a time when photography and painting were influencing one another quite freely. There were mutual benefits. To photographers came lessons of composition. To painters came lessons in accuracy and perhaps more significantly the license now to stop chasing an unattainable realism. Painters were left free to produce their art without the constraint of seeking accurate portraiture. Perhaps the only painters to suffer directly from the encroachment of photography were the miniaturists.

Galassi, a contemporary historian, has argued that "photography was

[75] *Ibid.,* p. 102, this volume.

[76] *Ibid.,* p. 109, this volume. (See Latour, *op. cit.;* and Cerise, M. (1865): Critique sur la *Mécanisme de la physionomie humaine. Journal des Débats,* 29 August.)

[77] A "Classic-Romantic Dilemma" preceded the rise of Realism in the mid-nineteenth century (see Boime, A. (1971): *The Academy and French painting in the nineteenth century:* London: Phaidon). In deciding that "Praxiteles" would not have marred the beauty of Niobe by portraying her in pain, Duchenne displays his romanticism: "Nothing is more moving and appealing than such an expression of pain on a young forehead that is usually so serene."

[78] Duchenne, G.B.A.: *op. cit.,* p. 110, this volume.

[79] *Ibid.,* p. 110.

[80] Scharf, A. (1968): *Art and photography.* London: A. Lane, p. 14.

[81] *Ibid.,* p. 13.

not a bastard left by science on the doorstep of art, but a legitimate child of the Western pictorial tradition," claiming that the ultimate origins of photography, both scientific and aesthetic, lay in the 15th-century invention of linear perspective. The use of optical aids for drawing long preceded photography and thus the introduction of the latter was not altogether alien. There was, before the introduction of photography, an "embryonic spirit of realism" in Europe, ". . . which painters had long been inventing and which photographers could not avoid."[82]

Duchenne's aim in the arts was to provide for greater naturalism in the representation of emotions on the human face, but by using photography he showed that this was no longer appropriately the task of contemporary painters or sculptors. The technologist in Duchenne could not resist demonstrating that photography was the most accurate means of presenting his scientific results. But in doing so, he demonstrated the futility of figurative painting as a means of accurate portrayal for its own sake. He thus sabotaged the besieged principle he had set out to defend.

"The camera could reproduce with ease those very images that academic painters struggled over, but it also recorded the blemishes, the pock-marked nose, the scraggly beard, the ill-fitting collar or the wrinkled waist-coat."[83] Photography revealed some of his models to be unfashionably ugly, and this made Duchenne uneasy. He used his scientific mission to justify his realist leanings. "I would certainly like to present only young and beautiful faces, but, above all, I had *scientifically* to demonstrate the *workings* of the lines of the face."[84]

Thus Duchenne unwittingly lent his weight to the realist movement. The champion of conventional figurative painting provided formal proof of the power and ease with which photography triumphed by most accurately portraying the emotions. While it is tempting to see Duchenne accelerating the decline of his preferred art form by advertising the consummate power of photography, he was ultimately a small player in a much broader revolution in Western art.

Science and contemporary aesthetics

The practice of 20th-century clinical neurology is based on Duchenne, and his original ideas on muscle action have become intimately incorporated into modern hand surgery and through the École des Beaux Arts the teaching of modern artistic anatomy.

[82] Galassi, P. (1981): *Before photography*. New York: The Museum of Modern Art, p. 11.
[83] Powell, T. (1972): Fixing the Face. In *From today painting is dead*. London: The Victoria and Albert Museum, p. 9.
[84] Duchenne, G.B.A.: *op. cit.*, p. 101, this volume.

Electricity, a profound knowledge of facial anatomy, the means of recording facial muscle contractions by photography, and an urge to modify the wayward course of French painting and sculpture, all contributed to his most quixotic book on the mechanism of human facial expression. The scientific findings of isolated and synergistic facial muscle actions, the linking of specific facial muscles with emotions, and a powerful illusion perceived by the viewer of the human face, all combine to mark this work as a classic document of experimental physiology. It is a book stamped with the presumption and genius of a nineteenth-century scientist.

Once published, *Mécanisme de la Physionomie Humaine* was eminently useful to painters and sculptors,[85] but paradoxically its influence was probably quite the reverse of that intended by its author. Duchenne's scientific observations, rather than his attempts to use them to influence contemporary aesthetics, stand today as his most original and lasting contributions.

[85] Being used even today at the École Nationale Supérieure des Beaux Arts (see the following chapter by J.-F. Debord in this volume).

2. The Duchenne de Boulogne Collection in the Department of Morphology, L'École Nationale Supérieure des Beaux Arts

JEAN-FRANÇOIS DEBORD

The original album of photographs

On the 15th of March, 1875, Duchenne (who was to die on the 17th of September of that year) presented us with the most precious evidence of his research on the Expression of the Emotions – his personal photograph album. Its dedication reads:

> "As a tribute to the École des Beaux Arts, the results of my first photographic experiments on the mechanism of human facial expression.
> Dr. Duchenne (de Boulogne),
> 15 March, 1875"

The dark green bound volume measures 31 by 44 cm. In gold capital letters as if it were a published book, the title is shown as "Mécanisme de la Physionomie Humaine par le Docteur Duchenne (de Boulogne). Album composé de 74 figures photographiées."

But there are only 58 photographs of various sizes pasted into the white pages of this album. The order differs little in the first part from that of the Album,[1] but gradually becomes more and more disordered. The first photographs are accompanied by a commentary that is not in Duchenne's hand. These notes soon become brief and then disappear completely. Forty-two of the photographic prints are rectangular and

[1] The published photographs that accompanied *Mécanisme de la physionomie humaine* and reproduced in this volume are referred to in this chapter as the "Album."

242

measure on average 17 cm in width by 23 cm in height and therefore correspond without doubt to the 18×24 cm negatives. Thirteen prints are oval-shaped enlargements measuring 28.5 by 20.5 cm, and the three other prints are of various shapes and subjects.

The 42 rectangular prints are the most precious, corresponding to some of the 56 illustrations in the scientific section of the published Album, and are taken from the same photographic plates. But while in the Album only the face and shoulders of the faradized subject and the tips of the electrodes are shown, the prints in Duchenne's personal album show the whole backdrop of the experiment: we see Duchenne himself, aided from time to time by an assistant, applying the electrodes with great concentration and delicacy to the face of his subjects [Figures 1 and 2].

Mathias Duval, who was the professor in charge of our Department from 1873 to 1903, devoted 30 pages of his "Précis d'Anatomie à l'Usage des Artistes,"[2] to the muscles of the face and to the work of Duchenne, which he considered to be the veritable foundation for the study of this subject. Mathias Duval recalled that: "By 1874 the anatomy course at l'École des Beaux Arts started to include some lessons to illustrate the vocabulary of human physiognomy. Pleased to see his work become part of this classic tradition of teaching, Duchenne bequeathed to the École des Beaux Arts the complete series of his original large-format photographs, which was never published in its entirety."

Twelve years earlier, the publisher of the Album, La Librairie Veuve Jules Renouard, had circulated notice of publication claiming that "a deluxe two part edition is also available in a grand-in-quarto edition of only 100 copies. The illustrations of the scientific section in this edition are the same size as the original plates. The price of this complete grand-in-quarto edition issued in a boxed set . . . 200 frs." We know that at this time darkrooms were usually designed to accommodate 18 by 24 cm collodion negatives.[3] Photographs in Duchenne's personal album were therefore made as contact prints from the original plates before these were reduced or masked to produce the prints found in the Album, which measure no more than 9 by 11cm.

None of the 100 copies of the deluxe grand-in-quarto edition, to our knowledge, has ever been found. Perhaps Veuve Renouard was anticipating events in claiming that "a deluxe edition *is* available." This does not seem to have been the case. The album donated to our school by Duchenne is "grand-in-quarto." It may have been a kind of rough draft for the planned but probably unpublished "de luxe grand-in-quarto edi-

[2] Published by Maison Quantin, Paris, 1881.
[3] We thank Michel Frizot of the Centre National de la Photographie, Paris for his expertise here.

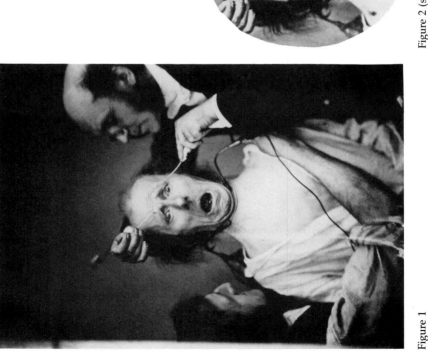

Figure 1

"Terror mixed with pain, torture . . ." as it was represented in the Album given to the École des Beaux Arts in 1875. h = 232mm, w = 169mm. From the École Na-

Figure 2 (small oval)

"Plate 64" from the Album of *Mécanisme de la Physionomie Humaine.* h = 111mm,

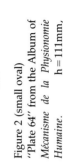

Figure 3 (large oval)

The same figure pasted onto stretched cloth to be used in teaching. h = 295mm, w = 215mm. From the École Nationale Supérieure des Beaux Arts

tion." The prints in our album were stuck at each corner onto white sheets of paper but on three of these sheets are only faint traces of glue, and the pictures are missing.[4]

In addition, our album contains the 13 oval photographs enlarged to life size devised as "teaching aids" [Figure 3].[5] The use of enlargements was unusual at this period (1856–57) and Duchenne was aware of the novelty of this technique.[6] Some of these oval photographs replace, while others accompany, the original rectangular prints.

The rest of the collection

In addition to the album, our Duchenne de Boulogne collection contains 78 oval photographs, of which 22 are duplicates, remounted with paste on cloth and mounted on stretchers [Figure 3]. Some have retained the movable mask, which allows the different expressions on each half of the face to be read clearly [Figures 4 and 5]. Some of the photographs still have a semicircular frame, which may prove that they were once hung.

The highest esteem in which Mathias Duval held Duchenne was most unusual for the time. Duval explained that "the works of Duchenne were not received with great favor in France at first. Physiologists, as well as artists, were somewhat mistrustful of a work that claimed to provide precise rules and scientific laws in a field where the custom was to draw laws and inspiration from fantasy and sentimental approximations."[7]

This negative response may have disrupted the plans of Veuve Renouard and Duchenne. They completed the publication of the Album, but cut short the "deluxe grand-in-quarto edition" and the oval enlargements. Perhaps the failure of these projects explains the disorder we find toward the end of Duchenne's personal album, which clearly had not had his full attention.

Our Duchenne Collection also includes the plaster casts photographed in Plates 66–73 in the Album, casts of the heads of antique sculptures, and castings corrected by Duchenne [Figure 6].

[4] Two of these three missing plates correspond to engravings that appeared in Charles Darwin's *Expression of the emotions in man and animals,* 1872. It is possible that Duchenne sent his own photographs at Darwin's request in order that the engravings could be made (see "Duchenne and facial expression of emotion," this volume, regarding the Darwin-Duchenne correspondence).

[5] According to the terms of the notice of publication, Duchenne, G.B.A. (1862): *Mechanism of Human Facial Expression*, p. 40, this volume.

[6] *Ibid.*

[7] *Précis d'anatomie à l'usage des artistes*, Baillière, Paris, 1882, p. 299.

Figures 4 and 5

"Plate 27" from the Album, mounted in oval frames with a moveable mask. Showing, on the left, with covering of the right eye, "an attentive gaze." On the right, now with the right eye uncovered, "painful concentration." h = 295mm, w = 215mm. From the École Nationale Supérieure des Beaux Arts collection.

Figure 6
A display case from the gallery of the Department of Morphology, École Nationale Supérieure des Beaux Arts, containing casts of the heads of antique sculptures and the casts corrected by Duchenne. From left to right: Niobe, Laocoön, and Arrotino.

Duchenne maintained that the lines drawn on the forehead of the *Laocoön* were physiologically impossible.[8] His naïvete makes us shudder. How could he dare to correct the forehead lines of antique sculptures and claim to assess scientifically the exactitude of a work of art? The unshakable convictions of certain successful artists, members of the Institute and Professors of the École des Beaux Arts at the time, were formidable. It took some courage for Mathias Duval[9] to demonstrate to the students of these traditionalists the significance of Duchenne's research in general and of these corrected plaster casts – veritable objects of scandal – in particular.

In our copy of *Mécanisme de la Physionomie Humaine* there is a hand-written note identifying the young man shown in Plates 4, 24, 25 of the Album. Described by Duchenne as a "talented artist and anatomist,"[10]

[8] Duchenne, G.B.A.: *op. cit.*, pp. 94, 98–99, this volume.
[9] Alexis Lemaitre in *L'École des Beaux Arts – dessinée et racontée par un élève*. Firmin Didot, 1889, described Mathias Duval's method of teaching and in particular his personality and sense of humor.
[10] Duchenne, G.B.A. (1862): *op. cit.*, p. 43, this volume.

Figure 7 (left)
A bust of Talrich in marble. On the pedestal is written "Jules Talrich sculptor, anatomical wax modeler 1826–   ." In the École Nationale Supérieure des Beaux Arts collection.
Figure 8 (right)
"Plate 16" from the album donated by Duchenne to the École Nationale Supérieure des Beaux Arts collection. Jules Talrich has been given an expression of "severity" by Duchenne. h = 232mm, w = 168mm.

he was a member of the Talrich family, who were modelers and anatomists in 19th-century Paris. In our Department, we still have the marble busts of two members of the Talrich family and some of their colored anatomical preparations. On the pedestal of the bust of Jules Talrich [Figure 7][11] we can read the date of his birth: 1826.[12] He was, therefore, in his late twenties when he appeared in Duchenne's photographs [Figure 8]. The marble bust is that of a stouter, heavier man, sporting a decoration on his lapel, but it is undoubtedly the same man. We can presume that this sculptor was perhaps present while Duchenne remodeled the foreheads of the antique *Arrotino* and *Laocoön.*

[11] Gabrielle Talrich relates in his memoirs: Dr. Duchenne needed several wax preparations to demonstrate the motor nerves of the face . . . These were requested of my father. Quoted from A. Jammes in the *Gazette des Beaux Arts,* December, 1978, p. 220.
[12] But not of his death.

The notion of beauty according to Duchenne

The description that Duchenne gives of the human beings upon whom he carried out his faradic experiments is often disturbing. Does this reflect the attitude of his age and the tastes of a certain society? The old man who seems so kindly, appealing, and interesting has features that, "without being absolutely ugly, approach ordinary triviality. . . ."[13] Duchenne apologized for the presence of the old man, adding that he did not believe that "in order to be true to nature one must show her imperfections . . ."[14]

At the same time the young Talrich, who appears somewhat ridiculous and almost fatuously sentimental in his attitude and expressions, would fit the "conditions that aesthetically constitute beauty."[15] A face, Duchenne felt, that was fit to portray the ecstatic recollections of love shown on the right side of his face and the expression of Christ on the left, in Plate 24.

One feels trapped in the quicksands of an aestheticism that today strikes us as strange. The old man was ugly in the eyes of contemporary critics. Duchenne quotes their condemnation for ". . . stripping art of its ideal of beauty and reducing it to anatomical realism along the lines of a certain 'Modern School' of art."[16] Nothing wounded our investigator more, he who shared the tastes of his critics. It was Duchenne's opinion also that realism "only shows us nature with her imperfections and even deformities and that it seems to prefer the ugly, the vulgar, or the trivial."[17]

Duchenne later took up this debate by adding the Aesthetic Section to his text: "In an attempt for those who possess a "sense of beauty," and wishing to please while at the same time teaching, I performed some new electrophysiological studies in which I hope the principal aesthetic conditions are fulfilled: beauty of form, associated with exactness of the facial expression, pose and gesture."[18]

Duchenne seemed blinded by his principles this time. In the previously published Scientific Section he gave us a very interesting lesson in observation as, armed with his electrodes, he remodeled on the skin of his "old and ugly subject," working with the style and bizarreness of a Daumier remodeling one of the busts of parliamentarians [Figures 9 and 10]. This comparison, although laudatory in our terms, would probably have been distasteful to him!

[13] Duchenne, G.B.A. (1862): *op. cit.*, p. 42, this volume.   [14] *Ibid.*, p. 42, this volume.
[15] *Ibid.*, p. 43, this volume.   [16] *Ibid.*, p. 109, this volume.
[17] *Ibid.*, p. 110, this volume.   [18] *Ibid.*, p. 102, this volume.

Figure 9 (left) appears as the 33rd plate in the album donated by Duchenne to the École. It shows an agreeable expression of admiration or surprise. From the École Nationale Supérieure des Beaux Arts collection.

Figure 10 (right) is a death mask by Daumier of the Comte de Keratry in plaster of Paris. h = 125mm. From the Musée d'Orsay, Paris. With permission from Robert Descharnes.

He had, it is true, been overwhelmed by Jules Talrich's facial expressions. But in this Aesthetic Section, where he arranges his "almost blind young girl" by seating her and draping her like a mannequin, we feel as if he is working for Madame Tussaud's or the Musée.

In 1760, a significant prize had been established entitled "Concours de la Tête d'Expression,"[19] and in 1861, the subject was "contentment of a mother after the recovery of a child." This may have been the stimulus for Duchenne publishing his Plate 79 the following year: "Joy of a mother who sees her child escape from a mortal illness." Duchenne never wished to be a member of the Institute.[20] Did he never dream of participating in the sessions of the "Academie des Beaux Arts" that decided on the subjects for that kind of competition and awarded the prizes? Duchenne organized public teaching sessions on "faradism," which were

[19] Founded by the Comte de Caylus, one of the instigators of the revival of antiquity, this prize claimed to promote "The art of demonstrating the expression of the emotions." See the catalogue of the exhibition: *La sculpture française au XIXe siècle*. Galeries Nationales du Grande Palais, Paris, 1986.

[20] Paul Guilly, *Duchenne de Boulogne*, Paris, Baillière, 1936, p. 220.

attended by "very distinguished artists."[21] He thus met artists "sophisticated," "skilled," and "eminent,"[22] but who were they? Was it Delacroix, or Bouguereau? According to André Jammes,[23] Duchenne's Album caused a sensation. It was a subject of conversation, and the Goncourt brothers related in 1864 that they had seen during a dinner party Sainte-Beuve's[24] facial expression change, "as if Dr. Duchenne touched the muscles of his face."[25] It would be interesting to know what Delacroix, who died in 1863, or Baudelaire, who died in 1867, thought of these experiments by Duchenne.

As for Duchenne's attitude to Delacroix, two sentences are particularly revealing: "Teaching the art of *correctly* painting the movements of human facial expression . . . can prevent or modify errors of the imagination."[26] "Isn't the exaggeration of morbid anatomical science one of the principal causes of the decline of art?"[27] We know that Delacroix had a predilection for the "errors of imagination"; and as for the "anatomical science!"

The passage that provides the most revealing insight into the thoughts and tastes of Duchenne is the one in which he attacks Carravagio. He admits to not being able to admire "this famous master's practice of always finding the models for his most sublime religious scenes in gambling dens and cabarets."[28]

Duchenne was in fact less interested in painting than in the subject, and the way in which the subject was treated, either suitably or badly. He tirelessly sought the nuances that separated "earthly love from celestial love" and reproached artists for having given the faces of saints and even virgins "the expression of sensuous pleasure."[29] And we must not forget the pages that Paul Guilly[30] wrote about Duchenne the believer: his religious education at the feet of Mgr. Haffreingue of Boulogne, his brother a priest . . . and his charity – days of free medical consultation. The originality of this character, his strength of conviction in his scientific research[31] sometimes makes us forget his provincial and religious roots. But this aspect bears heavily on his personality and his taste and,

---

[21] Duchenne, G.B.A. (1862), *op. cit.*, p. 67, this volume.
[22] *Ibid.*, p. 101, this volume.   [23] Jammes, A.: *op. cit.*, p. 217.
[24] Sainte-Beuve was a contemporary literary figure who was also born in Boulogne-sur-Mer.
[25] Jammes, A.: *op. cit.*, p. 218.   [26] Duchenne, G.B.A. (1862), *op. cit.*, p. 36, this volume.
[27] *Ibid.*, p. 33.   [28] *Ibid.*, p. 102.
[29] *Ibid.*, p. 111.   [30] Guilly, P.: *op. cit.*, p. 219.
[31] Cf. Leon Daudet, "Lamalou les Bains," Chapter V of *Devant le Douleur*, Librairie Nationale, Paris, 1915. Reprinted in *Souvenirs Littéraires*, Grasset, Paris, 1968, pp. 156–157.

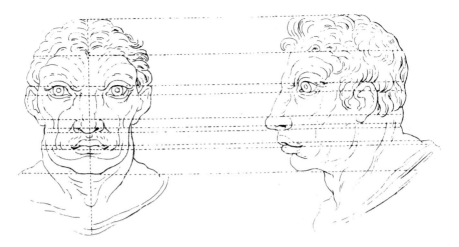

Figure 11
"A Human Figure Compared with that of a Cow" by Le Brun, taken from *l'Art de Connaître les Hommes par la Physionomie* by Gaspard Lavater, Paris, 1820, Volume 8, plate 562.

therefore, his aesthetic sense. He sometimes exhibited the most blatant adoration of church ritual for its own sake, for example, in Plate 77: "With her eye slightly obscured and turned obliquely upward and to the side, and with her smile and half-open mouth, with her head and body leaning slightly backward, and with her hands crossed on her breast, and with the little cross around her neck; . . . thanks to all this arrangement I have been able to photograph the pure pleasure of a soul devoted to God." In fact, the catalogues of the "Salon" of this epoch are filled with this type of religious nonsense.

"Applicable to the plastic arts"?

Daumier (1808–1879) was a contemporary of Duchenne and a master of his art form well before the publication of *Mécanisme de la Physionomie Humaine*. Throughout his life, there is clear evidence of a concern with morphology in many of his drawings and sculptures. Judith Wechsler[32] has demonstrated that the facial expression drawings of Le Brun [Figure 11] were used by Daumier throughout his career [Figure 12].

Degas was interested in the photographs of Muybridge and took account of them in drawing the legs of race horses. They are definitely not copies, however. Today, Bacon or Velickovic have used Muybridge in

---

[32] *Human comedy*, Thames and Hudson, 1982, pp. 160–161.

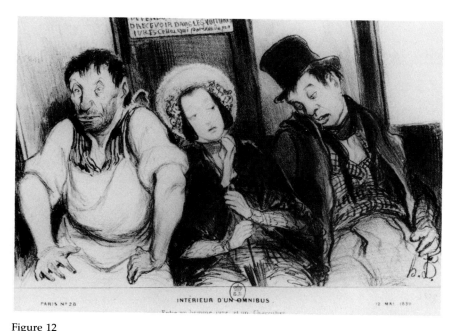

Figure 12
"The Interior of an omnibus" by Daumier, "Between a drunkard and a butcher." 12 May 1839, photograph from the Bibliothèque Nationale, Paris.

transposing certain photographic sequences directly into their paintings.

Duchenne was known in some contemporary Parisian artistic circles,[33] but there is no evidence that he was an inspiration to any contemporary or recent artist; there is no tangible proof of any direct use of his work, as Le Brun was used by Daumier or Muybridge by Bacon. But what about more discreet influences – such as the use of Muybridge by Degas? There were only a limited number of copies of Duchenne's Album and the tiny photographs of the 1876 edition were very difficult to memorize. And this rare *Mécanisme de la Physionomie Humaine,* after the grand period of phrenology and physiognomy in the nineteenth century,[34] never saw a revival. Neither the Impressionists nor the Nabis entertained this type of curiosity. And although the Symbolists gave it its romantic swan song, the Expressionists gave short shrift to such subtleties.

Only the École des Beaux Arts continued to demand that their unfortunate young students[35] should make the heros of antiquity grimace.

---

[33]Jammes, A., *op. cit.,* p. 217.   [34]Wechsler, J.: *op. cit.,* pp. 30–31.
[35]One of whom was Alexis Lemaitre (*op. cit.*), who relates how the students really didn't

Figure 13
Prix de Rome, 1883. "Oedipus
with his daughters Ismène and
Antigone at his side, cursing his
son Polynice." A detail from the
painting in the École Nationale
Supérieure des Beaux Arts collection.

A glance at the list of subjects of the Prix de Rome competition shows
that continuity was still the rule. But even in this domain, things were
to evolve, and if in 1883 Oedipus was still cursing his son [Figure 13], a
calmer source of inspiration slowly took over.

By 1906 the subject was "The Family." In 1907 it was "Inspiration,
Virgil contemplating the Roman countryside." The "Concours de la Tête
d'Expression"[36] also evolved. Toward the end of the nineteenth century, under the influence of symbolism, the fashion was for the "representation of the interior world" and the sentiments shown became more
and more discreet until it finally became a portrait competition.

If an editor had the idea of publishing Duchenne today in a paperback
edition, he would perhaps find a new public: The book would doubtless
be consulted by cartoon strip illustrators; and it would amuse the young
– like the students of the École des Beaux Arts.

At the École, we perpetuate the tradition of Mathias Duval and each
year present the *Mechanism of Human Facial Expression* as part of a lecture
series, which was followed this year by a questionnaire. The responses

take the notion of antiquity seriously. And then any remaining decorum was lost at the
"Bal des 4 Z'ARTS"!
[36] See above.

Figure 14
This photograph of the 28th plate in the Album donated by Duchenne to the École des Beaux Arts shows the "little 6-year-old girl," with an expression of pain on the right side of her face.

are quite astonishing in their diversity. Some students find the photographs "a veritable treasure trove." Others reject with disgust and irony that they might be useful. If some find them morbid, just as many think the opposite. Some related them to silent films, to *Frankenstein*, to *Nosferatu*; others find Duchenne "quite moving in the delicacy with which he placed the electrodes: He was someone who loved humanity and who tried to get as close as possible to people." Another remarked that Duchenne, captured in the larger-format photographs in the École Collection, was "more expressive than his guinea pigs, and thereby became the subject of his own experiments."

The poses of Jules Talrich and the "scenes" that Duchenne "wished to paint" in the Aesthetic Section, seem to the students to leave a "disagreeable after taste!" But none can forget the toothless old man; the possessed drunkard; the old lady in crinoline with one eye staring at us while the other seems to be obeying the electrode; the young woman who is always asymmetrical; and the young girls, so attractive in their melancholy [Figure 14].

Duchenne's importance is beyond questions of the aesthetic value or usefulness of *Mechanism of Human Facial Expression*. He has a profound effect on students, who ask questions about the sincerity or hypocrisy of emotions in general, as if the electrodes produce a perfectly frank, direct, and open expression that can be interpreted, whereas certain faces encountered in real life leave the same students confused.

Duchenne revealed himself very much more of an artist when he was simply himself – an investigator whose genius was to blend anatomical knowledge with scientific faradism and photography – than when he tried consciously to be an artist.

3. Duchenne today:
Facial expression and facial surgery

JOHN T. HUESTON

Their debt to Duchenne is rarely realized by surgeons who operate to restore facial expression. Whether dealing with muscle dysfunction or the aging process, our work rests on the foundation of Duchenne's studies. That this area of supreme psychological significance should owe so much to one of the founders of neurology, the mentor of Charcot and, therefore, ultimately of Freud, should give us all much food for thought.[1] The triad of Duchenne's advances has survived largely unchallenged: the application of electrical stimulation to facial nerves and muscles, his introduction of clinical photography,[2] and his profound analysis of the form and function of the facial musculature.

Electrical stimulation of muscles and nerves is still widely practiced, even during operations. Although his photographs are only snapshots from the process of facial movement, the evolution to recording the animation of the face on film and video was inevitable. Interpreting facial function in terms of muscle action rather than mere morphology, Duchenne revolutionized the understanding of expressive facial movement, and helped prepare a firm foundation for modern techniques of facial reanimation. Duchenne's "mask of muscles" has been recently restudied, confirming the relationship between individual facial muscles and total facial function.

Surgical advances in the management of both asymmetry and aging of the face are indirectly indebted to Duchenne. His description of secondary creaselines masking primary expression lines explains the rejuvenating effect of facelifting operations and their psychological value by restoring an illusion of youth.

[1] Hueston, J. T., and Cuthbertson, R. A. (1978): Duchenne de Boulogne and facial expression. *Ann Plast Surg*, 1: 411.
[2] Cuthbertson, R. A. (1978): Duchenne de Boulogne – the first published clinical photographs? *The Practitioner*, 221:276.

Surgery for asymmetry: Facial palsy and facial spasm

Facial palsy

When the facial nerve is congenitally deficient or later becomes unable to activate the muscles of the face, these muscles are paralyzed. This can happen spontaneously (Bell's palsy) or after injury to the nerve.[3] More than half of the patients with Bell's palsy recover completely within a few months; unfortunately, the others do not.[4] While awaiting nerve recovery and facial muscle action, the treating surgeon may try to limit the inevitable atrophy of unused and denervated muscles by the faradic stimulation introduced by Duchenne. Passive stretching of the paralyzed facial muscles can be minimized in this waiting period by the patient wearing a plastic sling supporting the angle of the mouth. The active pull across the midline is thus statically opposed.

Failure of recovery from Bell's palsy or from a facial nerve injury may also leave the patient with a total paralysis or a partial paralysis involving only one area of that side of the face. When the orbicularis muscles around the orifices of the face are weak or paralyzed, the effect is most noticed during the expression of emotions by distortion of eye or mouth. Later the effects of aging and gravity will add to the deformity of any weakened region of the face.

Facial palsy is often masked in the static face of a child by the skin's dermal elastic tissue passively supporting the weaker side like a sling. The muscle imbalance is unmasked on movement [Figure 1 A & B].

Because the facial deformity is produced by the unopposed action of the intact muscles of the opposite side of the face, early operations tried to control this displacement by fixing the tissues of the weak side; grafting a static sling suspending the orifices of emotional expression to a fixed bony point such as the malar (cheek) bone in front of the ear[5] [Figure 2 A & B]. This solution, of course, provides no movement but reduces the passive displacement and hence the deformity. Cutting of nerves to the muscles on the intact side of the face by superselective neurotomies – or even myectomies where normal facial muscles are excised – is often added to reduce the displacing muscle power. The stronger side is thus weakened to lessen the asymmetry.[6]

[3] Bell, C. (1844): *The nervous system of the human body*, 3rd ed., London.
[4] Taverner, D. (1955): Bell's Palsy. A clinical and electromyographic study. *Brain*, 78: 209.
[5] Gillies, H. (1934): Experience with fascial autografts in operative treatment of facial paralysis. *Proc Roy Soc Med*, 27:1372
[6] Niklison, J. (1964): Facial paralysis: "moderation of non-paralysed muscles." *Brit J Plast Surg*, 18:397.

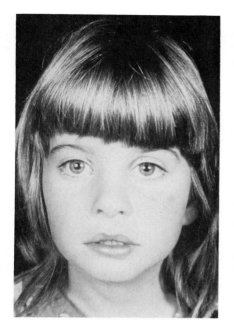 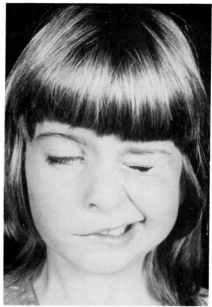

Figure 1
Congenital right facial palsy in 10-year-old girl. A. (left): The palsy being incomplete, good muscle tone remains; the facial integument being young, the effect of gravity is controlled by the elastic dermis at rest. B. (right): Contraction of the intact left side produces the deformity. (Patient of Dr. W. Morrison)

In older patients loss of this dermal elasticity allows gravity to display the deformity even at rest [Figure 3A]. Surgical treatment of the paralyzed half of the face may consist of living or inert slings, nerve or muscle transfers, and nerve or muscle grafts [Figure 3B].

Loss of *m. orbicularis oculi* allows the lower lid to sag and epiphora is common. A lateral tarsorrhaphy including some lid margin shortening[7] is useful to lessen these unpleasant features [Figure 2 B]. Inability to close down the upper lid is more dangerous to the exposed cornea and the weight of the small metal beads[8] [Figure 3 B] or magnets[9] has been found to be more reliable than the earlier metal spring of Morel Fatio in

[7]McLaughlin, C. R. (1953): Surgical support in permanent facial palsy. *Plas Reconstr Surg*, 11:302.
[8]Smellie, G.D. (1966): Restoration of the blinking reflex in facial palsy by a simple lid-load operation. *Brit J Plast Surg*, 19:279.
[9]Mühlbauer, W. (1973): Restoration of lid function in facial palsy with permanent magnets. *Chir Plast*, 1:295.

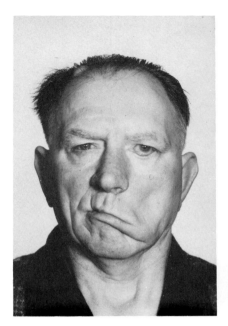

Figure 2
Total left facial palsy showing effects of gravity. A. (left): Lateral eyebrow ptosis (which in fact masks lagophthalmos); lower lid ectropion from *m. orbicularis oculi* loss and drooping heavy cheek and left angle of mouth with nose and philtrum pulled to intact side.
B. (right): Static fascial slings to zygomatic arch and *m. temporalis* have supported the cheek tissues and the angle of the mouth and centralized the nasal tip and philtrum. A lateral tarsorrhaphy has reduced the ectropion. Two simple "antigravity" ameliorative procedures. (Patient of Dr. Ian T. Jackson)

overcoming this lagophthalmos.[10] Active closure by introducing a free muscle transfer is nearer the ideal.

An even more sophisticated approach is to add some movement to the weaker side as well as to limit the pull of the opposite intact muscles. This was attempted using part or whole of one of the muscles of mastication, fully functional because they are innervated by the trigeminal (fifth) and not the facial (seventh) cranial nerve.[11] But this is physiologically illogical. Only by clenching the teeth can these muscles of mastication mimic the lost facial movement. But who clenches their teeth when smiling? Normal smiling involves relaxation of these masticatory mus-

[10] Morel-Fatio, D., and Lalardrie, J. P. (1964): Palliative surgical treatment of facial paralysis – a palpebral spring. *Plast Reconstr Surg*, 33:446.
[11] Brown, J. B. (1939): Utilization of temporalis muscle and fascia for facial paralysis. *Ann Surg*, 109:1016.

Figure 3
A. (left): Right facial palsy with gross asymmetry of mouth from atonic right cheek muscles – and lagophthalmos.
B. (right): Active masticatory muscle transfers using *mm. temporalis* and *masseter* have restored facial balance and movement on clenching the teeth. Lagophthalmos has been reduced by gold implants along the border of the upper lid. (Patient of Dr. Ian T. Jackson)

cles, often with the mouth open. The lips and eyelids are gently curved and new creases appear in areas we recognize as expressing a relaxed contentedness – even mirth. To convey the movement of a smile by clenching the teeth can be learned in front of a mirror or a camera by intensive training but it more often appears as a grimace. Furthermore, in the uncalculated freedom of natural emotional display the transplanted masticatory muscles relax, immediately revealing the deformity.

Primary or secondary repair of the facial nerve is used after nerve injury. When this has failed or proved impossible, more complex methods have been used. The commonest example is after the accidental intracranial destruction of the facial nerve during surgical resection of an acoustic neuroma on the immediately adjacent auditory (eighth) cranial nerve trunk. Suture of the intact hypoglossal (twelfth) cranial nerve trunk (which normally activates the massive muscles of the tongue), to the nonfunctioning facial (seventh) cranial nerve trunk can reinnervate the

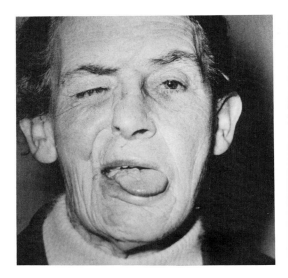

Figure 4
Hypoglossal nerve transfer into right facial nerve trunk after intracranial surgical section of latter during acoustic neuroma resection. Facial muscle tone is retained but movements are en masse from *mm. orbicularis oculi* to *platysma* – uncoordinated with the intact side. The asymmetry is enhanced by the tongue atrophy.

paralyzed facial muscles.[12,13] But the rationale for this reanimation technique is defective. The tongue is now paralyzed on the same side as the facial muscles, making mastication and speech even more difficult. The only advantage is that the tone in the facial muscles is restored by such reinnervation, providing a static muscular sling and better facial balance at rest. But when the tongue is protruded the whole half-face of facial muscles is thrown into an incoherent unsightly mass contraction [Figure 4].

Duchenne, who stressed the value of individual muscle movement in the expression of the emotions, would certainly be critical of this mass action where movement cannot express emotion. We should guard against the grotesque.

Cross-face nerve grafts and microvascular free muscle transfers conform more closely to Duchenne's proposition of individual muscles for

[12] Trumble, H.C. (1939): Nerve (hypoglossal-facial) anastomosis in treatment of facial paralysis. *Med J Aust*, 1:300.
[13] Conley, J., and Baker, D.C. (1979): Hypoglossal facial nerve anastomoses of the paralysed face. *Plast Reconst Surg*, 63:63.

emotions. In a cross-face nerve graft[14,15] some branches of the facial nerve on the intact side of the face are linked by long grafts of a fine (sural) nerve from the leg to the nonfunctioning distal fibers of the facial nerve on the paralyzed side. Some axon fibers of the intact nerve will grow through these long thin cable grafts across the face and into the final fibers of the injured nerve. Such are the hazards of this long journey of nerve regeneration over 20 cm, through the surgical scars of two nerve suture lines into long-atrophied muscles, that the outcome is often a poor recovery or total failure. Success can, however, restore the symmetry of the facial muscle movements and effortless symmetrical spontaneous expression of emotions. The muscles of both sides of the face are activated now by the same single intact facial nerve. Emotions, and not mere movements, may now be expressed [Figure 5 A & B].

Cross-face nerve grafts alone offer the theoretical ideal of restoring the individual or small-group muscle actions stressed by Duchenne. But the atrophy of long denervated muscles militates against full recovery. Microsurgical techniques now allow the joining of tiny blood vessels as well as nerves, so that an entire healthy muscle can be taken from the leg, the foot or the arm, and transferred, still living, into a long-paralyzed side of the face. There is no point in joining its nerve supply to the nonfunctioning facial nerve; so it must be joined to the opposite side's intact facial nerve using the long and hazardous cross-face nerve graft. When reinnervated, this new muscle will contract synchronously with the muscles of the intact side of the face. Although it may be split into several tongues to be able to move both mouth and eyelids, it is still only one muscle.[16,17] This restoration of "one muscle for several emotions" still contravenes Duchenne's "one muscle for each emotion." However, this rough approximation is the encouraging present state of the surgical art [Figure 5].[18,19,20,21,22]

[14] Smith, J.W. (1971): A new technique of facial animation. In *Transactions of the Fifth International Congress of Plastic Surgery* (J.T. Hueston, Ed.). London: Butterworth, p. 83.

[15] Anderl, H. (1974): Reconstruction of facial palsy through cross-face nerve transfer. *Chir Plast*, 2:17.

[16] Harii, K., Ohmori, K., and Torii, S. (1976): Free gracilis muscle transplantation, with microvascular anatomoses for the treatment of facial paralysis: a preliminary report. *Plast Reconstr Surg*, 57:133.

[17] Harii, K. (1979): Microvascular free muscle transplantation for animation of facial paralysis. *Clinics in Plastic Surgery*, 6:361.

[18] Hamilton, S.G.L., Terzis, J.K., and Carraway, J.T. (1988): Surgical anatomy of the facial musculature and muscle transplantation. In *Combating Facial Paralysis* (J.K. Terzis, Ed.), in press.

[19] O'Brien, B. McC., Franklin, J.D., and Morrison, W.A. (1980): Cross-facial nerve grafts

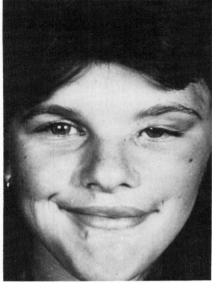

Figure 5
A. (left): Congenital left facial palsy with lagophthalmos and ectropion and epiphora; and severe displacement of upper lip and alar bases to the pulling intact side. The lower lip has largely escaped.
B. (right): One year after microvascular free *m. gracilis* graft, which has given control of both ocular and oral orifices with good balance of upper lip and central philtrum. Cross-face sural nerve grafts have been used to allow synchronous symmetrical facial movements – a natural expression of emotions is restored. (Patient of Dr. W. Morrison and Dr. B. McC. O'Brien)

The next step in surgical evolution may be to attempt multiple individual muscle transfers by microvascular techniques and to have them better nerve-linked to work harmoniously with the intact side. The microneurovascular transfer of other facial muscles, for example, *m. platysma*, *m. frontalis*, and *m. occipitalis* is another logical step under examination.[23]

Behind the challenge of facial reanimation lurks the "illusion" of

and microneurovascular free muscle transfer for long established facial palsy. *Brit J Plast Surg*, 33:202.
[20] O'Brien, B. McC., Lawlor, D.L., and Morrison, W.A. (1982): Microneurovascular free muscle reconstruciton for long established facial palsy. *Ann Chir Gynae*, 71:65.
[21] O'Brien, B. McC., and Morrison, W.A. (1987): Facial palsy. In *Reconstructive Microsurgery*, Edinburgh and London: Churchill Livingstone.
[22] Tolhurst D.E., and Box, K.E. (1982): Free neurovascularised muscle grafts in facial palsy. *Plast Reconstr Surg*, 69:760.
[23] Terzis, J.K. (1987): Ninth International Congress of Plastic and Reconstructive Surgery, New Delhi.

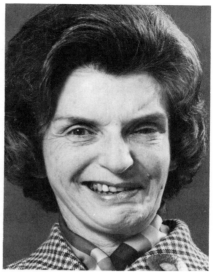

Figure 6
Left-sided facial spasm in a 50-year-old woman, following soon after recovery from left Bell's palsy 10 years before. A. (left): There is mild skin puckering of the forehead (*m. corrugator supercilii*) and the chin (*m. mentalis*) on gently smiling. B. (right): Gross over-action of *mm. orbicularis oculi* and *oris* with narrowing of the orifices on laughing; *m. platysma* is also increasing the distortion and asymmetry of the lower face.

Duchenne. He brilliantly demonstrated that movement of a single facial part provides a visual "cue" to the observer sufficient to create the illusion of the whole face moving in emotional expression. If only the mouth were well reanimated then the casual observer might – by the illusion of Duchenne – be able to "fill in" or subconsciously complete the other facial movements normally occurring in, say, smiling.

Facial muscle spasm

Another unpleasant "experiment of nature," the opposite of paralysis, is spasm of the facial muscles. The muscles are unable to relax or to contract in a sequential pattern. Movement occurs, but it passes beyond the range for which it was initiated. Instead of a gentle eyelid closure in smiling, a gross winking or even blinking occurs. This exaggerated activity produces disharmony and deformity of the facial features [Figure 6].

Perhaps spasticity would be a better term, as the face is balanced with good tone at rest, but on spontaneous expression of, say, happiness, the muscles of that side of the face contract excessively in a gross and uncoordinated way. This is the mass action that Duchenne abhorred as inimical to proper expression.

Even though relapse is common, partial denervation of the affected muscles in hemifacial spasm is a sound principle of treatment.[24] Each facial muscle has more than one motor nerve branch, so that a margin of safety exists when one branch is purposefully divided to weaken the muscle action. Preoperative testing using local anaesthetic allows temporary muscle paralyses and identification of the optimal branches to be divided. This simple clinical experiment is the reverse of Duchenne's faradic stimulations.

Logic suggests that the restoration of symmetrical expression in facial spasm could be achieved by linking the spastic muscles to the motor nerves from the intact normally innervated side. Such ruthless division of the entire facial nerve and cross-face nerve transfer has not yet been reported. Only when this cross-linking of neuromuscular control is more predictable can this be reasonably offered to these unhappy patients.

Surgery for the aging process

The loss of the elastic component of the skin from aging, aggravated often by sun exposure, allows a gradual process of stretching of the skin. Two forces act constantly to stretch the skin – muscle movement and gravity. Aesthetic surgery is mainly antigravity surgery.

Exaggeration of the secondary skin folds described by Duchenne[25] occurs with aging and is reduced by tightening the skin of the face, leaving only the primary skin creases [Figure 7]. Such restoration of the illusion of youth usually improves self-esteem.[26]

Both primary and secondary lines are caused by the constant action of the facial muscles. With age these secondary lines become permanent across the forehead (*m. frontalis*) and as "crow's-feet" around the outer canthus (*m. orbicularis oculi*). M. zygomaticus major in the cheek causes "smile lines." Finally, in the neck, the anterior border of *m. platysma* on one or both sides can cause long vertical skin ridges. In just the same way as Duchenne showed that *m. platysma* contraction exaggerates whatever emotion the face is portraying,[27] it is an everyday observation much loved by cartoonists that the anterior neck folds of *m. platysma*

[24] Wagasugi, K. (1972): Facial nerve block in the treatment of a spasm. *Arch Otolaryn*, 95: 356.

[25] Duchenne, G.B.A.: *Mécanisme de la Physionomie Humaine*, p. 34, this volume.

[26] Hueston, J.T., Dennerstein, L. and Gotts, G. (1985): Psychological aspects of cosmetic surgery. *J Psychosomatic Obstet and Gynae*, 4:335.

[27] Duchenne, G.B.A.: *op. cit.*, p. 89, this volume.

Figure 7

A. (left): Advanced combined effects of dermal aging, muscle contraction, and of gravity on the facial integument: Duchenne's "secondary lines of expression." B. (right): Rejuvenating effect of mobilizing and resecting excessive facial skin, leaving only Duchenne's "primary lines of expression." Eradication of most secondary lines by antigravity surgery: brow, cheek, and neck lifting, with excellent effect of *m. platysma* tightening. (Patient of Dr. Gwyn Morgan)

exaggerate the appearance of aging. A direct surgical transverse tightening or even division of platysma is now incorporated in the lifting procedure to counter this exaggeration of the aging process.

The weight of the facial integument is not insignificant.[28] As the aging skin is actively stretched by the muscles of facial expression, it is also being passively stretched by its own weight and that of the facial muscles. When a patient is lying supine, the facial integument slides down posteriorly and lies in folds about the fixed points – the ears. The supine face looks younger when viewed from above.[29] This simple observation demonstrates the mechanism of improvement provided by a facelift. The slack skin is removed in the same backward direction that it falls into when the face looks upward.

The immediate effect is rejuvenating. Duchenne's secondary lines of (aging) expression have been erased. Further aging, further facial mus-

[28] Hamilton, S.G.L., Terzis, J. K., and Carraway, J.T.: *op. cit.*

[29] Indeed this was a ruse in postoperative photography by less than scrupulous authors of aesthetic surgical techniques until editorial edicts were introduced to prohibit this faking of facial improvement.

cle action, and further effects of gravity, all slowly stretch the skin again, with some inevitable relapse.

Duchenne redefined facial muscle anatomy using localized electrical stimulation. He saw the face as responding to a "mask of muscles" whose nerve supply was of more practical importance than the ill-defined morphological boundaries between these muscles. Paris has once again been the source of highly original anatomical concepts in facial muscle function. The term "superficial musculo-aponeurotic system" (SMAS) was coined in 1974 for an allegedly continuous sheet of facial fibromuscular tissue enclosing the face like a mask, continuous from *m. frontalis* down to *m. platysma*. Its protagonists claimed that this linking fascial sheet "could be an amplifier of the contractions of the facial muscles."[30] They go on in more detail:

> The SMAS acts as a distributor of all facial muscular contractions to the skin: each muscle contraction follows one preferential direction in the network. An infinite number of resultant actions is possible because (1) the SMAS relays the contractions of the facial muscles along the longitudinal network parallel to the skin plane and (2) SMAS transmits the resultant effect in a perpendicular direction toward the facial skin, through the fibrous expansions from the SMAS to the dermis.

But they dispute whether Duchenne's hypothesis of "one muscle for each emotion" could provide "the human face with its wonderful ability to express so many different nuances and shades of expression."

This idea of SMAS has recently been revised and refuted – again from Paris. Jost and Levet have described a concept of the planes of the facial musculature that is much simpler than SMAS.[31] The two planes of muscles found in apes are, although fibrous in many regions, still present in man. The important deep enveloping "sphincter colli profundus" includes all the subcutaneous muscles grouped into the three orbicularis muscles, looking rather like a helmet or medieval mask of mail armor. These muscles have bony attachments, necessary for their active reshaping of facial orifices in the expression of the emotions.

Outside this envelope of powerful musculature is what Jost and Levet call the "primitive platysma." This covers the face and neck and in apes is strongly attached to the parotid fascia and the auricular cartilages. In man it is represented by four muscles – the true *m. platysma*, *m. risorius*,

[30] Mitz, V., and Peyronie, M. (1976): The superficial-musculo-aponeurotic-system (SMAS) in the parotid and cheek area. *Plast Reconstr Surg*, 78:80.
[31] Jost, G., and Levet, Y. (1984): Parotid fascia and facelifting: a critical evaluation of the SMAS concept. *Plast Reconstr Surg*, 74:42.

m. triangularis oris, and *m. auricularis posterior* – linked by the parotid fascia. The most distinctive and functionally most important feature of this external mobile sheet of facial musculature well known to Duchenne is that it has no bony attachment. This is the layer to be tightened surgically if lasting lifting is sought.

Their great debt owed by modern plastic and reconstructive surgeons to Duchenne de Boulogne is seen in the lasting value of his trilogy of expositions – faradism, photography, and facial anatomy revisited.

4. Duchenne and facial expression of emotion

PAUL EKMAN

> Armed with electrodes, one would be able, like nature herself, to paint the expressive lines of the emotions of the soul on the face of man. What a source of new observations![1]

It is only recently that I had the pleasure, through Andrew Cuthbertson's translation, of being able to read Duchenne's book with ease. Because of my rusty college French, my initial introduction to Duchenne was selective. My access to Duchenne had been aided by Harriet Oster, a postdoctoral fellow working with me in the early 1970s. With her background in French literature, and an interest in measuring facial behavior, Harriet carefully checked Duchenne's description of the muscles responsible for particular changes in facial appearance. I was then, with my colleague Waly Friesen, deeply immersed in constructing a tool for measuring facial behavior based on the anatomy of facial movement. Duchenne's book was an invaluable resource. His identification of the particular muscles producing specific changes in facial appearance provided the groundwork for those who measure facial behavior today. Duchenne's study of the mechanics of facial movement and the objective assessment of facial activity are, therefore, of great historical importance.

Most recently I have become fascinated by Duchenne's ideas on the nature of facial expression of emotion, having been quite unfamiliar with some of them until reading the translation in full. The photographs made by Duchenne provided, as he says in the quote above, a rich basis for observations.

Universality

Duchenne simply asserted:

> In the face, our Creator was not concerned with mechanical necessity. He was able, in his wisdom, or – please pardon this manner of speaking – in pursuing a divine fantasy, to put any particular

[1] Duchenne, G.B.A.: *Mechanism of Human Facial Expression*, p. 9, this volume.

muscle in action, one alone or several muscles together, when he wished the characteristic signs of the emotions, even the most fleeting, to be written briefly on man's face. Once this language of facial expression was created, it sufficed for him to give all human beings the instinctive faculty of always expressing their sentiments by contracting the same muscles. This rendered the language universal and immutable.[2]

It is only recently that evidence for the universality of certain facial expressions of emotion has been obtained[3] and there are still some anthropologists who reject such a claim.[4] Of course, the current explanation of universality is based on evolution, not our Creator. Charles Darwin, in his copy of Duchenne's book, put an exclamation mark in the margin next to the section I have just quoted. Darwin then wrote in the margin:

> Good to show how theory fails. Praise his book, well known for other excellent treatises and adds much. In my opinion, by [compared to?] other writers a vast step in advance.[5]

Character and facial appearance

People have long believed that they could derive information about personality or character from the face, usually based on physiognomy. While such interpretations of the size and shape of the facial features was respectable in the eighteenth and nineteenth centuries and continues to reappear in popular books today, it has no scientific credibility. Duchenne offered another possible means – apart from physiognomy – by which character might be revealed in facial appearance.

> In the newborn, the soul is bereft of all emotion and the facial expression at rest is quite neutral; it expresses the complete absence of all emotions. But, from the time that the infant can experience sensations and starts to register emotions, the facial muscles portray the various passions on his face. The muscles most often used by these early gymnastics of the soul became better developed and their tonic force increases proportionately.

[2] Duchenne: *op. cit.*, p. 19, this volume.

[3] For a recent review see Ekman, P.: The argument and evidence about universals in facial expressions of emotion. In *Handbook of psychophysiology: the biological psychology of emotions and social processes.* H. Wagner and A. Manstead (Eds.), London: John Wiley Ltd., 1989.

[4] Lutz, C., and White, G.M. (1986): The anthropology of emotions. *Annual Review of Anthropology* 15:405.

[5] I am grateful to Andrew Cuthbertson for giving me Darwin's comments on Duchenne's book, which I draw upon here and elsewhere in this chapter. This copy is in the Cambridge University Library, where access was kindly provided by Mr. Peter Gautrey.

> The face in repose must undergo some modification by the tonic force of these muscles . . . [to] be the image of our habitual sentiments, the *facies* of our dominant passions.[6]

Birdwhistell made a similar suggestion, although he did not cite Duchenne.[7] No one has seriously studied this matter using facial electromyography, in either longitudinal or cross-sectional developmental studies, to relate measures of emotion to any particular pattern of maintained facial muscle tonus. One of the problems with Duchenne's theory is that it presumes the facial muscles to be a dedicated system for emotion. My own studies[8] suggest that even in highly emotional situations, emotional facial expressions are outnumbered by facial actions that regulate the flow of conversation and illustrate speech as it is spoken. I have called these facial movements *conversational signals*. If there are changes in facial appearance due to usage, they will have to reflect the type of conversational signals deployed, not just the frequency of specific emotional expressions.

Perception of faces

Unlike his assertion of universality in expression, Duchenne provided evidence for his observation that the movement of a single muscle could create the impression that the entire expression had changed.

> From early in my research I had noticed that the isolated contraction of one of the muscles moving the eyebrow always produced a complete expression on the human face.[9] [Duchenne goes on to explain that at first he thought this was due to a reflex action spreading the effect across other muscles, until he made a lucky discovery.] And then a fortunate accident occurred that showed me that I had been the victim of an illusion. One day I was exciting the *muscle of suffering* and at the moment when all the features appeared to be contracted expressing pain, the eyebrow and the forehead were suddenly masked (the veil of the person on whom I was experimenting falling over her eyes). Imagine my surprise in seeing that the lower part of the face was not displaying the least contraction!

[6] Duchenne: *op. cit.*, p. 31, this volume.
[7] Birdwhistell, R.L. (1970): *Kinesics and context*. Philadelphia: University of Pennsylvania Press.
[8] Ekman, P. (1979): About brows: Emotional and conversational signals. In *Human ethology*. (M. von Cranach, K. Foppa, W. Lepenies, and D. Ploog, Eds.). Cambridge: Cambridge University Press, p. 169.
[9] Duchenne: *op. cit.*, p. 13, this volume.

I repeated this experiment several times, covering and uncovering the forehead and the eyebrow alternately; I repeated it on other subjects, and also on a fresh cadaver, and always got identical results. That is to say, I saw complete immobility of the features of those parts of the face below the eyebrows; but at the instant the eyebrows and the forehead were uncovered, so that one could see the whole facial expression, the features of the inferior part of the face seemed to take on an attitude of suffering.[10]

In his book on expression, Darwin commented on this discovery by Duchenne, including it in his list of reasons why it is so diffuclt to study expression.[11] More than a hundred years later, before being aware of Duchenne's discovery, we rediscovered and illustrated this point.[12]

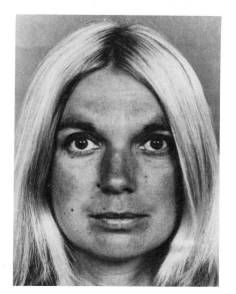 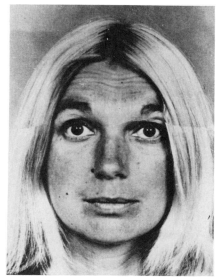

Figure 1 a&b

"[The figure] reveals something else that is very important when looking at facial expressions. Patricia [the name of the model] seems to show doubt or questioning across her entire face; but this is a composite photograph. The brow is the only part of the face that has been changed from the neutral picture on the left. If you cover the brow with your hand, you can see that this is so. With many facial expressions a change in just one area gives the impression that the rest of the facial features have changed as well."[13]

[10] *Ibid.*, p. 13, this volume.

[11] Darwin, C. (1955): *The expression of the emotions in man and animals.* New York: Philosophical Library, p. 13. (Originally published 1872.)

[12] Ekman, P., and Friesen, W.V. (1975): *Unmasking the face: a guide to recognizing emotions from facial cues.* New Jersey: Prentice Hall.

[13] *Ibid.*, p. 39.

Voluntary versus involuntary expressions

Duchenne not only electrically stimulated the face to produce expressions, but he also asked his subjects to make expressions. He discovered that some facial movements are very difficult to make voluntarily. Duchenne noted that one of his most gifted subjects (Plate 4), who could make nearly all facial muscle movements voluntarily, still could not move *m. procerus*, which lowers the skin between the eyebrows. More generally Duchenne claimed that "[t]he muscles that move the eyebrows, of all the expressive muscles, are least under the control of the will; in general, only the emotions of the soul can move them in an isolated fashion."[14]

Darwin considered the identification of those muscles difficult to control voluntarily to be one of Duchenne's most important discoveries.

> He has also, and this is a very important service, shown which muscles are least under the separate control of the will.[15]

Duchenne noted that all of the facial muscle actions would occur involuntarily, but only some could be produced deliberately. This dual control of at least some facial expressions agrees with the modern clinical neurology literature, which describes how lesions may differentially affect either voluntary or involuntary expressions while leaving the others intact.[16,17,18] If the lesion is in the pyramidal system (for example, the precentral gyrus), the patients cannot smile deliberately but will do so when they feel happy. Lesions in the nonpyramidal areas produce the reverse pattern; patients can smile on request, but will not smile when they feel a positive emotion. The pyramidal or voluntary motor pathways are more recent phylogenetically than the extrapyramidal or involuntary pathways.

While current research substantiates Duchenne's general observation that some muscles are more subject to voluntary direction than others, Duchenne wrongly asserted that the eyebrows cannot be controlled voluntarily. He may be correct about *m. procerus* (Friesen and I have never found anyone who voluntarily can produce that muscle's movement), but there are other eyebrow movements (for example, contracting the

---

[14]Duchenne: *op. cit.*, p. 43, this volume.

[15]Darwin: *op. cit.*, p. 5.

[16]Miehlke, A. (1973): *Surgery of the Facial Nerve*. Philadelphia: Saunders.

[17]Myers, R.E. (1976): Comparative neurology of vocalization and speech: proof of a dichotomy. *Annals of the New York Academy of Sciences*, 280:745.

[18]Tschiassny, K. (1953): Eight syndromes of facial paralysis and their significance in locating the lesion. *Annals of Otology, Rhinology and Laryngology*, 62:677.

entire *m. frontalis*) that everyone can produce voluntarily. Other movements of the eyebrows are difficult for most people to enact voluntarily, for example, raising just the inner or just the outer portions of the brows, but 10 to 20 percent of the population can produce these movements. Duchenne also failed to note other lower facial muscles that few people can move voluntarily (for example, tightening the inner strands of *m. orbicularis oris* or *m. zygomaticus minor*).[19]

Duchenne did note that:

> . . . certain people, comedians above all, possess the art of marvelously feigning emotions that exist only on their faces or lips. In creating an imaginary situation they are able, thanks to a special aptitude, to call up these artificial emotions.[20]

I interpret this quote as suggesting that some people have the theatrical ability to imagine emotional scenes and, when they do so, can produce expressions otherwise impossible when trying voluntarily to move specific muscles. This, of course, fits current thinking about the way actors using the Stanislavski technique retrieve sense memories to generate not just the expression but also the physiology of emotion.[21]

Smiling

Duchenne took matters one step further in asserting:

> But it will be simple for me to show that there are some emotions that man cannot simulate or portray artificially on the face; the attentive observer is always able to recognize a false smile.[22]

That is quite an assertion! Darwin wrote in the margin next to that passage "no evidence." Now, more than 100 years later, there is *some* evidence, but it is not as strong as Duchenne claimed, and differs in some details. Before summarizing these recent findings, let me describe in more detail Duchenne's discussion of smiling, for he was quite specific about how to distinguish the genuine smile of enjoyment from the feigned smile.

> The emotion of frank joy is expressed on the face by the combined contraction of *m. zygomaticus major* (I, Plate 1) and the inferior part

[19] See Ekman, P., Roper, G., and Hager, J.C. (1980): Deliberate facial movement. *Child Development* 51:886, for empirical findings on the development of the ability to voluntarily contract specific muscles.

[20] Duchenne: *op. cit.*, this volume, p. 30.

[21] For recent evidence of this see: Ekman, P., Levenson, R.W., and Friesen, W.V. (1983): Autonomic nervous system activity distinguishes between emotions. *Science*, 221:1208.

[22] Duchenne: *op. cit.*, p. 30, this volume.

of *m. orbicularis oculi* (E, Plate 1). The first obeys the will, but the second (the muscle of kindness, of love, and of agreeable impressions) is only put in play by the sweet emotions of the soul. Finally, fake joy, the deceitful laugh, cannot provoke the contraction of this latter muscle.[23]

Duchenne described his discovery of the crucial role played by *m. orbicularis oculi* in distinguishing a true from a false smile, in discussing Plates 30, 31, and 32. Of *m. orbicularis oculi*, which produces the movement of the lower eyelid observable in Plate 32, he said:

[without it] . . . no joy could be painted on the face truthfully . . . [it] does not obey the will; it is only brought into play by a genuinely agreeable emotion. Its inertia in smiling unmasks a false friend.[24]

He further discussed the role of the smile that lacks *m. orbicularis oculi*, recognizing that it can be used simply in politeness or to deceive.

You cannot always exaggerate the significance of this kind of smile, which is often only a simple smile of politeness, just as it can cover a treason. . . . We, in other circumstances and in normal intercourse with society, politely smile with our lips at the same time as being malcontented or when the soul is sad. When I did the experiment that is the subject of Plate 84, my model was in a very bad mood; her gaze was cold and the corners of her mouth a little lowered (cover on the left side the half of the mouth and the lower part of the cheek). As soon as I had produced the slight contraction of *m. zygomaticus major* on the left (cover the same parts on the opposite side), the false smile of Lady Macbeth in the above described scene [when concealing her plan to assassinate King Duncan], is portrayed on the face.[25]

Darwin substantiated Duchenne's interpretation of these photographs by showing Duchenne's Plates 31 and 32 (reproduced below) to people. Darwin reported that everyone recognized Plate 32 as happiness but Plate 31, in which there was only *m. zygomaticus major* activity without *m. orbicularis oculi*, was not said to be a smile of enjoyment.

In describing how one can recognize the true smile, Duchenne emphasized the effect of *m. orbicularis oculi* on the skin below the eye. Darwin added that this muscle produced changes in raising the upper lip and in slightly lowering the eyebrow.

We found[26] that some of the actions of *m. orbicularis oculi* – for ex-

---

[23] *Ibid.*, p. 126, this volume.   [24] *Ibid.*, p. 72, this volume.   [25] *Ibid.*, p. 127, this volume.

[26] Ekman, P., and Friesen, W.V. (1978): *The facial action coding system*. Palo Alto: Consulting Psychologists Press.

Figure 2 A & B

ample, producing the change in the skin below the lower eyelid, raising the cheeks, and the crows' feet wrinkles – were reliable only when the action of *m. zygomaticus major* was slight to moderate. When the smiling action produced by *m. zygomaticus major* was broad, these changes in appearance occurred even without the action of *m. orbicularis oculi*. With the broad smile it was only the lowering of the brow and the change in the appearance of the eye cover fold that remained as a reliable sign of *m. orbicularis oculi* activity.

Our studies of how readily people could voluntarily move each facial muscle[27] suggested a further modification to what Duchenne and Darwin suggested would differentiate the smile of enjoyment from the social or feigned smile. Most people can readily contract the inner portion of *m. orbicularis oculi*, which tightens the eyelids (pars palpebralis), but few can voluntarily contract the outer portion, which raises the cheeks and draws skin from around the eye inward (pars lateralis). We have identified those instances in which *m. zygomaticus major* was accompanied by *m. orbicularis oculi* pars lateralis as the smile of enjoyment. In his honor we have called this *Duchenne's smile*.[28] Duchenne's idea that one could tell from the smile itself whether it was one of enjoyment, or polite or feigned, is supported by recent evidence.

There have been nine studies. Ekman, Friesen, and Ancoli found that

[27] Ekman, Roper, and Hager (1980): *op. cit.*

[28] In an earlier paper (Ekman, P., and Friesen, W.V. (1982): Felt, false, and miserable smiles. *Journal of Nonverbal Behavior* 6:238) we referred to this as a *felt smile*.

Duchenne's smiles occurred more often than three other types of smiles when people watched pleasant films;[29] and only Duchenne's smiles correlated with the subjective report of happiness. Ekman, Davidson, and Friesen[30] also showed that Duchenne's smile, but not other smiling, differentiated which of two positive experiences was most enjoyed. Ekman, Friesen, and O'Sullivan[31] found that Duchenne's smiles occurred more often when people were actually enjoying themselves, as compared with people feigning smiling to conceal negative emotions. Fox and Davidson[32] found that in 10-month-old infants Duchenne's smiles occurred more often in response to the mother's approach, while other types of smiles occurred more often in response to the approach of a stranger; and only Duchenne's smiles were associated with left frontal EEG activation, the pattern of cerebral activity repeatedly found in positive affect. This EEG pattern of cerebral activity associated with Duchenne's smile was replicated by Ekman, Davidson, and Friesen[33] in adults who were watching amusing films. Matsumoto[34] found that depressed patients showed more Duchenne's smiles in a discharge interview compared with the admission interview, but there was no difference in the rate of other kinds of smiling.

The possibility that these differences between types of smiling might be universal was raised in the next four studies, all of which were conducted in Europe. Steiner[35] found that the frequency of Duchenne's smiles, but not other types of smiles, increased over the course of psychotherapy in patients who were judged to have improved. Ruch[36] found that Duchenne's smiles were sensitive to the amount of humor felt by German adults when responding to jokes or cartoons. Schneider[37] found

[29] Ekman, P., Friesen, W.V., and Ancoli, S. (1980): Facial signs of emotional experience. *Journal of Personality and Social Psychology,* 39:1125.

[30] Ekman, P., Davidson, R., and Friesen, W.V. (1989): Duchenne's smile: emotional expression and brain physiology II. Under review.

[31] Ekman, P., Friesen, W.V., and O'Sullivan, M. (1988): Smiles when lying. *Journal of Personality and Social Psychology,* 54:414.

[32] Fox, N.A., and Davidson, R.J. (1988): Patterns of brain electrical activity during facial signs of emotion in 10-month-old infants. *Developmental Psychology,* 24:230.

[33] Ekman, Davidson, and Friesen (1989): *op. cit.*

[34] Matsumato, D. (1986): *Cross-cultural communication of emotion.* Doctoral dissertation, University of California, Berkeley.

[35] Steiner, F. (1986): Differentiating smiles. In *FACS in psychotherapy research* (E. Branniger-Huber and F. Steiner, Eds.). Zurich: Department of Clinical Psychology, Universitat Zurich, p. 139.

[36] Ruch, W. (1987): Personality aspects in the psychobiology of human laughter. Paper presented at the Third Meeting of the ISSID, Toronto.

[37] Schneider, K. (1987): Achievement-related emotions in preschoolers. In *Motivation, intention and volition* (F. Hahseh and J. Kuhl, Eds.). Berlin: Springer.

that Duchenne's smiles distinguished whether young children had succeeded or failed in a game. Krause and Steiner[38] found that Duchenne's smile occurred more often during interviews with healthy subjects than in interviews with schizophrenic patients.

One qualification must be remembered. In all of these studies, Duchenne's smile was distinguished from other smiles by very precise facial measurement using repeated and often slow motion viewing.[39] It is not yet known whether an observer looking at real time can distinguish Duchenne's smile from other smiles.

Interpretation of particular muscle actions

Unlike Darwin, who checked his own impressions by showing photographs to others, Duchenne relied on his own judgment. Often his interpretations have been borne out by recent research findings. Most notable were his judgements that:

- *m. zygomaticus minor* was involved in sadness and pain, not happiness;
- *m. platysma* activity added to the intensity of any negative emotion shown on the face;
- *m. buccinator* signaled irony.

Duchenne also noted that by combining muscular actions, each of which are associated with different emotions, a blend of the two can be created. For example, he described combining a smile with the raising of the inner corners of the eyebrow to create the look of compassion. In recent times, Plutchik,[40] Tomkins and McCarter,[41] Izard,[42] and Ekman and Friesen[43] have all elaborated on this idea of blends, although none cited Duchenne.

Methodological contribution

Duchenne's discoveries using electrical stimulation of the face to determine exactly which muscles produce specific changes in facial appear-

---

[38] Krause, R., and Steiner, E. (1989): Facial expression of schizophrenic patients and their interaction partners. *Psychiatry*, under review.

[39] Ekman, P., and Friesen, W.V. (1976): Measuring facial movement. *Journal of Environmental Psychology and Nonverbal Behavior*, 1:56; and Ekman and Friesen (1978): *op. cit.*

[40] Plutchik, R. (1962): *The emotions: facts, theories, and a new model.* New York: Random House.

[41] Tomkins, S.S., and McCarter, R. (1964): What and where are the primary affects? Some evidence for a theory. *Perceptual and Motor Skills*, 18:119.

[42] Izard, C.E. (1971): *The face of emotion*, New York: Appleton-Century-Crofts.

[43] Ekman, P., and Friesen, W.V. (1969): The repertoire of nonverbal behavior: catagories, origins, usage, and coding. *Semiotica*, 1:49.

ance provide the basis for contemporary facial measurement in the behavioral sciences. To understand the nature of his contribution I will briefly describe the different approaches to measuring facial behavior and then the role of Duchenne's discoveries in current work.

There are two approaches to studying any aspect of nonverbal behavior[44,45,46]: measuring judgments about one or another message and measuring the sign vehicles that convey the message. Take for example the question of whether facial expressions vary with psychopathology. Suppose a sample were available of facial behavior during interviews with patients who have a diagnosis of schizophrenia or depression and with a control group displaying no psychiatric problems. To use the *message judgment* approach, the facial movements in these interviews would be shown to a group of observers, who would be asked whether each person they viewed was normal, schizophrenic, or depressive. If the judgments were accurate, this would answer the question. In using the *measurement of sign vehicles* approach, some or all of the facial movements somehow would be classified or counted. If we found, for example, that depressives raised the inner corners of the eyebrows more than the other two groups, whereas schizophrenics showed facial movements that very slowly faded from the face, this would answer the question affirmatively. The measurement of sign vehicles approach tells us about differences in facial behavior, but it cannot tell us whether observers (who are not using a measurement technique) can recognize those differences. Conversely, the message judgment approach would tell us that observers can recognize differences in facial behavior, but it would not tell us what those differences might be.

Both approaches are useful, but only by measuring the sign vehicles, the facial activity itself, can we learn which facial actions provide information. Until 10 years ago there were relatively few studies measuring facial behavior. There was no objective, comprehensive tool for making such measurements. Each scientist started anew, rarely making use of the work of predecessors.

Every investigator proposed a list of facial actions such as brow raise,

[44] Ekman, P. (1964): Body position, facial expression and verbal behavior during interviews. *Journal of Abnormal and Social Psychology*, 68:295.

[45] Ekman, P. (1965): Communication through nonverbal behavior: a source of information about an interpersonal relationship. In *Affect, cognition and personality* (S.S. Tompkins and C.E. Izard, Eds.). New York: Springer, p. 390.

[46] Ekman, P. (1982): Methods for measuring facial action. In *Handbook of methods in nonverbal behavior research* (K.R. Scherer and P. Ekman, Eds.). New York: Cambridge University Press, p. 45.

nose wrinkle, lip corners down, and so on. Measurement included noting the presence of any action or combination of actions, when they began and ended, and their strength. The question has been what to put on the list of facial actions, how an investigator, confronted by the complex flow of facial activity, decided upon what to put on the list of facial behaviors to score.

One investigator[47] tried to select facial behaviors to parallel linguistic units. Another proposed a list based on the function of each action.[48] However, most of these lists have been incomplete and imprecise. Most authors described facial actions by changes in the shape of the features and the appearance of wrinkles, disregarding the anatomical basis for these changes. Often these descriptions were vague and unable to deal with individual differences in appearance and differences associated with age.[49]

I started by listing those facial actions that theory or findings suggested were relevant to one or another emotion,[50] trying to achieve precision by photographically, rather than verbally, depicting each action on the list. I learned from Wade Seaford, an anthropologist who had studied facial anatomy,[51] that we had inadvertently left out the raising of the lower lip due to *m. mentalis*. This convinced me that the only way to build a tool for measuring facial behavior comprehensively was to base the list of actions on the anatomy of facial movement.

The anatomy texts provided relatively little description of how each muscle changes appearance. As Washburn pointed out,[52] the sections on the face in most anatomy texts was a dead, rather than a live, anatomy, naming muscles as one sees them when the skin has been removed, rather than classifying muscles by their action. Duchenne had discovered 100 years before:

> Anatomy has grouped some muscles under the same name that possess independent actions when electrically stimulated . . .[53]

[47] Birdwhistell, R.L. (1952): *Introduction to kinesics*. Louisville, Kentucky: University of Louisville Press.

[48] Grant, N.G. (1969): Human facial expression. *Man*, 4:525.

[49] See Ekman (1982): *op. cit.*, for a critical review of fourteen techniques for measuring facial behavior.

[50] Ekman, P., Friesen, W.V., and Tompkins, S.S. (1971): Facial affect scoring technique: a first validity study. *Semiotica*, 3:37.

[51] Seaford, H.W. (1976): Maximizing replicability in describing facial behavior. Paper presented at the Annual Meeting of the Americal Anthropological Association, Washington, DC.

[52] Washburn, S.L. (1975): Personal communication.

[53] Duchenne: *op. cit.*, p. 23, this volume.

Friesen and I borrowed extensively from Duchenne, and from a contemporary anatomist, Hjorstjo,[54] who did not cite Duchenne but whose work embraced Duchenne's discoveries by specifying the muscles that produce specific changes in facial appearance. Using both Duchenne's data and his method, I tested the activity of a number of muscles of whose action I was uncertain. I was my own subject, putting needles into my face either to stimulate electrically a particular muscle or to record electrical changes when I voluntarily contracted a muscle.

The needle was not pleasant, and Friesen and I mostly used our voluntary performance of specific muscle movements to film the changes produced by different combinations of muscle actions. Our contribution, building on Duchenne, was to explore many more combinations of muscle movements than he or anyone else had considered. We performed, photographed, and analyzed nearly 10,000 combinations of facial muscle movements. Using the information about how these actions changed appearance, we constructed a measurement technique that allowed the user to decompose any observed facial movement into the muscular actions that produced it. Our Facial Action Coding System – FACS[55,56] – is now being used by several hundred scientists.

Unknown to us when we were developing FACS, Ermiane and Gergerian[57] were developing a very similar technique to measure facial movement comprehensively in anatomical terms. They too built upon Duchenne and acknowledged his important role. Soon afterward, Izard published a third anatomically based measurement system.[58] It is similar to FACS, but only attempts to measure those facial movements Izard thought were related to emotion.

The last approach to measuring facial behavior has been to record electrical activity in different facial regions with electromyography (EMG). This technique promises to monitor emotional activity when there is no visible facial movement.[59] It too depends upon the knowledge provided

[54] Hjorstjo, C.H. (1970): Man's face and mimic language. Lund: Student-Literature.

[55] Ekman and Friesen (1976): *op. cit.*

[56] Ekman and Friesen (1978): *op. cit.*

[57] Ermiane, R. (1949): *Jeux musculaires et expressions du visage*. Paris: Libraire le François. Ermiane, R. (1970): *Visages et caractères*, 6th edition, mimeographed. *Atlas of facial expresions (Album des expressions du visage)* by Roger Ermiane (1976), translated by Edmund Gergerian. Paris: La Pensée Universelle.

[58] Izard (1979): *op. cit.*

[59] Cacioppo, J.T., Martzke, J.S., Petty, R.E., and Tassinary, L.G. (1988): Specific forms of facial EMG response index emotions during an interview: From Darwin to the continuous flow hypothesis of affect laden information processing. *Journal of Personality and Social Psychology*, 54:592.

by Duchenne, and those who followed him, about the muscles that produce specific changes in facial activity.

The current flurry of research measuring facial behavior – whether visible facial expression or EMG measurement of facial activity – rests upon the mechanics of facial movement pioneered by Duchenne. In almost all respects Duchenne's findings have been validated. The one disagreement regards the activity of *m. corrugator supercilii,* to which Duchenne attributed the raising of the inner corners of the eyebrow. Friesen and I[60] claimed instead that *m. corrugator supercilii* draws the brows down and together. We attributed the drawing-up of the inner corners of the eyebrows to the inner portion of *m. frontalis,* which may sometimes be joined by *m. corrugator supercilii.* Duchenne failed to note that the inner and outer portion of *m. frontalis* can act independently. Darwin and Hjorstjo agreed with our, not Duchenne's, explanation of how these muscles function.

I want to remind the reader who has survived this discussion of methodology that Duchenne was a marvelously gifted observer. Quite apart from the importance of his discoveries on how the facial muscles work, he contributed a variety of fascinating ideas about emotion and expression, many of which I have described in the first part of this chapter. Duchenne often asked questions that still are unresolved by those who study emotion today.

Seemingly perplexed by the large list of emotions described by such writers as Plato, Aristotle, Cicero, Descartes, and Hobbes, Duchenne commented:

> Perhaps it isn't given to man to express all his emotions on his face, especially when we consider the many different emotions that have been named and arbitrarily classifed by the philosophers.[61]

It does appear that there are more words describing emotions than distinctive facial expressions, although some of these variations may be due to differences in intensity of the same, or the blending of more than one, emotion. I have argued[62] that a pancultural facial expression is *one* of the distinguishing characteristics of an emotion, and that phenomena that do not have a distinctive, universal expression should not be considered emotions, but instead may be moods, attitudes, or preferences.

---

[60] Ekman and Friesen (1978): *op. cit.*
[61] Duchenne: *op. cit.,* p. 28, this volume.
[62] Ekman, P. (1984): Expression and the nature of emotion. In *Approaches to emotion,* (Sherer, K., and Ekman, P., Eds.). Hillsdale, New Jersey: Lawrence Erlbaum, p. 319.

Duchenne, a few sentences later, points to what I still believe may provide us with an answer to the question of "what are the emotions?"

> One day, perhaps, these electrophysiological studies on the different modes of expression of human "physionomie" will serve as the foundation for a better classification of the emotions founded on the observation of nature.[63]

[63] Duchenne: *op. cit.*, p. 29, this volume.

Index